DATE DUE			
GAYLORD			PRINTED IN U.S.A.

S.H.S.W.

HERBERT A. KELLAR

IN SUPPORT of CLIO
ESSAYS in MEMORY of
HERBERT A. KELLAR

Edited by

William B. Hesseltine   and   *Donald R. McNeil*

STATE HISTORICAL SOCIETY OF WISCONSIN

MADISON   1958

48,274
Nov. '64

Manufactured in the United States of America
by the Vail-Ballou Press, Inc., Binghamton, N. Y.

PREFACE

*T*O THE solemn strains of an academic march, the procession slowly moved from the new, functionalistic Memorial Library at the University of Wisconsin across the mall toward the Renaissance structure which, for fifty years, had housed the libraries of the University and the State Historical Society of Wisconsin.

It was Rededication Day and the academic procession, splashed with the vivid colors of hundreds of academic hoods that crisp October day in 1955, marched to commemorate the renovation of the Society's building–after fifty-three years of "temporary" joint occupancy with the University. Members of the procession and hundreds of spectators heard John D. Hicks give the dedicatory address. As the University band played, the black-robed figures rose from their seats and filed into the newly remodeled building for a tour.

As members of the procession and the spectators chatted in the corridors, a secretary from an upstairs office rushed up to a staff member and breathlessly told the bad news: "Mrs. Kellar called from home. Dr. Kellar just died."

PREFACE

It was a singular misfortune that at the moment of rededi-
cating one of the finest depositories of manuscripts and books
in American history, one of America's most dedicated supporters of historical studies should pass away. For many years,
Herbert Kellar made a distinguished contribution to the study
of history by aiding and abetting scholarship. He was perhaps
best known as a resourceful and energetic collector of manuscripts, the creator and guardian of his beloved McCormick
Collection, housed since 1951 at the State Historical Society
of Wisconsin. But this indefatigable servant of Clio found innumerable other ways to advance the cause of history. His
varied and numerous activities were all predicated on the
belief that the ancillary contributions to historical scholarship
were as important as historiography itself.

As author of *Solon Robinson, Pioneer and Agriculturist*,
numerous articles, book reviews, and significant reports on
source materials, Kellar knew the problems confronting the
historian. But his energy and zeal was spent in support of
history rather than in the writing of it. A member of countless
committees of every major historical organization in the country, Herbert Kellar used the force of his personality to foster
scholarship through new channels of experimentation and expression. An intense interest in new horizons–microcopying,
the Historical Records Survey, library co-operation, restorations, creation of new historical organizations, plus his organizational work, formed the pattern of Herbert Kellar's career.
He served on the councils of the Association for State and
Local History and the Society of American Archivists, and
was president of the Agricultural History Society and the
Mississippi Valley Historical Association. Equal to his interest
in new ideas and methods was his interest in the younger mem-

bers of the historical profession. Scores of them are indebted to his generous aid and wise counsel.

These essays are not about Herbert Kellar's career. They were suggested by his multi-facet career, are ascribed to his memory, and illustrate the contribution of those who labor in Clio's fields, sowing and cultivating, but who do not reap by writing.

In the days when formal history was new, and when the first full-time professional historians appeared on the scene, Edward A. Freeman's dictum that history was past politics established limited boundaries within which the historian might function. Under so narrow a scope as past politics, the materials of the historian were relatively simple. Those of the Freeman tradition could fulfill the obligations of their craft by using the materials already gathered in archives, by presenting accounts of the progress of governmental institutions, by tracing the political developments of reigns and administrations with never a thought of the economic and social background of those political developments or of the intellectual climate in which they took place.

There was, of course, even in the days of Freeman a different and a broader tradition of history in America. Springing from purely American roots, finding their rationale in the very mainsprings of American Democracy, there were historians who conceived of their province as including all the activities and relationships of mankind's past. In Wisconsin, Lyman C. Draper, founder and guiding spirit of the State Historical Society, understood the broader aspects of history and contended as early as 1869 that his Society should gather not only the records of the nameless pioneers who had "hewn down with dauntless heart and sturdy arm the trackless forests," but also of those "adventurous companies who planned and executed . . . noble improvements." He wanted information on the "genesis and upspringings of our Social Sytem," of "religious, literary, and humanitarian institutions," of industrial, agricultural, and mineral resources.

In time, owing to the work of John Richard Greene in England and John Bach McMaster in the United States, Draper's concepts found new advocates in the proponents of a 'New History' which reached far beyond past politics and past political leaders to include the common man–the "nameless pioneers"–as well as the 'adventurous companies' and all other things which could throw light on the 'genesis and upspringings of our Social System.' Despite its claim to novelty, the 'New History' was a vital part of the American tradition. Its fresh advocacy marked the merging of the older, American concept of history as an expression of the democratic experience, and the newly-imported, professional concept of history as an aid to political studies.

But the new history, as Draper so clearly foresaw, involved the gathering and collecting of records beyond those of governments. Archives, depositories, statutes, and the formal pronouncements of public men were insufficient for the broader concepts of history. Other materials needed to be gathered; men needed to be directed into newer fields of study; new and old historians, amateurs and professionals, needed to be encouraged to undertake investigations into social and economic matters, such as industrial history, business history, agricultural history. And, with the new and more bulky materials for investigation, there came a need for the exploration of new methods of research, a need for greater financial support if historians were to realize their goal. Other needs were for new and different media for reporting the results of research and interpretation and for adapting modern technology to the ever-growing task of fathering, collecting, collating, and utilizing the mounting tons of material which threw new light upon the ages of man.

In time, of course, the broadened nature of history, the new materials and methods of research, the new depositories of the historic record, the new aids to historical study all became so complex that even the best informed historian was scarcely able to keep abreast of the newer tools of his craft. The increased collections of the libraries, the multiplication of collecting agencies, the lengthening shelves of bibliographies, the museum, the "restored" villages, the microfilm, the microcard, even the IBM machines tended to become the special domains of technicians, who almost forgot their basic function as ancillaries to history and tended to develop into exclusive "professions" of their own crafts.

It is in the hope that some of these enlarged aspects of history and of historical study may be brought to the attention of lay and professional historians that these essays on some of the "aids" to history have been brought together. They are conceived as a memorial to a man who, in his lifetime, did more than any other single historian of his generation to encourage the use of new materials and new techniques, and at the same time to collect, to stimulate interest in new 'fields' of study, and to foster organizations devoted to historical study.

Herbert A. Kellar gathered a great and important collection of historical materials, pioneered in the application of scholarly methods to historical restorations, was in the forefront of the advocates of microfilming and microcarding, edited a

viii   *PREFACE*

collection of historical papers, and prompted libraries and governmental agencies to promote historical study. Fundamentally, he gave meaning and substance to the concepts of the 'new'–which was really very old–and he built many bridges across the inevitably widening gaps between historical students and the technicians and activities upon whom they depend.

The editors wish to express their appreciation to Mrs. Herbert A. Kellar for her aid and counsel, and to Miss Alice E. Smith, Jesse E. Boell, and Clement M. Silvestro for reading several of the essays. A further and deeper debt of gratitude is owed to O. Lawrence Burnette, Jr., Book Editor of the State Historical Society of Wisconsin, because of his skillful blue pencil, sense of organization, and feeling for words.

WILLIAM B. HESSELTINE

University of Wisconsin

DONALD R. McNEIL

State Historical Society of Wisconsin

CONTENTS

ix

CONTENTS

IN SUPPORT OF CLIO

THE W.P.A. HISTORICAL
RECORDS SURVEY

by DAVID L. SMILEY

Wake Forest College

*T*HE most extensive program of governmental support of historical research in America was the Historical Records Survey, sponsored as a relief measure by the Works Progress Administration. Born of economic crisis and justified only as a means of employing the jobless, the Records Survey was but a small part of the vast New Deal battle against unemployment. Federal Emergency Relief Administrator Harry Hopkins put the nation's unemployed to work at such disparate occupations as heavy construction, grass-cutting, sewing, and producing plays.

But among the many projects designed to change the face of the land, or merely to make work for unfortunate people, the Historical Records Survey stood out as an unusual experiment. The Survey's objective was to catalog and to protect public and semi-public records of the past, and thus to simplify the task of the historian. Its intent was to produce scholarly work of lasting value, and, therefore, it was unique among the emergency organizations of the New Deal. Work-

3

relief was as old as the Pyramids, Survey spokesmen were fond of saying, but "white-collar" relief for the educated was an American innovation; indeed, that was the New Deal's contribution to the tactics of recovery. Among the "white-collar" agencies, the Historical Records Survey was a highly successful venture. Without direct national precedents, and using clerks from relief rolls, Director Luther H. Evans trained and organized a corps of workers, tackled the immense chore of surveying public records in every state and county in the United States, and in the course of five years amassed an incredibly large collection of useful information.

The surveys contained the basic ingredients for the rewriting of local history, and therefore for a fresh analysis of national development. They have also been of value to lawyers and others who must work in public files, to students of genealogy, and to archivists laboring to dispel public apathy toward record-keeping. It was the most important federally-sponsored aid to historical research the American government had yet attempted, and was the most extensive bibliographic project any group has ever planned. An experiment in socialized scholarship, the Historical Records Survey made a significant contribution to the bibliography of source materials, and at the same time provided a valuable lesson in what such public projects could accomplish in subsidizing the routine drudgery of research.

It was surprising that such a program should ever have operated at all. The W. P. A. was a complex organization with an internal division of authority which made it seem at times like a headless monster. Certainly, scholarship and aids to research were far from its primary objectives. The Survey was the result of a combination of factors: the broad view which Harry Hopkins took of relief work; the difficulty in finding "useful" labor for the white-collar urban unemployed; and the zeal of Survey proponents.

For some years before the establishment of the project, persons interested in archives had seen the need for public assistance and national co-ordination in the task of listing state and county public documents. Organizations of scholars and librarians had established committees to work on the problem. In 1930 the American Council of Learned Societies and the Social Science Research Council established a Joint Committee on Materials for Research, with Dr. Robert C. Binkley of Western Reserve University as chairman. Dr. Theodore R. Schellenberg, of the National Archives, was executive secretary of the Binkley committee and later became chairman of the American Historical Association's Committee on Historical Materials. Dr. Joseph Mayer was chairman of the Library of Congress' Commission on National Archives Survey, and Lt. Col. J. Marius Scammell of the National Guard Bureau was working energetically to organize a survey of state militia records. Dr. Francis S. Philbrick of the University of Pennsylvania Law School chaired the American Historical Association's Committee on Legal History. Each of these men had a vital interest in records surveys. Furthermore, many librarians and custodians of state records, notably in Alabama, Connecticut, Florida, Minnesota, Ohio, Pennsylvania, Rhode Island, and Wisconsin, were already cataloging the public records under their jurisdictions. The recent opening of the National Archives in Washington drew public attention to the world of public records and promised training and professional careers to a burgeoning corps of workers.

Among scholars there was a widespread sentiment for records surveys which needed only leadership to become a potential force. The original suggestion for a nation-wide, coordinated survey of state and local archives with relief labor came from Professor Philbrick in January, 1934. Binkley, as chairman of the Social Science Research Council-American Council of Learned Societies' Joint Committee on Materials for Research, called a conference in Washington which was attended by librarians, historians, and others interested in records-keeping. With the aid of Dr. Schellenberg, his executive secretary, Binkley drew up plans for the project.

On the basis of these plans, custodians of state records requested funds from the Civil Works Authority and the Federal Emergency Relief Administration. Dr. Mayer of the Library of Congress' consultative staff, and Col. Scammell tried to unite these state efforts into a nationally-co-ordinated program, but the Senate by one vote refused to allow any but state projects under the C. W. A. program. The senatorial decision discouraged nascent survey leaders who expected national direction and assistance for their projects. Col. Scammell fumed that they sat back and waited for a "federal Santa Claus" to bring them gifts. "They need a Moses to lead them in the wilderness," he said, shifting his metaphor, "but unfortunately, in this case, Moses was *not* picked up by a daughter of Pharoah, and is still in the bulrushes!"

Not everyone was discouraged by the Senate's denial of funds for a co-ordinated survey. "The gospel in regard to archival surveys has been spread and it will bring forth fruit in due season," Schellenberg promised. It was too early to despair of using federally-allocated relief funds for a survey project, he said. "Another winter may bring us the opportunity, arising out of the distress of the white-collar class and the need for national relief," Schellenberg went on. "Personally I wouldn't welcome this opportunity, but we must make the most of the evil days that have fallen upon us."

It was not until the dark days of June, 1935, that survey advocates were able to reap any encouragement from the whirlwind of calamity. By the time Harry Hopkins became Federal Emergency Relief Administrator, Americans generally had accepted the necessity of national relief programs. Hopkins faced the task of quickly finding work for unemployed people; work which would require little training, equipment, or supervisory budget; and work which might be justified as worthwhile governmental activity. An archives survey met all those requirements, and was particularly suited to the difficult white-collar unemployment problem.

Thus the survey of state and county archives, which became a part of the W. P. A., was not the child of any one person. It was an outgrowth of the state records projects and the ideas of Binkley, Schellenberg, Philbrick, and others, for a nationally-co-ordinated program, and it was carefully shepherded into being by its future director, Dr. Luther H. Evans. Evans was born in Bastrop County, Texas in 1902, and liked to point out that he had attended a one-teacher rural school, worked on a farm while a school-boy, and yet graduated as valedictorian of his class. But his background left its mark upon him; years later one of his teachers asserted that as a college student Evans did not have a "wide range of knowledge and outlook." Nevertheless he made an enviable record, and by the age of 25 he had received the doctorate in political science from Stanford University and had spent a summer in Europe studying the League of Nations. For three years he taught political science in American colleges, and in 1930 he became Assistant Professor of Politics at Princeton University.

After his release at the end of the contract period at Princeton, in the spring of 1935 Evans was looking for a job. New York's Brain-Trusting editor, Raymond Moley, was induced to help Evans get a government position. Moley obliged with a "Dear Harold" letter to crusty Secretary Ickes of the Interior Department. Evans was "an exceedingly promising man with a grand personality," Moley said, and he "fits precisely into the picture in Washington." It turned out that Interior could not use Evans, but the rapidly-expanding F. E. R. A. might. In June, Evans was in Washington for an interview with Hopkins.

The amiable Hopkins told Evans that there were many old records in the capital that needed binding and cataloging, and he asked Evans to write up a project to care for them. The young professor exceeded Hopkins' request; not only did he report on the Washington project, but he also proposed a survey of federal archives in state depositories to be made under the supervision of the Archivist of the United States, Dr. R. D. W. Connor. This project began in 1936 as the Survey of Federal Archives, directed by Dr. Philip M. Hamer.

When Evans submitted the report on the federal archives inventory, Hopkins asked him to prepare another report on a survey of state and county archives, but he made no offer of a position and Evans was becoming desperate. On July 11, 1935, he informed Hopkins that he had to have a position within a week. "I am deeply interested in these projects," he told the relief administrator, "and would find work in them absorbing." Evans attached to his letter a brief memorandum outlining a national survey of state and local records. The proposal interested Hopkins, and he asked Evans to study the matter further and report a more detailed plan to him. After about ten days, Evans returned to Hopkins with a memorandum which became the outline of the Historical Records Survey. For his report Evans made use of advice from Binkley, Schellenberg, Philbrick, and others.

The memorandum, dated July 23, 1935, outlined the organization of a projected survey of "state and local archives and other historical materials." To justify the expenditure, Evans cited evidence that such surveys would provide work for white-collar workers, and that they required high labor and low materials cost–a prerequisite for W. P. A. projects. To establish the need for the project he quoted from Binkley and from the Public Archives Commission of the American Historical Association. In 1900 the Commission had declared that "it may be doubted if in any country in the world archives of relatively so much value are so lightly regarded or carelessly kept." Binkley agreed. "The condition of local archives in this country is such as to cause the United States to be classified . . . with the backward nations," he said.

To remedy the situation, Evans proposed that Hopkins appoint a "National Co-ordinator of State and Local Archives Surveys." The national co-ordinator would have ten assistants and an advisory committee of ten members. The national co-ordinator would appoint a director of the survey in each state, usually the state librarian or some other similar official charged with the responsibility of maintaining state records. Evans expected the state director to serve without federal compensation. But an executive secretary was provided to relieve the state director of administrative duties, and there should be stenographic assistance for both. The organization was completed by five examiners for each state, one regional supervisor for each seven and one-half counties, a supervisor for each county, and three archival workers for each county. Evans estimated the total cost of such an ideal personnel allocation at $15,480,660.

The projected work was subdivided into six categories: a preliminary survey of archives, classification and physical renovation of the archives, an identification inventory of the records, editorial work on the inventory reports, survey of storage space, and the possible rebuilding of records containers. For all of these tasks Evans was sure that qualified workers would be easily available from the relief rolls.

Except for minor changes in detail, and the reduction of Evans' proposed personnel as a result of allocation cuts, the project outline became the Records Survey. Though Evans did the actual work of preparing the outline, he received assistance from people who had experience in directing large-scale archival surveys. To that extent, therefore, the Historical Records Survey was an outgrowth of the earlier projects, such as Binkley's survey and indexing of newspapers in Cleveland and Cuyahoga County, Ohio; a project directed by Dr. Curtis W. Garrison under C. W. A. in Pennsylvania; and a Rhode Island survey under Dr. Herbert C. Brigham.

After submitting the report, Evans had to learn the necessity for patience. He waited two months before he learned that the project would be approved and that he would become the National Director. "By virtue of a fortuitous concatenation of circumstances too complicated and irrational to be explained here," he wrote Philbrick on October 16, 1935, "it seems that I am to direct the harvesting of the rich crop which you sowed in your letter of January 11, 1934, to Binkley." In 1937, explaining how he got the directorship, Evans said: "I walked in at the critical moment, gave Hopkins a sales talk and he gave me the job of setting up the national project. Politics had nothing to do with it, except that Professor Moley got Mr. Hopkins and myself together."

However Evans got the appointment, the record is clear that he handled exceedingly well the routine of setting up the national organization and of directing its work. Before any surveying could begin he had to prepare instructions and inventory forms. "I am at present engaged in the uninspiring task of writing the forms and instructions to cover the whole project," he told Philbrick in October. He found "particularly difficult" the problem of reducing to routine a complex mass of information about records in many categories and with varying titles. In this phase of the project Evans labored diligently, making use of the sound advice he received from Binkley, Schellenberg, and Verne E. Chatelain of the National Park Service, and he produced an excellent set of plans.

Evans' administrative imagination enabled him to foresee many of the problems which might arise in the actual cataloging process, and his innate skill as a politician helped him handle the inevitable personality clashes within the organization. Occasionally he had to crack a disciplinary whip over his subordinates: "I have turned the heat on so much in some places that I find that some of my field supervisors run around turning off the radiators, but we are getting results," he told a Chicago conference of historical society executives in 1937. All of these qualities made Evans an excellent choice for the national directorship.

On November 15, 1935, President Franklin D. Roosevelt

established the Historical Records Survey of the Works Progress Administration by Presidential Letter No. 1090. The directive set forth in broad terms the functions of the Survey: to locate and measure local records, to study ways of preserving them, and to make recommendations concerning filing, classifying, and cataloging them, and also concerning means of facilitating their use. At the same time the President authorized the expenditure of $1,195,800 on the project, with a specific amount allocated to each state. Evans was disappointed with the allocation. His original request had been for more than fifteen million dollars, but he was eager to begin the project. The reduction was "terribly disappointing, particularly as the National Office will have only $44,000," he told Binkley. But, he added, "there may be more where this came from, provided we do a bang-up job."

Evans immediately set himself to the task of doing a "bang-up job." There were multitudes of decisions to be made, some petty and some far-reaching in their consequences, and always he requested advice from the experts. He consulted with an official of the American Library Association, for example, about the size of the inventory forms he was designing: "I have debated the question of having the inventory forms to be 5″ x 7″ and it is possible that the final decision may call for the 5″ x 8″ size," he said.

But far weightier matters also confronted him, such as the basic question of what aspect of the work the survey should attempt first. From the beginning, Evans and his advisors planned the project with an eye to extending it. Even before the original allocation was approved, they were looking to the day when they would get a second grant. Philbrick was explicit with his advice: "Better *complete* throughout the country, or even only in scattered representative states, one portion of your project than begin everything and complete nothing," he counselled. "Also, since performance may be a leverage for further grants, and the influence of local 'statesmen' may be of great importance, it seems to me . . . that it would probably be wise to begin with public archives." It might seem wise to complete all the work in a state once an organization was established in it, "but . . . no widespread support would be gained for further appropriations."

Since survey leaders understood the requirements for additional grants, they planned the early course of the project with that in mind. On December 3, 1935, Evans called an organizational policy meeting in Washington and invited the men who had agreed to serve on his Advisory Committee. Many influential scholars were present. Dr. Arthur R. Newsome of the University of North Carolina, formerly archivist of the state, was chairman. Others included Binkley, who was vice-chairman, Dr. Solon J. Buck and Dr. T. R. Schellenberg of the recently-established National Archives, and Verne E. Chatelain, Chief Historian of the National Park Service.

Most of those present agreed with Philbrick that the survey should begin with an inventory of county records or some other selected category of records found throughout the country, and the committee advised Evans to plan accordingly. The attitude and work of the advisory group encouraged Evans, and he began to make optimistic statements about the forthcoming work of the Survey. It would demonstrate, he said a few days after the committee meeting, "that certain unsuspected possibilities for social science research lie hidden in the dusty attics and damp basements which now house the records of local governments."

Other men in the country also saw possibilities in the Survey; Herbert Kellar, curator of the McCormick Collection in Chicago and a man of vision and inspiration, was among them. At Christmas, 1935, at the Chattanooga convention of the American Historical Association, Kellar, with characteristic enthusiasm, supported the project and spoke at length to Evans of its potentialities. He suggested people who might serve as state project directors, and offered counsel and advice on many practical problems. Years later, Evans declared that Kellar "was an invaluable source of guidance and encouragement."

Faced with the prospects of using untrained and perhaps uninterested workers to do a work of great significance to archivists and to historians, Evans' most difficult but effective task was planning. In January, 1936, he published a mimeographed "Manual of the Survey of Historical Records," a clear statement of the project's purpose and a concise set of procedural rules to govern its activity.

Evans' instructions directed the Survey first to obtain a complete list of depositories of public records and historical manuscripts in each state. The state directors would then seek the permission of local custodians before beginning inventories. Before any workers were assigned to a project, state directors would instruct them fully in the preparation of the inventory forms. When they received their first field assignment a supervisor should accompany them for further instruction. After they had been at work for several days, the supervisor should visit them again to discuss any special difficulties which might have arisen.

Evans described in detail the general procedure the clerical workers were to follow in making an inventory. They should begin with the recent records of an administrative unit, for they were generally in the best order. By handling the current records, the workers would become familiar with the records of that agency. They should then go to the room in which the oldest records of the office were housed, and then work through the records chronologically. As the Survey was no stronger than its weakest researcher, the director provided for close supervision. "We have not ignored difficulties inherent in undertaking inventory work with relief labor," he said at the beginning of the project. He planned for workers to go out in pairs so that each could check the work of the other, and he also provided for additional checking in state and national offices.

Anticipating many problems in advance, by mid-January, 1936, Evans had the Survey in operation. Sargent B. Child was National Field Supervisor and Evans' chief assistant. Throughout the country, men interested in the project continued to make suggestions. In Chicago, Herbert Kellar plied Evans with questions: "Would you advise me as to the present situation in Illinois concerning these surveys? Who have you selected to direct them in the Chicago district? Who is interested in this subject in Chicago? With whom may I get in touch to further activities in an advisory capacity?"

Nudged by such interest and driven by his own energetic nature, Evans pushed forward rapidly. His reports were extensive and critical; he pulled no punches and spared his organization no sharp words when he deemed them appropriate, and he was capable of recognizing mistakes when they were made. "I am paying more and more attention to the causes for the estimated 15% error rather than the hoped for 85% success," he told Kellar in 1936. In many states, the project got off to a slow start because the national director had made no arrangements for local organization. He made no apology for his own failures, but he assumed responsibility for the mistakes he made. The reports also reflected the countless personality clashes involved in a national project. In Michigan, Mississippi, Missouri, Tennessee, and Florida, local officials would not, at first, co-operate with Survey officials. In other states, such as Wisconsin and Illinois, state directors complained of dictation and encroachment of local W. P. A. officials in their work. And in New Jersey (whence he had come to Washington) Evans made his only major political blunder when he appointed a Republican, George J. Miller, the Assistant State Attorney-General, as State Supervisor. That mistake corrected itself, however, as the state Democratic officialdom reluctantly agreed to let Miller remain in the job.

Elsewhere, state organizations and project plans ran more smoothly, and outstanding scholars and librarians agreed to direct the work in their states. At the beginning of the Survey, some of the state supervisors were Lester J. Cappon (Virginia), Christopher C. Crittenden (North Carolina), Curtis W. Garrison (Pennsylvania), Alston G. Field (Illinois), Thurston J. Davies (Colorado), James A. Robertson (Maryland), Milo M. Quaife (Michigan), T. C. Blegen (Minnesota), Edward P. Alexander (New York), William D. Overman (Ohio), and Miss Alice E. Smith (Wisconsin) until July 1, 1936, when she was succeeded by Jesse E. Boell.

As Evans worked out the problems of procedure and personality, the program began to move faster. On March 1, 1936 there were 600 persons employed on the project; by May 15 there were 1,450 at work. From 1936 to 1939 the national average was around 3,000 per month. Though most of the clerical workers were unskilled in historical research, they produced a worthwhile product because of the self-explanatory forms, the extensive instruction, and the careful supervision. "We believe that our organization is competent to furnish the needed supervision," Evans told a gathering of American librarians in May, 1936, "and that the product which we are turning out is capable of meeting the tests of critical historical scholarship."

As the project gained momentum, Kellar continued to advise and encourage Evans. At a Washington dinner in May, 1936, Kellar came to Evans' support. "Needless to say, I felt very much flattered by the confidence placed in me by yourself," Evans wrote Kellar. "I feel that you took a good chance and won, on your daring undertaking to analyze me, warts and all, in the presence of those who attended our . . . dinner. . . . You were perfectly grand to do what you did, and I shall be forever in your debt for doing it." Two weeks later, at a regional conference in Chicago organized by Kellar, he urged Evans to expand his activities to include cataloging manuscript collections. The director asked Kellar to "amplify" his remarks and write out "detailed suggestions for proceeding with the manuscript collection work."

Kellar complied, and included sample blank forms to be used in the inventory. His "Suggestions for the Survey of Manuscript Collections" was a masterpiece of simplicity and detail, carefully written with the untrained layman in mind. Kellar defined and described various types of manuscripts, explained how they might be located, and how they might be preserved and cataloged. "In answer to the question, what is a Survey of a Manuscript Collection—it may be defined as an examination of a group of manuscripts for the purpose of obtaining information of such character that when recorded it will serve as a guide to anyone who wishes to know reasonable detail about the collection or to make use of its materials." Kellar suggested that clerical workers first list the location, present ownership and custody of the collection, and how and where the various items in the collection originated; then individual items should be listed. From his long experience with the McCormick Collection, he even offered advice on the delicate task of gaining access to manuscript holdings. The supervisor should assemble as much information as possible about the prospect and his interests, he said. "Frequently such information will throw light on the proper method with which to make the contact and will also offer suggestions as to what to say after the initial approach is made."

The Manuscript Survey suggestions indicated the type of advice Kellar offered to Evans and the Historical Records Survey, but they did not stop there. Kellar was a man of ideas, and the magnitude of the Survey project appealed to him. In his work with the McCormick Collection he had had to do without trained help for filing and noting, so he was familiar with the problems of teaching untrained people to do historical and library work. He knew people all over the country who were interested in record surveying and collecting, and was able to offer sound advice as to personnel appointments.

On the basis of Kellar's ideas on the manuscript survey, in August, 1936, Evans proposed that the Historical Records Survey be enlarged to include such projects. The survey of public records was nearly complete, Evans said, but still there was wide-spread unemployment among white-collar workers in urban areas. No more useful work could be found, he said, than indexing newspapers and manuscripts. "I assure you that this proposal is made reluctantly and not because of over-weening ambition," Evans assured Mrs. Ellen S. Woodward, Assistant Administrator for Women's Work in the W. P. A. organization. "My recommendation is made with the conviction that the Survey can assist in the rapid employment of a large number of clerical white-collar workers . . . and produce a highly useful product," he explained.

Thus a new project began, and Evans prepared an instruction manual to outline it, based on suggestions made by Kellar, Binkley, Solon J. Buck, and Miss Grace L. Nute of Minnesota. "We already have most of the general ideas of purpose and . . . procedure, and it merely remains to gear such ideas to W. P. A. workers," he told Binkley. When he finished a draft of the manual, Evans sent copies to Kellar and others for their comments.

In his response, Kellar continued to praise the survey projects. Of the manuscript inventory, he said that it would bring to light an "amazing amount of first class material." He was highly pleased with the public records survey. "The gigantic task of surveying the county records in the more than three thousand counties of the United States . . . bringing to light and making available basic information relating to the local governments of our country, is one of the most worthwhile and valuable of governmental activities in recent years," he told Evans. Kellar also wrote Harry Hopkins to compliment Evans' work. "The inventory of the records of each county," he said, "has been prepared with efficiency and accuracy, and in conformance with the best historical standards."

As Kellar indicated, the Historical Records Survey had gone

a long way in a short time and was ready to turn out its finished product. In most of the 3,066 counties in the United States, relief workers in court houses and other depositories filled out the forms describing the various records. "We have sent one or more workers into every courthouse in the entire country," Evans announced in 1938 (though in his final report in 1942 Sargent B. Child estimated that the field work was complete in only ninety per cent of the nation's counties). These workers took down the information on printed forms regarding "all the records that can be found of every agency of county government from the beginning of the county's history." The completed forms went direct to state headquarters. (The ideal organization Evans had envisioned in the beginning, including district supervisors in the states, had disappeared when his allocation was drastically cut.) At state headquarters highly trained workers edited them into an inventory of county archives. They added a brief historical sketch of the county, a political analysis of the county government, and an essay on the care and housing of its records. Though not every county inventory received such treatment, that was the ideal which Survey leaders set for themselves. Each inventory did contain a classified descriptive list of the county's records, and that was the most valuable part of the booklet, which was generally mimeographed for a limited distribution. For every set of county records inventoried, there was available a list by title, dates, quantity, description of contents, arrangement, indexing, size, and location of all records.

The county inventories attracted wide-spread attention among scholars. An early report was of the records of Muskogee County, Oklahoma, which Survey leaders offered as a sample of the work the project could do. Similarly, the Survey of Manuscript Collections offered as an example the inventory of the papers of William Walker in Louisiana. "I believe that our project can do this quality of work in most of the states of the Union, after we have had an opportunity to complete our manuscript instructions and to train a limited corps of workers," Evans told Kellar. W. P. A. regulations prohibited the printing of these booklets, so unless local officials could locate a sponsor to bear the cost of publication, they were mimeographed in Survey offices. They were then deposited in selected libraries in each of the states and in several foreign countries. The mimeographed guides to county records, church records, and manuscript collections proved to be the most valuable contribution of the Historical Records Survey.

In addition to its work in public records and manuscript collections, by late 1937 the Survey had branched out into other areas of activity. It was directing inventories of Early American Imprints, under the supervision of Douglas C. McMurtrie; listing portraits in public and semi-public depositories; and surveying the records of some 235,000 churches in the country. Other major surveys of the W. P. A. were the Historical American Buildings Survey and the Historical American Merchant Marine Survey. Indeed, so diverse and so important had the Historical Records Survey's work become that W. P. A. officials feared they would lose control of the project. "Confidentially, I had a brief chat with Mr. Hopkins," Evans wrote Binkley in March, 1937. "He thinks we should keep our chickens under our own roof, rather than having them stray off to the Archives or Library of Congress."

The Records Survey was engaged in a broad program, but Kellar's active mind was yet dissatisfied. Other projects the Survey should undertake, he told Hopkins, were digests of newspaper files and indexes for unpublished records of the U. S. Census and of the Federal Land Office. Binkley, another man of ideas, was likewise unsatisfied; he envisioned a national survey of elections with analyses down to precincts, to obtain a more accurate picture of political trends. There was still much work to be done as the depression abated, but the Survey personnel began to drift away to other jobs. In 1939 Evans resigned as National Director to take a position in the Library of Congress, where he subsequently became chief librarian. Evans was succeeded in the Survey by his assistant, Sargent B. Child, and during the last year of its operation B. Alden Lillywhite was the National Director.

Evans did not leave the project until its transition to local sponsorship was successfully completed. With defense spending and war orders for the "Arsenal of Democracy," the need for federal relief was passed. A bill to abolish federal W. P. A. projects became law, and on August 21, 1939 they closed down. Theatre, writers, music and art, and historical records projects continued only as local projects in the states. Evans had foreseen the eventuality and had already obtained local sponsorship in each of the nine regions of the W. P. A. Local support for the work was obtained in every state, and most local organizations did not cease operating for a single day. "The Historical Records Survey is the only ex-Federal project which is operating everywhere in the United States today," Child reported in May, 1940. "I think that fact alone speaks eloquently of the determination and the tenacity of Dr. Evans' purpose. . . . Our inventories, keys, and guides are being issued at a more rapid rate, our program is larger, and we have a greater employment of certified workers." The Records Survey had been broken down into fifty-one projects, each under a local sponsor, and the work of the national director became largely that of maintaining editorial standards and publishing inventories. Indeed, with field work completed in most of the local administrative units, the work of publication was greatly increased. "I am *not* among those who believe that high standards of accuracy and form of presentation are incompatible with mass production," Child concluded.

Though the work went on in the states, the national Survey had come to an end. The mounting war tension and its insatiable demand for manpower cut increasingly into the rolls of the W. P. A., and the coming of the war in December, 1941 curtailed its operations. Administratively, the Records Survey came to an end in April, 1942, when the Service Division of the W. P. A. re-directed its program to the war effort. Permission was usually granted to complete projects (especially publication) which were in progress, but the major portion of the Survey's unfinished business was turned over to a housekeeping detail for safeguarding and deposit for the duration of the war.

The Survey made a great contribution in the identification and publication of aids to historical research. In five years its workers collected a remarkable amount of information, and much of it was published for the use of scholars. In a final report on the work of the Historical Records Survey, Child listed its tangible achievements. By 1942 the Survey had published 628 volumes of county archival inventories, 584 volumes of federal archives inventories, and 28 volumes of state archives inventories. There were 180 volumes of municipal and town archives, 107 guides to manuscript collections, 164 volumes of church archives, and 49 volumes of American imprints. A checklist of those publications compiled in April, 1943, required 85 pages to describe them.

There was also a great mass of undigested data, "tons of material," Child said, which was deposited in state archives and libraries by the housekeeping detail. Most of this information has remained undisturbed ever since. There were unpublished inventories of county records and transcriptions and abstracts of source materials. All of this material, though it was not incorporated in any of the Survey's publications, has unlimited potential value to the historical researcher. It is a bibliographical tool for future studies. "Ten times as much inventory and research material has been collected and placed in orderly arrangement as has been published," Child said. "A great deal of valuable work has been done in a very short time."

Prodigious accomplishment in a short time could well describe the entire operation of the Survey. It was the purpose of the W. P. A., Evans said in justification of the project, to create a "second library system" in the country by making unpublished documentary materials as readily available to officials and researchers as were printed materials. Of the published guides he said, "We like to think of them as being hand-books for the administration of the day-to-day business of the county and as guides to mountains of research data for historians and others." The Survey, he declared, not only produced inventories; it furnished the basis for an "historical renaissance in America."

Much of Evans' statement must be discounted as the enthusiastic observations of the project's pilot. If there has developed a "renaissance" of history in America, a proposition which might be debated, it could hardly be traced to the publication of county court records or indexes of census returns. But that in no way detracted from the real utility of the Survey's work. At its inception in 1936, Evans told historians that the inventories would serve American historical scholarship, and he realized that aim. Had the economic crisis lasted longer, or the war not come so soon, additional indexing and cataloging of source materials would likely have been completed. Whatever else it did, the Survey proved that high standards of accuracy were not incompatible with mass production, and that properly supervised clerical workers were capable of relieving scholars of much of the routine in research.

From the published guides, and from the masses of materials collected but not published, a new approach to local history was made possible. Authentic information of archival nature may document county and state histories, and will therefore permit more valid interpretation of the American past. Significant generalizations about election trends and local issues may replace the genealogical encomiums of a generation ago. The light such rejuvenated local histories could shed upon the development of national history is incalculable.

The Survey produced other indirect results. It aroused in localities and states an awareness of the value of records and the need of preserving them, and it encouraged the establishment of state archives departments. It also provided training for archival directors and workers; many state archivists, curators of state and local records collections, and National

Archives and Library of Congress staff members got their start in the Historical Records Survey organization.

There is evidence, however, that the fruits of the Survey, the printed and mimeographed guides, have not been as widely used as they might have been. A poll recently taken among thirty-five young historians from all parts of the country and representing the best graduate training in American history revealed that very few had used the Survey's guides, and some of them were even ignorant of their existence. Most of them explained that their research was not localized enough to justify use of the county inventories, but others admitted that it never occurred to them to consult the guides and that their graduate instructors had not suggested it to them. Evidence from so restricted a sample is not conclusive, but it is indicative of a blind spot in the use of bibliographical aids to research. The Survey's guides are only recently beginning to appear in essays on research materials and in manuals for instructing graduate students in research techniques. Perhaps this will stimulate more interest in these sources. Unless this happens, the painstaking work was done in vain, and any continuation of it would be difficult to justify.

Despite its notable achievements, the Survey did not complete its work. When it was disbanded, many of its projects, such as an annotated bibliography of American history, an atlas of congressional votes on specific issues, or a continuation of the compiled *Messages and Papers of the Presidents* from 1898 to 1938, lacked only a little work to make them ready for the printer. Others, such as an index to the *Official Records of the Rebellion,* and extensive newspaper indexes, were planned but not begun. Considering the unfinished work of the Survey, the judgment of a consultant to the W. P. A.

seemed valid. Speaking to the Society of American Archivists in 1942, Miss Lillian Kessler said: "The Historical Records Survey has come to an end but it was only a beginning."

BIBLIOGRAPHY

Blegen, Theodore C. "Some Aspects of Historical Work under the New Deal." *Mississippi Valley Historical Review,* 21: 195–206 (September, 1934).

Child, Sargent B. "What is Past is Prologue." *The American Archivist,* 5: 217–227 (October, 1942).

Evans, Luther H. "The Historical Records Survey." A statement on its progress and accomplishments presented to the Sub-committee of the Senate Committee on Education and Labor on March 1, 1938 and reprinted by the W. P. A.

————. "W. P. A. Fashions New Tools for Research." A paper presented at the 31st annual meeting of the Mississippi Valley Historical Association, Indianapolis, Ind., April 28, 1938 and re-printed by the W. P. A.

Historical Records Survey. General Project Correspondence, State Correspondence, Records Relating to the Origin of the Survey, all in Works Progress Administration section (Records Group 69) of the National Archives.

————. "Manual of the Survey of Historical Records." Mimeo-graphed by the W. P. A., 1936; Supplementary instructions were added to govern the Church Records Inventory, the Manuscript Collections Inventory, and the editing and publication of the in-ventory booklets.

————. "The American Imprints Inventory: A Preliminary State-ment of Plan." Mimeographed by the W. P. A., 1937.

Kellar, Herbert A. "An Appraisal of the Historical Records Survey of the Works Progress Administration," in A. F. Kuhlman, ed., *Archives and Libraries,* pp. 44–59. Chicago, 1940.

————. "The Historian and Life." *Mississippi Valley Historical Re-view,* 34: 3–36 (June, 1947).

Morrison, Perry D. "Everyman's Archive: Robert C. Binkley and the Historical Records Survey." *The Call Number,* 18: 4–9 (Spring, 1957).

United States Federal Works Agency. *Final Report on the WPA Program, 1935–1943.* Washington, n. d.

————. *Inventory: An Appraisal of the Works Progress Administration.* Washington, 1938.

United States National Archives (Betty Herscher, comp.). "Preliminary Checklist of the Records of the Historical Records Survey, 1935–1942." Mimeographed, 1945.

United States Works Progress Administration, Division of Service Projects. "Bibliography of Research Projects Reports: Check List of Historical Records Survey Publications." W. P. A. Technical Series, Research and Records Bibliography No. 7, prepared by Sargent B. Child and Dorothy P. Holmes, mimeographed, 1943.

MANUSCRIPT COLLECTING

by LUCILE M. KANE

Minnesota Historical Society

THE contemporary historian is so thoroughly grounded in documentation that he often takes for granted the manuscript resources he uses. Preoccupied in using the great institutional collections, he may be unaware of the saga of their evolution and their influence upon his discipline.

The chronicler of early America was not a scientific historian. His was a highly personal history, woven out of observation, recollection, and opinion. He frequently served the purpose of polemic rather than the advancement of truth. But his very quality of partisanship led him to seek documentary sources that would support and elaborate his preconceptions. Some became so fascinated with the search that they relished the hunt as much as the writing based on the search. These collector-historians personally saved from destruction many important manuscripts; they herded private papers into institutions; they fired historical institutions with their own collecting zeal; and they established a tradition of service to Clio.

One of the earliest of the collector-historians was Jeremy Belknap, a New Hampshire minister, who in the 1780's undertook a history of his state. Studying at Harvard under Thomas Prince, the famed collector of historical memorabilia, Belknap, too, soon turned collector to overcome the paucity of materials. Ferreting out the manuscripts he needed in public offices and the "garrets and ratholes" of old New Hampshire houses, Belknap developed the skill and persistence of a successful collector. However successful, Belknap was keenly aware of the loss and damage to records which had escaped him.

Belknap was also distressed at the tragedies that sometimes befell collected manuscripts. He had personal knowledge of the havoc wrought by the American Revolution. An angry mob had scattered Thomas Hutchinson's papers in the streets of Boston. Many of Governor John Wentworth's manuscripts had been burned in vengeance. But most tragic of all had been the destruction of the Thomas Prince collection when the British occupied the Old South Church. Conditioned by such losses, Belknap became a leading advocate of institutional manuscript libraries and actively sponsored the founding of the Massachusetts Historical Society.

A generation after Belknap, another collector-historian, Jared Sparks, followed in his predecessor's tradition. Sparks was absorbed in the Revolution, and like Belknap, he was forced to search for his own materials. His first major venture was editing George Washington's writings, to which he secured access through Bushrod Washington. Experience with the Washington manuscripts fired his interest in other materials of the period, and he tracked them in America and Europe. Sparks, Peter Force, and their contemporaries capitalized on the rising nationalism of the 1830's and 1840's to make documented history and manuscripts editions a paying proposition. Many of the manuscripts thus harvested were ultimately sold to institutional libraries.

Sparks and other similar collectors focused their attention on the grand political and military themes of eastern United States. They sought most eagerly the papers of statesmen and military men. Their heroes were Washington, Lafayette, Jefferson, Franklin, and Madison, men who had guided the nation through its birth and national crisis. Though the westward march had already begun to pass beyond the Ohio and Mississippi valleys, and Lewis and Clark had crossed the continent to the Pacific, the attention of eastern collectors was still fixed on the region east of the Appalachians. But a new age was coming. Historians with a fresh and dynamic inspiration to match the western pioneers were suggesting new dimensions for American history. Francis Parkman used the entire West to paint his epic of the struggle for the American heartland. William H. Prescott further enlarged the canvas by including Mexico and Peru. And Hubert Howe Bancroft dramatically reminded American historians that their nation stretched to the far Pacific.

Lyman Draper was among the advance guard of the collectors who broke out of the eastern orbit. Born in 1815 and raised in Lockport, New York, on the banks of the Erie Canal, Draper grew up on the tales of the West and its heroes. At seventeen he began writing historical articles for the Rochester *Gem*, and he continued to pursue his interest in western personalities through his classical education at Granville College, in Ohio. Before finishing college, Draper embarked on the collecting career that earned him the title of "Plutarch of Western History."

Draper did not write the books he envisioned on Daniel Boone, George Rogers Clark, and the other giants of the West. But the manuscripts he gathered in the backwoods of trans-Appalachia were monument enough to his historical contribution. The Draper Collection is the symbol of a new school of American history, a badge of western independence from New England's hold on American historiography.

As Draper was to the trans-Appalachian West, so Hubert Howe Bancroft was to the Pacific West. Born in Ohio in 1834, Bancroft was swept along in the restless tide of the westward movement. After stints as a clerk in a Buffalo book shop and as a book peddler in his native Ohio, at nineteen he shipped for California. In a few years he rose from poverty to wealth and prominence as California's leading book seller. His phenomenal business success gave him the wealth and leisure to indulge his own interests in collecting. His judgment, patience, and imagination made Bancroft the first great collector of materials on the Pacific West.

Bancroft's motivation for collecting was to write a comprehensive historical series on the Pacific Coast states. To gather the materials he needed he combed the book shops at home and abroad, appointed agents to buy entire libraries, and employed copyists to transcribe documents and manuscripts he could not acquire. Attracted by the drama of his enterprise, old California families added to Bancroft's growing store of personal papers, reminiscences, books, pamphlets, and newspapers. This grist was ground into the projected historical series, but more important, it was preserved for historical research when it was acquired in 1905 by the University of California Library.

From a modern vantage point, a contribution of the early

collectors as significant as their collections was their concern for adequate repositories. Belknap, hunting manuscripts for the Massachusetts Historical Society, expressed his belief that "there is nothing like having a good repository." Alarmed at the danger to research materials, Sparks observed that the best way to preserve them was through "societies in the several states established for the purpose." Draper, though keeping his collection separate from the Wisconsin Historical Society, made the Society an active collector in its area. And Bancroft's collection became intellectual equipment of a great university.

The agitation for repositories began to bear fruit in the latter half of the nineteenth century. After a faltering beginning, historical societies, special libraries, colleges, and universities by the dozen joined the crusade for records preservation. Their corporate nature gave them a permanence and a potency which even the most devoted individual lacked. Through their members, friends, and alumni, they aroused a widening circle of interest in an otherwise apathetic public. With private and public funds they constructed buildings, hired staffs, and purchased additional material. The regional and topical emphasis of their collections influenced the course of American historiography; but their close association with historians, in turn, exposed them to intellectual currents that broadened their collecting policies.

The number and variety of historical societies placed them in the most prominent position among institutional collectors of manuscripts. Beginning with the Massachusetts Historical Society, a myriad of state, local, and regional organizations spread with remarkable speed across the nation. By 1884, when the American Historical Association was formed, over two hundred societies were in existence.

Although many societies did not outlive the enthusiasm present at their founding, those that survived accomplished notable work. In the spirit of a crusade, they rescued manuscripts with varying degrees of diligence. Some followed Belknap's doctrine of active solicitation of materials. They circulated lists of materials they wanted, bombarded prospects with letters, and tracked prized papers through genealogical labyrinths. Into their vaults poured a stream of papers of local political leaders, businessmen, educators, and churchmen; the records of frontier industries, churches, clubs, and cultural groups; and the reminiscences of pioneer settlers.

Important as were the historical societies in practicing the gospel of manuscript collecting, their sins were numerous. Most of them were guided by antiquarians, whose narrow focus made their societies myopic; they often concentrated on the trivial and commonplace. Venerating "old" manuscripts, they neglected contemporary, indigenous material. Many, too, were absorbed in the political and military facets of history. When the late nineteenth century historians penetrated economic and social fields, the shortcomings of collecting institutions became increasingly obvious.

The organization of the American Historical Association in 1884 was attended by sharp criticism of historical societies. The movement was, in part, a protest by discontented scholars against the societies' stagnation and provincialism. At an early meeting of the Association, Moses Coit Tyler urged the societies to broaden their collections and to construct fireproof buildings in which to house them. In 1897, J. Franklin Jameson followed this gentle injunction with a stinging rebuke. He lamented the societies' passion for beginnings, "weak devotion" to genealogy, and ignorance of new historical fields. Few people, he alleged, "care a rush whether the Blue Boar Tavern stood in First street or Second street." He invited the historical organizations to pull out of stagnant waters into the main stream, taking as their province "American history locally exemplified."

To combat the lethargy that gripped research libraries, the Association in 1895 appointed a Historical Manuscripts Commission to broaden records preservation. It encouraged the deposit of privately owned manuscripts and urged repositories to collect the neglected sources for social, economic, and recent history. The Commission also prevailed against the disturbing practice of auctioning off collections by the piece. Too, it encouraged governmental units to preserve their records and publish their important documents. Following its own precepts, the Commission edited several series of manuscripts. Indeed, in later years, it concentrated more on manuscript publication than on collecting.

The expanding interest in manuscript collecting was also manifest in the growth of special libraries devoted to collections on a subject, period, area, or individual. Early America had produced such prototypes as the Essex Institute at Salem, the Filson Club at Louisville, and the American Philosophical Society at Philadelphia. Outstanding among the new special collections were the William L. Clements Library at the University of Michigan, the Clarence M. Burton Collection in the Detroit Public Library, the Hubert Howe Bancroft Library at the University of California, the Henry E. Huntington Library and Art Gallery at San Marino, the Baker Library at Harvard University, the Rutherford B. Hayes Memorial Library at Fremont, and the James Ford Bell Collection at the University of Minnesota. These libraries have immeasurably strengthened the nation's research resources, making available to American scholars choice materials that might otherwise have been held in private hands, obscured in general repositories, or lost to foreign institutions.

The McCormick Historical Association, founded in 1912, was a unique aspect of the movement for special libraries. Its distinction was that it was supported by a private family; its good fortune that it had an especially able director. Herbert Kellar, in the tradition of Bancroft and Draper, showed great zeal and vision in assembling his materials. He collected books, periodicals, pamphlets, almanacs, maps, and pictures, as well as a broad range of unpublished materials. Numbering over a million pieces, the manuscripts include papers of the Cyrus Hall McCormick family, collateral families, and records of firms absorbed by the International Harvester Company in 1902. Acquisition by the State Historical Society of Wisconsin insures the continuing preservation of the collection.

The growth of general and specialized manuscript repositories has not kept pace with the even more rapid expansion of the historian's interests. New fields of social, economic, and intellectual history have given new meaning to manuscript collecting. A case in point is church history. Freeing church history from the domination of sectarian churchmen, historians came to regard religious studies as guides to American character and intellectual development. Such studies obviously required the utilization of a vast accumulation of church records formerly of interest only to particular denominations. Fortunately, some of these records have been preserved by church-related historical societies, colleges, and other research libraries.

Among the religious groups most active in the preservation

of their records were the Presbyterian Church through its historical society founded in 1852, the Episcopal Church through its transcription of colonial documents in England, the Church of Latter-Day Saints through its genealogical collection at Salt Lake City, and the Catholic Church, famed for its network of parish, diocesan, and archdiocesan archives. However well motivated, some of these institutions have permitted improper housing and casual administration to endanger their valuable collections.

Of the many changed attitudes toward manuscript collecting, no developments have been more startling than those affecting business records. Repositories had incidentally collected sources for economic history in earlier years through personal papers and residual records of old firms. But it remained for the new economic interpretation of history to give business records a respectable priority on the collector's agenda.

The very bulk of business records created problems for institutions collecting them. The avalanche glutted storage areas and overwhelmed catalogers accustomed to more refined ore. Threatened by such massive quantity, collecting institutions became apprehensive of the future. To those who took a long view, it was clear that while research libraries might absorb eighteenth and nineteenth century records, they could not possibly house the essential documentation of the twentieth-century economy.

The only alternative to institutional collection of business records seemed to be the creation of company archives. The Firestone Tire and Rubber Company was the first large corporation to undertake the maintenance of its records under professional direction, and it was followed by such firms as the Connecticut Mutual Life Insurance Company, the Pennsylvania Telephone Company, and the Ford Motor Company. While progressive firms readily see the advantage of records programs, the novelty of the idea and the initial costs of installation have made progress slow.

Fortunately for the historian, archivists working with government records during World War II gained experience in managing collections of massive quantity and developed a strategy for fighting the battle against paper. In 1949, out of the co-operative efforts of businessmen, archivists, and historians, came the National Records Management Council. Under the imaginative leadership of Emmett J. Leahy, the Council developed efficient procedures for records control, which have reduced maintenance costs while improving accessibility.

Techniques for evaluating business records were important tools for discriminating collectors. The assimilation, however, did not take place without dislocations. To collectors trained in manuscript conservation, records destruction was difficult to accept. Although many had taken pensive tours through warehouses and had tried piecemeal to evaluate collections measured by the ton, it was hard for them to depart from the old ways. The transition was not made easier by the advocates of the new methods, who persistently lauded the "dollars and cents" benefits accruing from records destruction. Although most of them recommended preservation of a nucleus of important papers, they subordinated historical values to such an extent that collectors feared for the future.

The records of business are but part of the raw materials for the new economic history; the records of organized labor also gained attention. Several institutions, such as the University of Michigan, the State Historical Society of Wisconsin, and the John Crerar Library, have built collections of printed materials on the labor movement, and other research libraries collected some manuscript records. But as late as 1940 neither historians nor collectors were fully conscious of labor's records. In 1948 Lester J. Cappon wrote that the field was a "kind of 'no man's land' which has distressed the historian venturing into it much more than the archivist who has neglected it or the labor leader who seems blissfully unaware of its significance."

Signs of a change were evident in the years following Cappon's statement. In 1948 the Society of American Archivists turned its attention to labor records and soon a special Committee on Labor Union Archives devoted itself to the field. Other significant developments were the establishment of embryonic archives supported by labor unions, a labor-records survey by the State Historical Society of Wisconsin, and the appearance of articles stressing the importance of neglected sources for labor history.

The potential sources for labor history are vast. In a survey sponsored by the Ford Foundation, Vaughn Bornet found that the archives of labor include the files of 75,000 locals, 109 international unions, 50 state and territorial federations, 821 city central organizations of the A. F. of L., 33 unions of the C. I. O., 40 state industrial union councils, 247 city and county councils, and 73 railroad brotherhood and other independent unions. Citing the meager use that had been made of this material, Bornet reminded union leaders, as historians had reminded businessmen a decade before, that it is unhealthy for the history of an organization to be written without reference to its records.

Some observers see a virtue in the late start in collecting labor records. Previously ignored by collectors, many of these records are still in the possession of the unions. Thus they are immediately susceptible to a management program administered by the labor movement itself.

Stimulated by developments in the archival field and the vogue of institutional history, many colleges and universities have organized their own records on a professional basis. Some institutions have deposited their administrative files in their libraries, some have administered them with their historical manuscripts, while a few have established separate archives departments.

Other dimensions to manuscript collecting have been realized through the use of mechanical recording devices. Collectors and historians have always accepted the principle of supplementing written records with oral. The Library of Congress has built a magnificent collection of indigenous speech patterns and folk songs using the older phonograph records; and historians and collectors have used various techniques to record personal testimony. Magnetic tape, however, has brought oral history into flower. A research project at Columbia University led the way in developing criteria for selecting informants, techniques of interrogation, and processes for converting tapes into usable transcripts.

In their enthusiasm for the dramatic new medium, several institutions embarked on ambitious projects for recording interviews. They soon learned, however, that the production of good source material by this method was a time-consuming and expensive undertaking. The wider development of oral history must await the expansion of institutional budgets and support by foundations, businesses, and special groups.

Although shifting emphases and technical developments have altered the nature of manuscript collecting, the chase has lost none of its fascination. And though hunters of the past have captured great treasures, the supply seems undiminished. One collector submits that the pursuit of manuscripts "is possibly one of the most thrilling businesses a person can engage in, this side of swallowing fire, handling snakes at a Holy Roller meeting, or tracking down international spies." Illustrative of the adventure of collecting is the "Cornshucks Story" as told by Herbert Kellar:

"I had been quite successful in finding and securing manuscripts in Virginia to be added to the McCormick Collection and had spent considerable time in that state. Ulrich Phillips was intrigued with the idea of going on a manuscript hunt and proposed that we go together. This was finally arranged and we met one fall at the Dutch Inn in Lexington, where I customarily stayed. When Ulrich arrived he had with him Ryan McKissick of South Carolina who evidenced a desire to accompany us.

"I was feeling a bit on the spot, because I wanted to come through with some manuscripts, but you just can't pull them like a rabbit out of a hat. Looking through my notes I found that George Armentrout, who lived in an adjoining county, had once told me that he had some old papers in his attic. So we concluded to try him. We went on the train to Greenville then.

"We hired a car to take us to the Armentrout farm. When we reached the vicinity I discovered that there were several Armentrouts and that we had the wrong one. I asked about George and was told that the lady where we were was his sister and that George had died. So I asked the sister if he had

had any old papers. She said she thought there were some old papers in some sacks in his attic, which was some distance away. We expressed a desire to seem them so she said she would take us. However, she concluded our car would not make it over the rough roads so we had to take her model T. Ulrich was tall and thin. McKissick was very rotund, I was not thin as you know, and the lady was not thin either, but we all crowded into the old model T.

"It was an open car and I can still see Ulrich's long arms trying to hold the side curtains to keep out the cold damp wind which was blowing that day. When we neared the house we came to a creek and here Mrs. Armentrout said we must leave the car and cross the creek on a swinging bridge. The bridge had no hand rails and we all looked at it in dismay except McKissick who rashly started across. When he reached the middle or lowest part of the bridge, in he went. The water was very cold and quite deep, and poor McKissick was thoroughly soaked. When we got into the house, which had been closed up, Mrs. Armentrout made a fire for him to dry out. Then she went to the attic and returned very soon with a huge sack, like a cotton picking sack, which was full of manuscripts. I put in my hand and pulled out a manuscript dated 1795. We asked her if there were more and she said yes there were five sacks. Ulrich whispered to me, 'I think we should get them, what shall we offer?' I asked if she would be willing to sell them and she said 'yes' so I offered five dollars a sack sight unseen. She agreed. We then had to get them back across the creek to the model T. This was no easy job but was finally accomplished. We tied them to the top of the car and on the running boards and looking like a moving hay stack returned to the other farm and our own car. On the way we decided to send them by freight from the little town of Greenville to Lexington. We told the station agent what they were and after much search he said he could not take them because they were not listed in his book. We said he had to take them or we would take them in the passenger car. He protested mightily but finally had an inspiration. 'Do you mind if I call them corn shucks?' We did not mind so we paid thirty cents apiece for five sacks of corn shucks from Greenville to Lexington. Arriving at the Dutch Inn, Mrs. Owen, the proprietress, used to my vagaries, promptly rented us an extra room for the corn shucks and we spent the balance of the day and all the next going through our find.

"I had a nice pile of agricultural items, Ulrich had some slavery items and surprisingly McKissick had a few South Carolina papers. The last item I picked up was a receipt for locating some land in the 'Dark and Bloody Ground' and was signed by Daniel Boone."

Behind the dramatic acquisition of manuscripts lies long hours of patient planning and plodding routine. Every systematic collector relies on a file variously called the "master list," "possible accessions," "lead file," or "tips." Through careful study of his area, the collector enters names of important persons, institutions, events, and movements, which set a pattern for his collecting. He adds to his file data gathered in conversations, correspondence, telephone calls, and field trips. Collectors often keep records of their searches, for their experiences are guides to those who follow them, and the history of a collection is important to historians who use it. Planned collecting has reduced the element of surprise, but, fortunately, it has not eliminated it.

Once a collector has located desirable manuscripts he often

must assume the role of diplomat to acquire the material for his institution. Persons who have manuscripts often do not understand the historian's needs, and they do not give up their papers without considering how they will be used. A woman growing old in her ancestral home, surrounded by family mementos, values her personal ties with the past more highly than the advancement of historical knowledge. Or descendants may have an exaggerated sense of responsibility to protect family reputation. An old radical's son may hesitate to re-exhibit his father's political individualism by releasing his papers. A conscientious daughter may fear that an ancient scandal may live again to blemish the reputation of her father. Law firms ponder their ethical responsibilities to clients; doctors must protect the confidence of patients; businessmen and labor unions must guard their trade secrets and their competitive positions. Unless the collector overcomes these objections, he may witness the partial or total destruction of records. He is a vigilant and patient middleman who explains the historian's purpose to laymen, and the owner's dilemma to historians.

With the aid of legal counsel, the collector can usually solve the most intricate problems of donors. Agreements can be reached that protect the essential interests of all parties concerned. These agreements may provide for restricted access for a stipulated period, restriction on the use of specific items, or a system of family or organizational control. In formulating agreements, the collector's objective is to secure for the historian a full collection governed by minimum restrictions, while encouraging the donor to deposit papers rather than destroy them.

Although institutions acquire papers as gifts, manuscripts

are also valuable commercial items. In the United States there are more than a dozen outstanding dealers and numerous casual traders who carry on a brisk commerce. Institutions with funds often enrich their collections through purchases from dealers; those without money must watch items they covet being sold to the highest bidder. But more tragic than the commercialization of collecting is the dispersal of collections. Dealers, no matter how much they may be in sympathy with historical ideals, must market their wares to their best advantage. In the past profitable marketing often involved splitting collections. The situation is improving, however, as dealers have co-operated with institutions to limit the practice.

Modern life poses new problems for the historian who seeks to interpret it and for the institution which seeks to collect its documentary remains. Contemporary American society is indeed composed of "organization men," who work, play, worship, vote, and think as members of a group rather than as individuals. Even our leaders are swallowed up by the groups they head. The history of the contemporary age may be written more from records of organizations than from the literary remains of individuals.

Intensification of field work and co-operation among institutions give the greatest promise of overcoming the larger problems of collectors. The employment of trained field workers transfers the point of initial evaluation of manuscripts from the overcrowded and understaffed repository and results in greater selectivity in collecting. The success of institutions with staffs of trained collectors proves that rich historical treasures lie in wait for those who go out to find them. Limitation of space and a growing professional conscience has also replaced petty competition with friendly co-operation among collecting institutions. It is now rather common practice for collectors to consult one another when they locate manuscripts of primary interest to others, to transfer papers that rightfully belong in other areas, and to facilitate the microfilming of collections of wide use and great importance. Commenting on competition among institutions, the *Ad Hoc* Committee of the American Historical Association observed in 1951 that *"the important thing is to bring valuable manuscripts into a safe place where they will be most available to the largest number of users."* While varied interpretation of the principle allows latitude for healthy competition, wide subscription to the ideal is in Clio's best interest.

BIBLIOGRAPHY

American Association for State and Local History. *Church Archives and History*, Bulletin No. 10. Boston, 1941.

Bauer, Harry C. "Where Manuscripts Should Be." *Oregon Historical Quarterly*, 51: 163–167 (September, 1950).

Benjamin, Mary A. *Autographs: A Key to Collecting*. New York, 1946.

Bischoff, William N. "Tracing Manuscript Sources." *Oregon Historical Quarterly*, 51: 156–163 (September, 1950).

Blegen, Theodore C. "Our Widening Province." *Mississippi Valley Historical Review*, 31: 3–20 (June, 1944).

Bombard, Owen W. "A New Measure of Things Past." *American Archivist*, 18: 123–132 (April, 1955).

Bornet, Vaughn D. "The New Labor History: A Challenge for American Historians." *The Historian*, 18: 1–24 (Autumn, 1955).

————. "Oral History *Can* Be Worthwhile." *American Archivist*, 18: 241–253 (July, 1955).

Browne, Henry J. "Raiding Labor Records." *American Archivist*, 17: 262–264 (July, 1954).

Cole, Arthur H. and Cochran, Thomas C. "Business Manuscripts: A Pressing Problem." *Journal of Economic History*, 5: 43–64 (May, 1945).

Ford, Worthington C. "Manuscripts and Historical Archives." American Historical Association, *Annual Report* (1913), 1: 77–84.

Holmes, Oliver Wendell. "The Evaluation and Preservation of Business Archives." *American Archivist*, 1: 171–185 (October, 1938).

————. "Some Reflections on Business Archives in the United States." *American Archivist*, 17: 291–304 (October, 1954).

Hower, Ralph M. *The Preservation of Business Records*. Boston, 1941.

Jameson, J. Franklin. *The American Historian's Raw Materials, An Address . . . at the Dedication of the William L. Clements Library of Americana. . . .* Ann Arbor, 1923.

————. "The Functions of State and Local Historical Societies With Respect to Research and Publication." American Historical Association, *Annual Report* (1897), pp. 53–59.

Jennings, John Melville. "Archival Activity in American Universities and Colleges." *American Archivist*, 12: 155–163 (April, 1949).

Lewinson, Paul. "The Archives of Labor." *American Archivist*, 17: 19–24 (January, 1954).

Lovett, Robert W. "Business Records." *American Archivist*, 13: 303–305 (July, 1950).

McNeil, Donald R., ed. *The American Collector*. Madison, 1955.

Metcalf, Keyes D. "Coöperative Development of Research Collections in the United States." *American Documentation*, 2: 18–20 (January, 1951).

"Report of *Ad Hoc* Committee on Manuscripts Set Up by the American Historical Association. . . ." *American Archivist*, 14: 229–240 (July, 1951).

"Report of the Historical Manuscripts Commission." American Historical Association, *Annual Report* (1896), 1: 467–480.

"Second Annual Report of the Historical Manuscripts Commission of the American Historical Association." American Historical Association, *Annual Report* (1897), pp. 399–403.

Schiller, Irving P. "A Program for the Management of Business Records." Business Historical Society, *Bulletin,* 21: 44–48 (April, 1947).

[Sparks, Jared]. "Materials for American History." *North American Review,* 23: 275–294 (October, 1826).

Sweet, William Warren. "Church Archives in the United States." *American Archivist,* 14: 323–331 (October, 1951).

Tyler, Moses Coit. "The Neglect and Destruction of Historical Materials in This Country." American Historical Association, *Papers,* 2: 20–22.

Wilson, Dwight H. "Archives in Colleges and Universities. . . ." *American Archivist,* 13: 343–350 (October, 1950).

PUBLIC ARCHIVES IN THE UNITED STATES

by G. PHILIP BAUER

The National Archives

*A*RCHIVES, according to Theodore R. Schellenberg, are those records that have been made or accumulated in accomplishing some definite administrative, legal, business, or other social end, but that have been preserved for reasons other than those for which they were originally made. The latter standard assumes some secondary value, characteristically attached to records by historians, genealogists, antiquarians, and scholars in other disciplines. But secondary values are also found in records by a much larger class of ordinary citizens, who make use of archives for the purpose of establishing or maintaining their private rights.

In the English colonies during the seventeenth century there were few historians, genealogists, and antiquarians to be interested in the records of their provincial governments. Probably no one of that period would now be referred to as an archivist. The past of the colonies was too brief and their population too small to produce a great body of records. As a rule, colonial history was written as first-hand narratives by colonial leaders with little recourse to records or documents.

Colonial legislators, however, concerned themselves from a very early date with some of the secondary values of records. In 1639 the General Court of Massachusetts recited in a resolution that "many judgments have been given in our Courts, where no records are kept of the evidence and reasons whereupon the verdict and judgment did pass; the records whereof being duely entered & kept would bee of good use for president to posterity." Similarly in Maryland the lower house of the legislature complained in 1723 that several of the "Ancient papers, Records and Registries" of the towns were in the hands of private persons and passed an ordinance directing that all such records should be turned over to appropriate county clerks. In 1744 the same lower house noted that several of its journals were in the possession of the clerk of the Governor's Council, to whom they had been given as "a present" by a former governor. The House raised no objection to the gift but merely proposed to have copies made for its own use.

The records of chief interest to the colonists were naturally those that related to practical everyday matters such as land grants, deeds, wills, and licenses. Access to these was usually given without favor on the payment of stated fees. One of the early enactments of Massachusetts provided that every inhabitant of the country should have the liberty to search any rolls, records, or registers of any court or office except of the council, and to have transcripts made and certified for the customary fees. In North Carolina the instructions to Governor Edward Hyde in 1711/12 directed him "to take care that all persons may be admitted to Peruse ye Publick Records . . . provided they make such Perusal in the place where the same are Constantly kept & pay the Customary & usual Fees."

Records of the colonial governors and legislatures that dealt with policy determination were generally regarded as private and closed to the public. Governor Robert Hunter Morris of Pennsylvania expressed in 1755 the general view of governors by observing that "The King's Commands signified by a Secretary of State may be very proper for the Consideration of the different Parts of the Legislature, but are not always to be communicated to the Public." Yet, in Maryland in 1740 the lower house of the legislature had declared that all records of the government (except perhaps those of the Governor) were "the Right and Property of the People of Maryland" and that all persons had the right to examine documents and secure transcripts. The rising public interest in official records was generally met by selective admission to them.

Evidence of an awakening historical interest in the eighteenth century had appeared in the works of Thomas Prince and Governor Hutchinson of Massachusetts. And after the Revolution, patriotic fervor stimulated the general interest in history and historical sources. The Massachusetts Historical Society was founded in 1791, heralding the formation of many similar societies throughout the nation. All were active in collecting or encouraging the collection of historical records and archives.

Provisions by state governments, however, for the care of their public records continued to be inadequate. Most of the older records were left as a matter of course in the custody of the agencies that accumulated them. In some states the secretary of state was responsible for keeping the administrative records of the governor and the legislature as well as those of his own office. No state provided for the methodical concentration of its archives in a single, separately-administered depository.

Decentralized and desultory control prevented the states from preserving complete files of their own records, either in manuscript or in print. Some of the records were destroyed. Some were lost. Some passed into the possession of other states or the national government. Many early Maryland documents apparently disappeared in connection with the researches of the historian John Thomas Scharf and others went in the forays of Peter Force and Jared Sparks. Many New Hampshire documents passed into the hands of the Library of Congress when it purchased the private library of Peter Force in 1867. In Georgia, the volumes of colonial records that had been transcribed in London at state expense were lent in 1887 to Professor Henry Anselm Scomp for use in the preparation of his *King Alcohol in the Realm of King Cotton;* most of them were lost when fire destroyed his house.

Desultory measures, to be sure, were taken from time to time by state governments for the preservation of their records. New Jersey manifested an early concern for the fate of its records in 1784 when a committee of the legislature recommended that the records then in the secretary's office at Burlington ought not to be removed to Trenton until a suitable building should have been constructed to receive them. But the proposed bill in 1797 to prevent original papers from being taken from the secretary's office for any purpose whatsoever suggests that losses from this practice had probably occurred. In 1798 an act was passed "for the better security of the office of Secretary of State, and for arranging the irregular files of original papers in the Register's Office."

In 1805 and again in 1810 Governor John Langdon of New Hampshire pointed to the need of measures for the preservation of the original acts of the legislature and for the protection of state and county records against fire. Governor Isaac Hill in 1836 obtained authority for the recovery of papers that had passed out of the state's custody and for the appointment of someone to arrange and bind the state records. The following year the House of Representatives appointed a committee on public archives, which earnestly recommended continuance of the work of arrangement that had been begun.

The Governor of Georgia in 1810 urged that steps be taken for the preservation of the Revolutionary and other old records of the executive office. In 1823 funds were appropriated to enable the clerk of the house to compile an index to the thirty-one volumes of its records (1783–1809) and for the secretary of the senate to prepare a similar index to the twenty-three manuscript volumes of senate journals (1790–1821). In 1829 Governor John Forsyth was authorized to employ an indexer to perform a similar work on the books of record and other papers of the secretary of state, the treasurer, the comptroller general, and the surveyor general.

New York began in 1818 the process of translating its Dutch colonial records, producing twenty-four folio volumes, which were deposited in the office of the secretary of state. In 1881 most of the older archives were transferred to the State Library where they continued to suffer from crowding and fires. New York made no provision comparable to that of Massachusetts for the supervision of local custodians.

Consequently, public officials often knew and cared little about the older records in their charge and did not always take the necessary precautions to protect them against loss or damage.

Massachusetts, between 1836 and 1846, engaged the Reverend Joseph Barlow Felt to arrange and bind the colonial and Revolutionary records of the Commonwealth. In carrying out this assignment, Felt adopted an arbitrary system of topical arrangement that has been denounced for violating the natural order of the records; but he did achieve the physical preservation in 241 volumes of a most valuable collection. No significant correction of the system was made until 1891, when Secretary of State William M. Olin took steps to carry out some suggested improvements in indexing. Among the projects then undertaken and completed was a record index of 700,000 record cards, on which were abstracted information about the military service of every person mentioned in the ninety-seven volumes of Revolutionary rolls and 150,000 cards similarly indexing the personal data contained in the muster-rolls series covering the years 1710–1774. These card series (resembling in general plan and purpose the famous Ainsworth carded records of the United States War Department) made it possible for anyone to obtain the military record of his ancestors from 1710 to the close of the Revolution without consulting the original volumes.

Massachusetts also tried to improve the record systems of its local jurisdictions. Since 1884 a commissioner of public records has exercised some control over records of parishes, towns, and counties in the state. The effect of the commissioner's work, in the opinion of Andrew McFarland Davis, who reported on archival conditions in Massachusetts for the

American Historical Association's Public Archives Commission, was to awaken a sense of responsibility in custodians and gradually to induce an improvement in the conditions found unsatisfactory.

In South Carolina the clerk of the senate was directed in 1847 by legislative resolution to arrange the records in his charge from 1782 to date. This was accomplished and reported on in 1848, and in the same year a committee of the General Assembly, to which had been referred a resolution for the construction of rooms for legislative records, urged the collection and preservation of documents relating to South Carolina history, citing the destruction of legislative records by fire in 1843 and 1844 as proof of the need for a place of storage. In 1850, J. S. Green began to collect, arrange, and index the colonial and Revolutionary records of South Carolina in the various offices of the state.

Pennsylvania's colonial and state manuscript records were notoriously inaccessible, liable to destruction by fire, and subject to the ravages of rats, dampness, and dirt, and to mutilation and theft by unscrupulous persons who had access to them and realized their commercial value. In 1851 select committees of both houses of the legislature investigated and reported on the condition of the state's archives. The senate committee reported that the archives "in their present condition are useless and, indeed, fast perishing. . . ." To prevent further destruction the committee recommended a small appropriation for the classification and binding of the more important papers. In 1885 a law was enacted providing for the preservation and binding of the manuscripts used in the printed archives, and requiring that the manuscripts should be deposited in the State Library and kept for reference. But no marked improvement was made in the care and preservation of other manuscript archives. At the end of the century the Public Archives Commission reported in summary that many of the older manuscripts and records of the state were still in the condition described in the legislative reports of 1851.

In Virginia, although the governors repeatedly called for legislative action to preserve the state's archives, nothing was done until 1872, when an act was passed authorizing systematic work on them.

The early archives of Delaware, according to a report by Professor Edgar Dawson to the Public Archives Commission in 1906, had almost entirely disappeared on account of the carelessness and ignorance of officials or the dishonesty of students and antiquarians who had abused the confidence of the state officials. Most of the public archives that had been accumulated before 1873 were deposited along with a collection of branding and cropping irons, in the loft of the statehouse at Dover. While this building was in the process of being remodeled during the years 1873–1875 vandalism ran riot. What little remained of the collection was taken to the cellar, where it was used by the janitor to start fires. A box of these papers was rescued by public-spirited citizens and put away for safe-keeping. Dawson reported that the records of the counties were much more complete than those of the state.

Illinois in 1874 seems to have become awakened to the desirability of arranging and preserving its archives. In that year Secretary of State George H. Harlow outlined a plan to collect the files and records of the successive territorial organizations and the state and, so far as possible, to replace all missing papers with certified copies from the printed records or transcripts from the originals wherever they could be found. The legislature appropriated funds for indexing and removing the archives to the "new statehouse"; and a "department of indexes and archives" was set up within the office of the secretary of state.

The chaotic state of land titles in Tennessee put a premium on all its archives, which were at first crowded into the office of the secretary of state. Later some of them overflowed into the west crypt of the capitol. Here, according to a report of the Public Archives Commission, "they lay piled in masses on the stone floors, among old paint barrels, ashes, and trash of every description, dirt, and grime. They were wet and rotting, and . . . the janitor of the capitol burned up several cartloads because of the fact that they were wet and nasty and smelled bad." Many records had already been defaced by stamp and autograph collectors, and some valuable papers were undoubtedly sold. No real improvement in the situation occurred before the end of the century.

Throughout the nineteenth century the states placed greater emphasis on publication as a means of preserving and disseminating the contents of selected documents than on the arrangement and preservation of the larger body of original papers. Before the Revolution, Pennsylvania had published its *Votes and Proceedings of the House of Representatives* . . . (1682–1776). In 1836 the state began publication of a series of *Colonial Records,* which was completed in seventeen volumes by 1860. Concurrently with the *Colonial Records* the state published the first series (in twelve volumes) of the collection known as the *Pennsylvania Archives.* A second series of this publication in nineteen volumes was published between 1874 and 1893; and a third in thirty-one volumes between 1894 and 1899. Subsequent series brought the total number of volumes to 138 in 1949.

In 1764–1766 the *Journal of the . . . General Assembly of the Colony of New York* (1691–1765) had been printed. In 1820 the series was carried forward by the reprinting of the *Journal* for the years 1766–1776. Several series of colonial and state documents were translated, edited, and published in the latter half of the nineteenth century. Similar documentary publications were issued by Vermont beginning in 1823 and by Connecticut beginning in 1850.

In Massachusetts Governor Hutchinson had as early as 1769 brought out a *Collection of Original Papers Relative to the History of the Colony. . . .* But the first official publication of the state's archives was issued in 1853–1854. It was followed by many other volumes and series devoted to the records of the colony and the state.

Rhode Island published its colonial records in the period between 1856 and 1865, and was followed by New Hampshire, which began to publish its series of *State Papers* in 1867. The Maine Historical Society began publication of the state's *Documentary History . . .* in 1869.

Eleven volumes of documents called the *Calendar of Virginia State Papers and other Manuscripts . . .* (1652–1869) appeared between 1875 and 1893; the *Archives of the State of New Jersey, 1631–1800,* in thirty volumes, between 1880 and 1906; the first twenty-six volumes of the *Archives of Maryland,* between 1883 and 1906; *The Colonial and the State Records of North Carolina, 1662–1790,* in twenty-seven volumes, between 1886 and 1905.

Besides publishing the older records that were at hand, some of the eastern states hired agents to transcribe important papers of their colonial history in archival repositories abroad. The legislature of Georgia in 1837 appropriated funds to have records relating to its colonial history in the archives of the Board of Trade in London transcribed. In 1839 the New York legislature authorized the appointment of an agent to visit England, Holland, and France to secure copies of papers relevant to the state's colonial history; and J. Romeyn Brodhead was selected in 1841 to undertake the project. Ultimately he transcribed eighty volumes of documents–enough to fill fourteen printed volumes.

Efforts to persuade the New Jersey legislature to provide for Brodhead's employment as its agent to transcribe documents were unsuccessful; but the New Jersey Historical Society, by private subscription, in 1849 engaged Henry Stevens of London to make an index to documents in the British public offices relating to New Jersey. In 1858, with additional money raised by subscription, the Society published a volume entitled *An Analytical Index to the Colonial Documents of New Jersey, in the State Paper Offices of England.* . . . Finally in 1872 the legislature appropriated funds to procure, under direction of the New Jersey Historical Society, copies of colonial documents on file in London. This authorization was later extended to include the transcription of documents that might be found elsewhere; and in 1878 provision was made for arranging, collating, and publishing the transcripts obtained. They were included in the series of *New Jersey Archives.*

In South Carolina repeated efforts were made to gain legislative support for the transcribing of documents in the archives abroad, but nothing effective was done until 1891, when an act was passed establishing a Public Records Commission. This Commission selected an agent in London to transcribe all provincial papers in the colonial department relating to the Province of South Carolina from 1663 to 1719, and all papers or records from 1719 to 1775, except certain papers already available to the commission. By 1895 a total of thirty-six volumes of transcripts had been received.

While the state archives were being burned, lost, stolen, and sporadically printed, those of the federal government fared little better. In 1810 the House of Representatives passed a motion presented by Josiah Quincy for the appointment of a committee "to inquire into the State of the ancient public records and archives of the United States, with authority to consider, whether any, and what, provision be necessary for a more safe and orderly preservation of them. . . ." The committee, headed by Quincy, reported that it found all the public records of the period before the adoption of the Constitution in a state of great disorder and exposure; it expressed the opinion that immediate provision ought to be made for their preservation and orderly arrangement. The committee also reported that the records of the state, war, and navy departments were very inadequately stored in the garrets of the building which also housed those departments, just west of the new President's Mansion. It accordingly proposed the construction within the building of three additional fire-proof rooms, large enough to contain all the public papers and records of the departments of state, war, and navy and also a new building for the general post office and patent office. This proposal was embodied in a bill, which passed both houses and was approved by the President in 1810. Its effect was in no way to provide for an archival establishment but was merely to provide slightly more and better storage space for the older records of the departments.

As the government expanded its activities, especially during and after the Civil War, the quantity of its records increased far more rapidly than suitable space could be provided for storage. The departments had all they could do to keep in serviceable condition the records they needed for daily reference. Those that were not so needed were relegated to attics and damp cellars where they were subject to all the familiar archival hazards and because of their highly combustible nature became a menace to the buildings and to the lives of the clerks who worked in them. Between 1833 and 1915, according to J. Franklin Jameson, 254 fires occurred in buildings occupied by the national government.

The government's neglect to provide adequate housing for its older records was matched for a time by an easy-going, almost indifferent policy in granting public access to the records. Francis Lieber's *Encyclopedia Americana*, published in 1829, contains the statement that "The archives of the U. States are easily accessible, and proper recommendations will open them to anyone who wants to use them for scientific purposes." Four years earlier a clerk in the State Department wrote of his tribulations in producing documents for strangers who visited the Department; he apparently had no orders to refuse them.

But as the century advanced, the bureaus and departments became stricter about opening their archives to outsiders. The clerks found it difficult to do their regular work with unofficial searchers in their way. Although Secretary Bayard in 1886 granted George Haven Putnam access to the papers of Benjamin Franklin in the State Department on the ground that the historical archives were preserved by the government to serve the best interests of the people, the more characteristic attitude of the time was expressed in 1893 by the Chief of the Bureau of Rolls and Library, who wrote to a private researcher that the manuscripts and books deposited in the Library were primarily for the use of the Department. He grudgingly permitted an examination of the journals and papers of the Continental Congress only when they were "not required by the Department and the use of the Library." In 1910 Gaillard Hunt declared to the national Conference of Archivists that the archives of our government were opened with less freedom than were those of any other great country.

Like the states, the federal government during the nineteenth century placed greater emphasis on the publication of selected documents than on the care and preservation of originals. Ebenezer Hazard had set the pattern for this form of endeavor in 1792–1794 when he published, with some government aid, two volumes of miscellaneous documents ranging over the entire period from discovery and colonization to the end of the New England Confederation. Later a number of much more ambitious enterprises for the collection and publication of historical materials on a national scale began when Jared Sparks assembled copies of documents in the archives of all the first thirteen states, in foreign archives, and in private hands, which he published in 1829–1830, with a sizable government subscription, as the twelve-volume *Diplomatic Correspondence of the American Revolution*. His *Life and Writings of George Washington*, which filled twelve more volumes, were published between 1834 and 1837; his *Works of Benjamin Franklin; with Notes, and a Life of the*

Author, in ten volumes, between 1836 and 1840; and his *Correspondence of the American Revolution; Being Letters of Eminent Men to George Washington*, in four volumes, in 1853.

Contemporaneously (1832–1861) the federal government sponsored and supported publication of the thirty-eight volume collection of *American State Papers: Documents, Legislative and Executive* (1789–1838), which were brought out by the publishing firm of Gales & Seaton. Between 1837 and 1853 Peter Force, with the aid of a government contract, published nine volumes of documents relating to the American Revolution under the title of *American Archives . . . a Documentary History of . . . the North American Colonies*. The *Annals of Congress of the United States*, which reprinted contemporary newspaper reports of the debates in Congress during the period from 1789 to 1824 in forty-two volumes, was published by government subvention between 1834 and 1856.

Official publication of government documents increased steadily during the second half of the century. Not only did the volume of material issued through the Congressional series continue to grow, but in 1861 the State Department inaugurated its famous series of volumes now commonly referred to as *Foreign Relations*, and in 1880 the War Department published the first of 130 volumes of *The War of the Rebellion: a Compilation of the Official Records of the Union and Confederate Armies*.

Toward the end of the century the need for better maintenance and administration of our national archives became more and more apparent. In 1877 the President transmitted to Congress the report of a commission appointed to consider the security of the public buildings in Washington against fire, which raised the question: What provision should be made for the custody of non-current files? This report commented on the fact that all the departments held large numbers of papers no longer needed for constant reference, adding to the quantity of combustible material in the structures and the consequent danger from fire. It rejected the suggestion that papers should be destroyed instead of being merely pushed aside: "Every paper worthy at any time to be recorded and placed on the public files may be of value at some future time, either in a historical, biographical, or pecuniary way, to the citizen or the nation." It recommended "that a fire-proof building of ample dimensions be constructed for the accommodation of the archives of the government no longer required for constant use."

The Secretary of War in his annual report for 1878 endorsed a proposal of the Quartermaster General for the construction of an inexpensive but fire-proof hall of records. In this building it was proposed that the records not in daily use by the departments should be stored "under charge of competent superintendents and watchmen," so that "on telephonic order, any document needed in any public office could be quickly sent to that office." There was no suggestion here of a separately administered archives.

Each year for several years the Secretary of War repeated his recommendation without variation and was supported by the Secretary of the Treasury and other members of the cabinet. Bills were from time to time introduced in Congress to accomplish the purpose, but none was passed before the end of the century. As a partial relief to the congestion of government files, in 1889 Congress did pass an act providing for the lawful destruction of "useless papers." In 1903 it provided also that records of especial value in the departments might be transferred to the Library of Congress. But no effective provision was made for the preservation of the large body of occasionally useful records in the departments.

The first concerted effort by persons outside the government to improve the condition of archives and develop an archival profession in the United States began in 1900 when the Public Archives Commission of the American Historical Association set about methodically to survey the records of the states. The reports of this Commission's findings, published each year through 1917, stimulated interest in the subject and provided solid factual information to support the growing demand for better archival conditions. Herbert A. Kellar, an indefatigable advocate for archival reform, prepared the Commission's report (1916) on the archives of Minnesota.

The work of the Commission directly stimulated archival reform in the states. In some cases the reformation was in establishing archival departments or commissions. In others, the function was assigned to state libraries or historical societies. By 1909 twenty-four states had passed measures relating to the preservation and custody of their archives.

The Public Archives Commission also contributed to the professionalization of archivists and the establishment of good practices through the work of the annual Conference of Archivists, which was established in 1909. Under the leadership of such men as Herman V. Ames, J. Franklin Jameson, Victor Hugo Paltsits, Gaillard Hunt, and Waldo G. Leland, the Conference produced the preliminary draft of a "Manual of Archival Economy for the Use of American Archivists." And it particularly strove to establish the European principle of *provenance*, whereby archives are arranged according to the offices of their origin.

Through the efforts of the Public Archives Commission and others, legislative provisions for state archives continued to improve irregularly until the mid-thirties when the founding of the National Archives and the inauguration of large archival surveys by the W. P. A. gave new stimulus to the movement. These two events suddenly increased the number of persons actively engaged in archival work and drew the attention of many others to the value of archives for the nation. In 1937 there were enough interested people to form a professional organization, the Society of American Archivists. Herbert Kellar was among the charter members and early leaders of this society. One of the society's first major projects was the drafting of uniform standards for archival legislation in the states.

Although the Public Archives Commission was primarily concerned with the condition of archives in the states, the American Historical Association had much broader archival interests. In 1901 it formally endorsed the request of the federal departments for a national hall of records, and in 1908 the executive council appointed a committee, under the chairmanship of J. Franklin Jameson, to promote the movement for an archives building in Washington.

Jameson was active throughout his lifetime in promoting the cause of the national archives. In 1902 he recommended as an initial project for the Carnegie Institution of Washington a comprehensive survey of the government archives in Washington. This survey resulted in the publication of the celebrated Van Tyne and Leland, *Guide to the Archives of the Federal Government in Washington.* Later under Jameson's direction, the Institution's Department of Historical Research produced a series of guides to American materials in the archives of a number of foreign countries. Publication of a number of important documentary series was also undertaken.

From 1909 until 1928 Jameson was active in promoting a national archives building. He corresponded with the Secretary of the Treasury and various members of the Senate; he petitioned President Taft; he drafted bills for Congress; he circularized the historical societies of the country; he addressed the Daughters of the American Revolution and the American Library Association to enlist their support. At one time in 1913 it appeared as if the goal were about to be reached, but as the act passed in that year called for an inspection of foreign archives buildings before plans should be adopted, the European war shortly afterward foreclosed the possibility of accomplishing anything.

The idea of a hall of records to be used simply as a warehouse had gradually given place to the idea of a separately administered archives establishment. This new idea was expressed in a bill introduced in the Senate in December 1906, which proposed the creation of a "board of record commissioners," which should have sole legal custody of all records eighty years old or more of all the several branches of the government. It provided for a "suitable record office," a "record keeper," and deputy record keepers. A special feature of this bill that had no sequel was its provision for receiving into the national archives ancient state records, especially those of the colonial period.

Establishment of a national archives naturally raised the question of control of the records to be deposited. Leland's paper, "The National Archives: a Programme" in the *American Historical Review* (1912), helped to settle the issue of physical and legal custody by pointing out that the best European precedent indicated that absolute custody vested in the archives was preferable.

As spokesman for the American Historical Association, Jameson continued to campaign for an archives building. In 1921 he was joined by the powerful American Legion, which had a natural interest in the proper care and availability of war records. In 1923 the Hearst papers took up the crusade. Finally, President Coolidge presented to Congress a program that specifically provided for an archives building, and this program was embodied in an act approved on May 25, 1926. A site had yet to be chosen and the land condemned, a building had to be designed, and a general plan of organization had to be drawn up. All these things were accomplished in due course. On February 20, 1933, President Hoover laid the cornerstone of the building; and on June 19, 1934, the National Archives Act was approved by President Roosevelt.

In staffing the National Archives, R. D. W. Connor, first Archivist of the United States, accepted the views expressed by Leland a generation earlier in emphasizing historical training as the primary qualification of an archivist. A large proportion of the archivists first employed by the National Archives held graduate degrees in history.

The first major project was again to take an inventory, more complete than any previously taken, of the records held by all federal agencies. A group of deputy examiners surveyed and evaluated the records in the several departments and independent agencies in Washington. A W. P. A. project known as the Survey of Federal Archives outside the District of Columbia (S. F. A.), under National Archives sponsorship, made a parallel survey of federal records in the field. In its final phase, the S. F. A. was taken over by the larger Historical Records Survey.

Acquisitions moved slowly at first. But by July, 1938, they were coming in at a rate of nearly 50,000 cubic feet a year, almost as fast as they could be properly handled. The expansion of government operations to meet the threat of war in 1940–1941 stimulated many agencies to increase the rate and size of their deposits. By July 1, 1946, the building was nearly three-quarters full, with more than 730,000 cubic feet of records under its roof. These included the records of a number of temporary agencies of World War II as well as a majority of all records of the executive branch more than fifty years old.

The sudden increase in the production of records during the war brought the National Archives into the new field of records management. Members of the staff were sent into the temporary war agencies to study their organization and assist in developing plans for the disposition of their records when they should have to liquidate after the war. Some members of the staff accepted wartime appointments in various agencies to take full charge of their record programs and gained practical experience that they would not have otherwise received. The present Archivist of the United States, his Deputy, and the two Assistant Archivists of the United States all benefited from service in war agencies.

From the time of its establishment, the National Archives has studied the question of how best to arrange and describe its holdings so that they shall be truly available to scholars and others who have need to consult them. It has gradually developed a system of "finding aids," so called for want of a better name, which are methodical descriptions of classes of records rather than tools for identifying and locating records on particular subjects.

The most significant general fact about public archives is that nearly all of them bear a close relation to the functions and activities of some government agency; they can, therefore, be more fruitfully traced and studied through those functions and activities than through any other channel of approach. For this reason the National Archives places its record holdings in the stacks according to the rule of *provenance*. The rule, however, must be reasonably interpreted; the organizational entity chosen as the largest unit to be regarded must be neither so large as to be unworkable nor so small as to be meaningless. In the National Archives this unit, known as a "record group," usually consists of the records of a bureau or its organizational equivalent.

The first step of methodical description is the record group registration sheet, which is prepared as soon as possible after records are accessioned. Its purpose is to give immediately some measure of administrative control over all records brought into the building. In two pages or less it gives a summary historical account of the organization and functions of the agency, describes the records in broad terms with their inclusive dates, mentions other records of the agency that are elsewhere than in the National Archives or the originating agency, and calls attention to other nearly-related record groups.

The second step of methodical description is the comparatively detailed preliminary inventory, which sets forth in logical order (arranged either according to the agency's organizational structure or according to its functions) the record "series." Series derive their name from the fact that the documents comprising them are characteristically arranged in serial order, but the term is extended to apply to other small aggregations of records with no apparent internal arrangement, whose common source or form, or other common characteristic holds them in close association as a natural unit and distinguishes them from the records comprising other series. The fact that series are sometimes more or less arbitrarily delimited does not lessen their usefulness as units of description. Nearly 100 preliminary inventories have now been issued by the National Archives.

Other finding aids are prepared as convenience or necessity demands rather than as a matter of uniform procedure. These aids include special lists of individual documents or volumes; name, place, and subject indexes; and special subject guides. Two large subject guides to materials relating to Latin America and to genealogical research are being compiled.

A joint resolution of Congress in July, 1939, enlarged the functions of the National Archives to include the administration of the Franklin D. Roosevelt Library, which now houses the former President's papers and books, and a large collection of museum objects and other memorabilia relating to his life. It also holds and continues to acquire the papers of some of his associates.

In 1949 by act of Congress the National Archives with its appurtenant organizations was attached to the newly-created General Services Administration, where it was given larger responsibilities and bureau status under the name of the National Archives and Records Service. Its function of advising and assisting other agencies in their records problems was expanded and assigned to a new Division of Records Management co-ordinate with the National Archives, the Federal Register, and the Roosevelt Library. One of the first tasks undertaken by this new division (now called an "office"), carried out in collaboration with the National Archives and record officers in the agencies, was to have all federal agencies submit for approval comprehensive schedules identifying the small portion of their records that are worth permanent preservation and setting time limits on the retention of the rest. This initial task having been accomplished, the refinement and periodic revision of schedules will be carried out chiefly by the agencies in co-operation with the National Archives. The Records Management Office is now concentrating much of its attention on the problem of how to bring about greater economy and efficiency in the creation and maintenance of current records. It also supervises the operation of a system of regional record centers, which provide inexpensive space for the storage of semi-active and non-permanent records.

The Harry S. Truman Library in Independence, Missouri, was the second presidential library to be acquired by the Service. Similar establishments may hereafter be acquired as "part of the national archives system" under the authorization of an act approved on August 12, 1955. Provision is thus complete, in the words of the Archivist, Wayne C. Grover, for the "co-ordinated management of all Federal records and for the orderly preservation of all valuable records of the Government, in the field as well as in Washington, and also the papers of men whose high office imparts to their archives a quasi-public character."

The National Historical Publications Commission, long advocated by the American Historical Association and formally established by the National Archives Act of 1934, became active for the first time in 1950 when it was provided with an executive director, on the staff of the National Archives and Records Service. Its main function is to encourage and promote the publication of useful historical works, especially source materials; but it also regularly prepares under the Director's supervision the *Writings in American History* and will soon bring out a comprehensive guide to all manuscript depositories in the United States.

The selective publication of the *Territorial Papers of the United States* under the distinguished editorship of Clarence E. Carter, has been transferred from the State Department and is now one of the regular activities of the National Archives. The National Archives also carries on a much larger program of documentary publication by means of microfilm. Documents are microfilmed in series on negative masters, and positive copies are furnished on request at a cost substantially less than that of comparable volumes in print. There are now available on film for distribution in this way more than 7,000 rolls of microfilm publications reproducing about 5,000,000 documentary pages. In addition to these formally designated microfilm publications, the National Archives has under way a large-scale program for the reproduction on microfilm of series of disintegrating records whose intrinsic value is not sufficient to justify lamination but whose informational content is worth preserving. Positive copies of these microfilm series are available at the same prices as are the microfilm publications.

The National Archives has always striven to advance archival knowledge and techniques, producing a number of bulletins and pamphlets on various topics of professional interest to archivists. It has for many years co-operated in the academic courses and summer institutes given by the American University in the field of archives and related subjects, and since 1953 it has given a basic training course, primarily for its own employees but open to others, which is now accepted by the American University as creditable toward a degree. Dr. Schellenberg, Assistant Archivist of the United States for the National Archives, who has been principally responsible for the development of this course, has prepared a textbook on *Modern Archives: Principles and Techniques,* which emphasizes American archival problems. He has also conducted a series of seminar conferences of senior archivists for the purpose of creating a body of monographic literature on special problems relating to federal archives and record-keeping practices of the past.

The growing recognition that public records belong to the people, to posterity, and to Clio has precipitated a virtual archival revolution during the last two hundred years. Where documents were once allowed to deteriorate and disappear through official carelessness and irresponsibility, today they are preserved and protected by the skill of dedicated professional archivists; once housed as so much waste paper, they are now accorded the dignity of their importance. Their marble storehouses are temples to the muse of history.

BIBLIOGRAPHY

Bahmer, Robert H. "The National Archives after 20 Years." *American Archivist,* 18: 195–205 (July, 1955).

Bauer, G. Philip. "Recruitment, Training, and Promotion in the National Archives." *American Archivist*, 18: 291–305 (October, 1955).

Beers, Henry P. "Historical Development of the Records Disposal Policy of the Federal Government prior to 1934." *American Archivist*, 7: 181–201 (July, 1944).

Bemis, Samuel Flagg. "The Training of Archivists in the United States." *American Archivist*, 2: 154–161 (July, 1939).

Brown, Robert M. "The Development of an Archival Program in Minnesota." *American Archivist*, 16: 39–44 (January, 1953).

Cappon, Lester J. "The Archival Profession and the Society of American Archivists." *American Archivist*, 15: 195–204 (July, 1952).

Connor, R. D. W. "The Franklin D. Roosevelt Library." *American Archivist*, 3: 81–92 (April, 1940).

Eddy, Henry H. "The Archival Program of Pennsylvania." *American Archivist*, 12: 255–266 (July, 1949).

Flippin, Percy Scott, comp. The Archives of the United States Government: a Documentary History, 1774–1934. 24 vols. (Unpublished compilation in the Library of the National Archives).

Grover, Wayne C. "Recent Developments in Federal Archival Activities." *American Archivist*, 14: 3–12 (January, 1951).

Hill, Roscoe R. *American Missions in European Archives (Missiones Americanas en los Archivos Europeos*, II, Pan American Institute of Geography and History). Mexico, D. F., 1951.

Horn, Jason. "Municipal Archives and Records Center of the City of New York." *American Archivist*, 16: 311–320 (October, 1953).

Leahy, Emmett J. "Modern Records Management." *American Archivist*, 12: 231–242 (July, 1949).

Leland, Waldo G. "The First Conference of Archivists, December 1909: the Beginnings of a Profession." *American Archivist*, 13: 109–128 (April, 1950).

Newsome, Albert Ray. "Uniform State Archival Legislation." *American Archivist*, 2: 1–16 (January, 1939).

North Carolina Department of Archives and History. *The North Carolina Historical Commission; Forty Years of Public Service*. Raleigh, 1942.

Posner, Ernst. "The College and University Archives in the United States." Vatican, Bibliotica Vaticana, *Studie Testi*, 165: 363–374 (1952).

Public Archives Commission. Annual Reports, in *Annual Reports of the American Historical Association, 1900–1922*. Washington, 1901–1926.

Renze, Dolores C. "The State Archives of Colorado." *American Archivist*, 15: 303–308 (October, 1952).

Schellenberg, Theodore R. *Modern Archives; Principles and Techniques*. Melbourne, [1956].

United States National Archives. *Annual Reports of the Archivist of the United States* [for the fiscal years 1935–1949]. Washington, 1935–1949.

United States National Archives and Records Service. *Annual Reports on the National Archives and Records Service*, from the annual reports of the Administrator of General Services [for the fiscal years 1950–1956]. Washington, 1951–1957.

MECHANICAL AIDS IN HISTORICAL RESEARCH

by GEORGE L. ANDERSON

University of Kansas

*N*EW pieces of equipment are appearing on the campuses of many colleges and universities and in the studies of historical scholars. Microfilm and microprint readers have become a normal feature of library equipment. Some universities have established Computation Centers and filled them with electronic computers, punch-card machines, and electrical sorters. Highly skilled operators are on hand to help the researcher with his problem. In individual studies, scholars who have reached the writing stage may be "taping" preliminary versions of manuscripts or listening to recorded data.

While these specialized pieces of equipment or machine services have not become commonplace, they are assuming an increasingly significant role in the routine activities of the research scholar. And, indubitably, there is more to come. Automation seems to be invading cloistered studies and libraries. In a recent advertisement for trained librarians by the Rand Corporation, the following sentence appears, "Rand's System Development Division utilizes the largest advanced electronic digital computers for the exploration and development of the latest automation techniques and systems." In quite another area of activity, mechanical translators seem to be moving beyond the experimental stage, and a machine that can collate disparate texts is a reality.

Although the appearance of the "mechanical messiahs" has caught many historical scholars unawares and unprepared, many others are in a receptive mood. They have been conditioned by the ever-increasing flood of prime source material, by the sight of stack after stack on level after level of archival documents, and by the knowledge that the records of a single governmental agency are described in hundreds of running feet of shelf space. They have talked of sampling techniques and have tried them. They have used research assistants. They have narrowed their fields of research until they are vulnerable to the charge of seeking to know more and more about less and less. The more devoted and disciplined have adhered rigidly to their high standards by working longer days and even longer years, but plainly the problem of coping with the mounting mass of material is an acute one. More extensive use of mechanical aids may provide a part of the answer.

The older members of the historical profession and the younger ones who have hailed the appearance of new techniques will have no difficulty in recalling the names of those pioneers who two decades and more ago called attention to the significance of mechanical aids. Robert C. Binkley, Herbert A. Kellar, and Edgar L. Erickson comprise a select group of individuals whose original, imaginative, and eminently practical projects have enriched and enlarged the scholarly opportunities and productivity of the entire profession. In a later generation Allan Nevins, Lawrence A. Harper, William T. Morgan, Barnes F. Lathrop, Grace Lee Nute, Murray G. Lawson, and Vaughn Davis Bornet have made significant original contributions or have stimulated and encouraged others to do so. Thus historians of today are the direct heirs of the originative thinking of a relatively small group of their colleagues. The disciples of Clio are also the beneficiaries of the far-sighted vision of several men outside of the profession who discerned the possibilities of the oak while it was yet an acorn, or as one writer has put it, while mechanical aids were still but 'a gleam in the eye' of Robert C. Binkley. The publishing world has provided men such as Albert Boni, of Readex, the persuasive advocate of microprint; Eugene B. Power of University Microfilms, the successful promoter of microfilm as a form of publication as well as reproduction; and R. S. Ellsworth of Filmsort Inc., who has provided one answer to the "scroll" problem in the use of microfilm. Historians have reaped rich rewards as a result of the enlightened interest of many librarians and archivists expressed in the activities of the Library of Congress, the National Archives, and a long list of state historical societies. The names of Julian P. Boyd, Luther Evans, Theodore R. Schellenberg, and Vernon D. Tate appear frequently in the literature on mechanical aids. The editors of, and contributors to, such journals as the *American Archivist, American Documentation, Journal of Documentation*, and the *Journal of Documentary Reproduction*, have made countless contributions to the development of mechanical aids. The specialized library periodicals such as *College and Research Libraries, Library Trends, The Library Journal*, and the *Library Quarterly* have paid consistent attention to the subject during the past several years. Of the professional groups the most active in exploring the possibility of a mechanical answer to complex bibliographical problems has been the American Chemical Society.

Historians have probed the possibilities of mechanical help in their research problems much more cautiously than the librarians and the scientists. Several sessions devoted to the subject of mechanical aids have been presented at the annual meetings of the major historical associations during the past quarter of a century. At the New Orleans meeting of the Southern Historical Association in November, 1938, Barnes F. Lathrop of the University of Texas gave a first-hand report on "Microfilming Materials for Southern History." The opening remark of Professor Lathrop, "To historians the unknown quantity in this project is microfilming," is a sharp reminder of the tremendous developments that have occurred in less than two decades.

By 1941 microcopying had become so important that the American Historical Association devoted a full session to it. The session was chaired by Herbert A. Kellar and included a paper by Edgar L. Erickson of the University of Illinois entitled "A Program for the Microcopying of Historical Materials" and discussion by Julian P. Boyd, librarian of Princeton University, William T. Morgan of Indiana University, and Richard W. Hale, Jr., of Newberry Library. The program of the New York meeting of the American Historical Association in 1946 also included papers on "Mechanical Aids in Historical Research," by Murray G. Lawson of the College of the City of New York and "Microphotography for Scholars," by Vernon D. Tate, then of the National Archives. In 1947 and again in 1952 progress reports were made on the American Historical Association and Library of Congress

Joint Program for Microfilming Historical Source Materials. On the former program domestic developments received the major emphasis whereas on the latter, reports were made on the problems and accomplishments of overseas projects, especially in France and Italy. A similar program was presented at the 1947 meeting of the Mississippi Valley Historical Association in Columbus during Herbert Kellar's term as president of the Association. This singularly appropriate program under the chairmanship of E. J. Leahy of Remington Rand, Inc., featured papers by Louis Knott Koontz and Edgar L. Erickson and remarks by Eugene B. Power, Earl N. Manchester, Albert Boni, and Warner F. Woodring.

Papers and reports on the use of mechanical aids including those presented on the programs of historical associations characteristically have found their way into print in journals other than the principal historical ones. The *Journal of Documentary Reproduction* published the Lathrop paper and Grace Lee Nute's "Microphotography at the Minnesota Historical Society" in June, 1939; William T. Morgan's, "Suggested Materials to be Filmed for the use of Historians" in 1941; and Erickson's descriptive report in 1942. Lawson's provocative and history-centered essay and Vaughn Davis Bornet's "Oral History *Can* be Worthwhile" appeared in the *American Archivist*; John M. Blum's "Editor's Camera: The Letters of Theodore Roosevelt" and Erickson's "The Sessional Papers Project" in *American Documentation*; Max Savelle's "History, Photography, and the Library" in the *Library Journal*, and Dean Albertson's "History in the Deep Freeze: The Story of Columbia's Oral History Project" in *Columbia Library Columns*.

By comparison only a few articles on mechanical aids by

historians have appeared in historical journals. Omitting the
"service" items that appear as regular features of several
journals, Lawrence A. Harper has published "Microphotog-
raphy and History" in the *Pacific Historical Review;* Francis
C. Huntley described a keysort system in "A Bibliographical
Method for the Individual Scholar" in the *Historian;* W. Burlie
Brown summarized developments in microfilming in his
brief, but important "Microfilm and the Historian" in the
Mississippi Valley Historical Review in 1953; and Herbert A.
Kellar devoted several pages to the general subject of mechanical aids in his presidential address before the Mississippi
Valley Historical Association, "The Historian and Life,"
which appeared in the *Review* in 1947. Kellar's comments on
mechanical aids were more suggestive and provocative than
analytical and conclusive. He did not go beyond a brief argument for the duplication of perishable documents, a challenge
to explore the use of punch-cards and machine sorting of research data, and a plea for advisers to familiarize their graduate
students with the new methods and encourage their use. From
this survey of the reaction of the historical profession to
mechanical aids to research, it seems possible to conclude that
either they have been taken for granted, as in the case of
microcopying, or largely ignored as inapplicable as in the case
of machine sorting. Or perhaps historians have been too busy
digesting the blessings of the machines to prepare interpretive
and descriptive discussions of their use. The published literature does not justify the conclusion that the younger mechanical cousins of the fountain pen and typewriter have
been tried and found wanting.

Apart from material in the scholarly journals, two men have
made particularly notable contributions in bringing the sig-

nificance of new mechanical developments to the attention of the historical profession. The pioneer and most original contributor was Robert C. Binkley; the most important in matters of co-ordination and organization was Herbert A. Kellar. The *Manual of Methods of Reproducing Research Materials* prepared by Binkley in 1936 is still cited in discussions of the subject. It has been suggested that it needs to be brought up to date, but thus far no one has attempted the task. Meanwhile it continues to be the most compact source of information on a great variety of methods of publishing research materials. In addition to the *Manual*, Binkley wrote a number of essays on various phases of mechanical aids. Fortunately such titles as "The Problem of Perishable Paper," "New Tools for Men of Letters," and "The Reproduction of Materials for Research," have been brought together in Max H. Fisch, *Selected Papers of Robert C. Binkley*.

A measure of Herbert Kellar's service in bringing the machine to the attention of the historian is found in his chairing several significant committees. In 1939 he succeeded Theodore R. Schellenberg as chairman of the Committee on Historical Source Materials of the American Historical Association. He continued to serve in this capacity until 1946. The most detailed report of the committee was made in 1939. It included a sub-section on "New Technical Processes of Reproduction of Records" and another on the "British Sessional Papers." In each instance Kellar undertook to summarize the principal developments and to elicit from his colleagues their interest and support. A considerable portion of the 1940 report of the committee was devoted to describing the development of the emergency program to microfilm historical materials threatened with destruction by the war.

Herbert Kellar's effective and significant contribution in developing a wantlist of historical materials in the war zone made him the logical person to become director of the Experimental Division of Library Co-operation of the Library of Congress by appointment of Archibald MacLeish, Librarian of Congress. The most tangible product of the work of the Division which was financed by the Carnegie Foundation is a fifty-two page *Memoranda on Library Co-operation* prepared by Kellar. This document contains a summary of his thinking on matters of research materials, their availability, and their handling by libraries. In Part III, entitled "Documentary Reproduction," Kellar invited the attention of his colleagues and associates to the potentialities of mechanical developments. Among other things he suggested the near-print processes of microphotography, hectograph, mimeograph, multilith, photostat, Ozalid, and photo-offset for inexpensive reproduction of research materials and for limited publication of specialized historical research. Kellar fully anticipated resistance to these new forms of publication, "since the fetish of form rather than content is still strong in the academic world."

The point of departure for the discussion of the mechanical aids that bears a recognizable relationship to the task of the historian is the formulation of A. T. Maierson and W. W. Howell: "The use of machinery is considered desirable where it will relieve a thinking human from non-thinking activities." In elaborating this principle the authors equate mechanical storing with memory; matching with selecting; copying with copying; and collating with rearranging. If copying is interpreted broadly to include publishing, and storage is expanded to include the placing of either primary source material or an intermediate version of the final manuscript on tape or disc, then the principal categories of the uses of mechanical aids are copying, storing, and selecting. It will be readily recognized that this restrictive approach will result in the omission of a very large number of machines from this discussion. There is considerable literature on IBM and PSM composing type-writers as well as on the DSJ Vari-Typer and the Justowriter. A few writers are undertaking to keep abreast of the developments in the field of mechanical translation. It has been nearly ten years since *Gone With the Wind* was transmitted by Ultrafax a considerable distance in two minutes and twenty-one seconds. At the conclusion of this successful demonstration of the union of the principles of television and photography, Luther Evans, then Librarian of Congress, stated that it was conceivable that a ton of letters and manuscripts could be transmitted in facsimile from New York to Los Angeles in a matter of minutes and be reduced to a spool of film in the process. The mere mention of these devices both actual and potential is sufficient justification for concentrating in this brief discussion upon microphotocopying, oral recording, and mechanical sorting.

Almost every writer on the use of photography for copying documents calls attention to the fact that it is as old as photography itself, the earliest reference being by Francois Arago in 1839. The perfecting of the process about 1870 and its use by the besieged defenders of Paris during the Franco-Prussian War is a fairly well-known story. But more than sixty years were to pass before the scholarly world was to explore seriously and continuously the applications of the process to research. In a very brief period of time historical scholars became aware of its applicability to their work. Writers have appraised the development of the process in superlative terms. In his *Memoranda on Library Co-operation* Hebert Kellar remarked that "Microphotography . . . has been the means of reproducing out-of-print and unique materials for research purposes . . . A substitute in many cases for interlibrary loan . . . [and] the bridge whereby copies of valuable research materials are being conveyed to this country from Europe." According to R. S. Ellsworth, "Microfilm is the wonder tool of our time. In cost, physical characteristics and technological potential microfilm surpasses other record mediums." A few years later Vaughn Davis Bornet concluded that, "The use of microfilm to reproduce books, newspapers, and manuscripts [is] possibly the most important technical step forward in the scholarly world since the invention of the typewriter. . . ."

Microphotography has been made available to historical scholars in two principal forms, microfilm and microprint. Both forms are in reduced facsimile, but the former appears as a roll of film on a spool, and the latter most characteristically as a number of small prints on a card. The relative merits of the two forms have been debated at considerable length. The comparative advantage of microfilm is alleged to reside in better reading equipment, simpler storage facilities, and greater speed of processing. On behalf of microprint it is claimed that it offers greater economy in space, greater savings in production, and greater flexibility in use. A variant method of presentation known as Filmsort combines both index and record on the same card which can be adapted for use with mechanical sorting equipment. The developer of Filmsort claims to have solved the outdated format of microfilm which he says, "resembles the papyrus scrolls of Ancient Egypt."

The "wonder tool" has been utilized in many ways by the scholarly world. Eugene B. Power, of University Microfilms, has provided a fairly inclusive list of uses: Protection against loss or unnecessary use of rare or irreplaceable books, manuscripts, and documents; securing permanent copies of material of ephemeral nature; economically obtaining copies of material in distant depositories; radically reducing space occupied by any collection; original publication of scholarly or technical material in limited editions; and republishing material in short supply or out of print.

In spite of the apparent lack of interest of members of the historical profession, it is clear that the labors of Binkley, Kellar, Erickson, and Power had borne fruit by 1950. An analysis in that year of the *Union List of Microfilms*, possibly a product of the fertile mind of Herbert Kellar, showed history leading all the other disciplines in microfilm titles with a percentage of twenty-six per cent. Languages and literature was in second place with only fifteen per cent of the total. Much of the credit for the strong representation of history in microfilm holdings was due to the work of the Joint Committee on Historical Source Materials and the Committee on Documentary Reproduction of the American Historical Association and to the development of microcopying projects both large and small by departments of history, state historical societies, and individuals.

In many ways the most dramatic filming program was associated with the outbreak of the war in Europe. This project originated in a conference on Microcopying Research Materials in Foreign Depositories held in Washington, D. C. in June, 1940, under the sponsorship of the Library of Congress and the American Council of Learned Societies. It was concluded that because of the European war, the center of learning would shift to the United States and that a plan should be developed to bring microfilm copies of source materials from all parts of the world to this country. A continuation committee was created with Keyes D. Metcalf, director of Harvard University Library, as chairman. Herbert A. Kellar was given the task of compiling a "want list of historical materials desired by American scholars." Some 332 persons were circularized producing 562 pages of titles of materials in 35 different countries, there being 200 pages of titles for England alone. No more eloquent evidence of the indefatigable energy and devotion of Herbert A. and Lucile O'Connor Kellar to the historical profession can be found than the Emergency Want Lists of Historical Source Materials in the War Zone, in nine volumes comprising over 1,000 typewritten pages, which was completed between June 6 and September 25, 1940. The arrangement by depositories as well as by countries was intended to facilitate the task of microfilming the material. In January, 1941, the Rockefeller Foundation made a preliminary grant of $30,000, and Herbert Kellar was made chairman of a sub-committee on the selection of materials for microfilming. In appraising the gigantic salvaging operation, Edgar L. Erickson has said, "To the Rockefeller Foundation and to those who have made the plan for its realization, and especially to Mr. Kellar who has shouldered most of the burden of preparing the want lists, historians are deeply indebted."

A project which has something in common with the one just described is the production under the editorship of Edgar L. Erickson of a microprint edition of all of the publications of the House of Commons during the years 1801–1900 inclusive with the exception of *Hansard's Debates*. When completed the project will include in microprint 6,000 quarter and folio volumes totaling more than 4,000,000 pages. The price will be approximately $1.25 per 1,000 pages.

Of great significance to American historians whose research interests are in Medieval and Modern European History is the Vatican Library Microfilm Depository at Saint Louis University. This tremendous undertaking is being financed by the Knights of Columbus. In addition to materials relating to the general history of the periods covered, there are special collections in the fields of medicine, physical science and mathematics, Roman and Canon law, and on classical languages and literatures.

By far the widest historical use of microfilm has involved American materials; reels of film have issued from such depositories as the Library of Congress, the National Archives, and many of the state historical societies. The *Union List of Microfilms, Newspapers on Microfilm: A Checklist*, and the *List of National Archives Microfilm Publications* are indispensable guides to this mass of material. Supplementary listings of microfilm projects are carried in the scholarly journals. Some of the outstanding special projects have been the filming of Early American State Records, a joint undertaking of the Library of Congress and the University of North Carolina, and the filming of the Draper Collection and other holdings by the State Historical Society of Wisconsin.

An illustration of the use of mechanical aids in gathering and collating historical data is provided in the Theodore Roosevelt Research Project, sponsored by the Massachusetts Institute of Technology and directed by John M. Blum. The ultimate objective is an edition of some 10,000 letters selected from a total of 100,000 pieces gathered from 130 manuscript collections in the United States and England. After stating that the use of microfilm had resulted in "substantial savings of time and money and ensured a continuing standard of accuracy" Blum credits the Contura copying device developed by Frederick Ludwig with a greater usefulness than film for many purposes, and concludes that "Scholarship, like other pursuits of twentieth century man, has harnessed technology."

Leaving aside certain mechanical shortcomings it may be concluded that the development of photoduplication techniques has produced a wholesome and stimulating revolution in the realm of historical scholarship. Almost everyone agrees that they have provided an effective solution to the twin problems of scarcity and maldistribution. No longer is it true that the seasoned veteran on a campus graced by a well-stocked library has a monopoly of research opportunities. He has been helped by accessibility to rare and significant archival and manuscript material, but it is the rising young scholar on a relatively remote campus with scarcely any library holdings of research quality who has benefited most. Up until a decade and a half ago he could plead his situation as a reason for abandoning his scholarly career. But today if the scholarly Mahomet cannot go to the mountain, enough of the mountain can be moved to enable him to develop a career of scholarly productivity. Basic materials in almost every field are available. The increasing flow of finding aids and bibliographies makes it possible for almost everyone to locate material within the range of his research interests. No longer are expensive and time-consuming trips to Washington, New York, and Boston an absolute prerequisite for a productive research program. Indeed for the cost of one such trip the scholar can acquire a modest quantity of material on film and a machine to enable him to use it.

The effects upon colleges and universities could be as dramatic. Many more of them are already offering work toward advanced degrees. Clearly by the older standards, their libraries cannot be said to be adequate. But just as the six-shot Judge Colt was the great equalizer in the early days of "triggernometry," so microfilm and microprint materials have become potentially the great equalizers of research opportunities. College libraries with small budgets can build up modest holdings of basic materials in restricted fields while those with larger budgets can fill gaps in more inclusive collections. There will be many "side-effects" as the use of microfilm catches on even more widely with more people. The smaller, more remote schools will not be so seriously handicapped in securing promising young men and women for their staffs. A wider range of completed research should flow from a larger group of writers to the professional journals. Because historical scholars will be able to stay in fairly intimate contact with significant source materials, teaching should improve, and graduate students should be guided into more significant lines of research. Staff members should be stimulated to make fairly regular visits to major libraries and depositories to consult material unavailable on microfilm and to arrange for additions to the supply available to him on his campus. The overall results in the course of a few years may include the abandonment of well-ploughed fields, the opening up of new lines of approach in method as well as subject matter, a greater degree of accuracy in the use of source materials, and the general enrichment of the body of historical literature.

It should be clear to historical scholars that the blessings of microfilm are not wholly unmixed with potential hazards. One possible difficulty is the human tendency to take too much of everything that is obtained easily. As John M. Blum has observed, "By increasing the temptation to overaccumulation of data, photoduplication, it has been argued, both delays and inhibits the final organization of digested material. Selective notetaking, on the other hand, presumably hastens the ultimate organization." The problem of the overaccumulation of data is more apparent than real if applied in limited terms to a particular project that is well formulated. The basic question resides in the matter of delimitation when the initial steps are taken. In some fields of research there is literally more material available on even a limited phase of a subject than an historian can consult in a lifetime. Knowing this to be the fact and knowing that obtaining microcopies of the great bulk of the material is a real possibility, the historian must define his area with precision. Scholarly starvation in the midst of an abundance of data is a real possibility. As a minimum, the historical scholar who is confronted with a surfeit of data is obligated to maintain the professional standards that were formed by the discipline of poverty.

A second danger of relying upon microcopies of books, manuscripts, newspapers, and periodicals is that the historian will lose a degree of the intangible quality of the period in which he is working. A microfilm copy of a book several centuries old cannot convey the same impact as the book itself. In the case of manuscripts there is an even greater loss. There is an indefinable value in noting the kind and quality of paper used, its size and form, and even its state of preservation. Some may argue that the historian should be immune to such subjective influences, but it is difficult enough to equip one's self with the mental furniture of a period without installing a microfilm curtain between the historian and the period. The qualitative difference between reading an original manuscript and a film copy is roughly akin to the difference between seeing a great masterpiece of painting and a photograph of it. Quite obviously the remedy is not to reject microfilm, but to supplement it whenever possible with the use of originals. Just as photographs and recordings whet the artistic appetite for the seeing and hearing of original compositions, so the use of microcopies should stimulate the historian to seek out and use original documents.

The great success of microcopying in assembling and preserving materials has prompted its suggestion for speedy and economical publication of very small editions. This was the main theme of Binkley's *Memorandum on Auxiliary Publications*, as well as of his *Manual of Methods of Reproducing Research Materials*. Herbert Kellar adverted to the idea on several occasions. In the publication of doctoral dissertations, microfilming has become acceptable. There has been much discussion of the feasibility of publishing only abstracts of research papers in the learned journals with a reference to the availability of a microfilm copy of the entire article from a specific depository. The American Documentation Institute provides such a service. It is said that this form of publication complies with the copyright laws and that it has the very considerable advantage of getting the product of a particular piece of research promptly to the small, but interested group of scholars who want it. Over against the advantage of quick and immediate availability there must be weighed the possibility that microfilm publication may short-circuit the critical judgments by editors and reviewers, and fail in sufficiently publicizing the product.

Members of the historical profession have been much slower in realizing the potentialities of electronic recording devices than of photoduplication. The basic equipment is familiar to everyone; Dictaphones, Sound-Scribers, Voice-Writers or similar machines grace many administrative offices. The most obvious and direct use of these mechanical aids will be made by the historian who feels that it is faster or easier to dictate a first draft than to write it. Speed and effectiveness are not the only advantages of the system. The recording device is usually so light and compact that the scholar can take it with him on research trips either in this country or abroad and at his convenience he can dictate his manuscript and mail the discs or tapes back to his home base for transcription. It is conceivable that where microfilming service is not available the scholar abroad could read the documents onto tape or disc for later recopying. Obviously the process does not guarantee the same degree of accuracy as photoduplication, but the dangers of inaccuracy are little greater than in copying material either in longhand or on a typewriter. The great advantage of the system is that the research scholar can be going forward with his work while at the same time his typist is reducing the material on disc or tape to a typed draft.

The second major use of recording equipment lies in the area of securing accurate transcriptions of reminiscences and interviews. Immediately the oral history project sponsored by Columbia University, the project at Colonial Williamsburg, and tentative beginnings in the same direction by the State Historical Society of Wisconsin will come to mind. To afford some measure for judging the potential usefulness of the method it is only necessary to recall the significance that has been attached to Hubert Howe Bancroft's attempt to assemble first-hand information from surviving participants in historical events. Vaughn Davis Bornet has prepared and published what he describes as "Standards for the Manufacture of Reminiscences with a Recording Device." These ethical and procedural standards were devised for the guidance of individuals and organizations planning to use recording devices in order to prevent the wasting of time, to win the confidence of historians of the future in the method, and to protect the public from false and misleading information about the past. Adherence to the standards would require complete identification of the person interviewed, the interviewer, the place and date of the interview, and the name of the transcriber. In addition to a literal transcription of questions and answers, the final manuscript would contain a brief biographical sketch, a statement of why the person was interviewed, and a description of the interview written by the interviewer immediately following its termination. After suggesting other safeguards and procedures, Bornet concludes, "The true oral history product is the final typed memoir, the faithfully produced and standardized reminiscence, deposited in the archives for later generations."

Historians have made some use of machines for copying and collecting raw materials, but mechanical sorting, selecting, and storing of derivative data is *terra incognita* for the profession. The article by Lawson in the *American Archivist* and the one by Huntley in the *Historian* constitute the only published material on the subject. Many historians will say that this is the way it should be; that by definition, the scholarly historian who is loyal to the demands and traditions of his discipline is the thoughtful individual armed with pen, a pack of note cards, and a pad of paper; and that the historian inevitably becomes the social scientist whenever he attempts to apply mechanical techniques to the sorting and selecting of data. It is quite possible, on the other hand, that these processes may rescue the historian from the tidal wave of materials and provide him with a safe foundation for conclusions rather than assertions or assumptions.

If library administrators continue to place more operations on a punched-card basis, historians may be forced to study the basic processes in order to be able to utilize library services. Curiously enough two non-historians, Carl S. Wise and James W. Perry, have used the field of history as the point of departure for their discussion of "Multiple Coding and the Rapid Selector." They suggest that the historical dimensions of time, place, person, organization, and nature of action can all be coded into patterns of punched holes. To assist in the selecting process there are two levels of mechanical devices available: The manually operated Keysort system and the mechanically powered and operated International Business Machines and Remington Rand systems. Brief but competent and understandable descriptions are found in the Huntley and Lawson articles and extensive discussions in Howard F. McGaw, *Marginal Punched Cards in College and Research Libraries* and Ralph H. Parker, *Library Applications of Punched Cards*. Basically the procedure consists of four steps: Compiling of data, coding, selecting or sorting, and tabulating or printing. The McBee Keysort system requires very simple equipment, cards with holes punched around the margins, a simple punch, and a sorting needle. Data may be taken on the cards; the proper hole or holes slotted with the punch according to a prearranged subject classification and the cards sorted by passing the needle through the proper hole. It is claimed that more than four million non-conflicting items can be coded on one edge of a standard-size card and that the cards can be sorted at the rate of from sixty to ninety thousand per hour.

The completely machine-operated equipment includes specially designed cards, a numerical and alphabetical key punch somewhat resembling a typewriter, a sorting and counting machine, and the tabulating and printing machine. The basic pattern of operation is relatively simple. Once the data are accurately coded and properly punched into the cards the machines take over. All sorts of questions can be asked, whether factual, statistical, comparative, or correlative, and the correct answer will be forthcoming as a tabular statement or printed list.

It should be obvious that one of the least controversial of the applications of machine procedures of selecting and sorting is in the preparation of bibliographies. Both Huntley and Lawson emphasize this use by pointing out possible applications and calling attention to the enormous savings of time, money, and energy. For example, suppose that with the aid of a foundation grant all of the bibliographical information contained in the many volumes cited in Griffin's *Writings on American History* were to be placed on punched cards and the resultant file housed in a central depository. In a matter of minutes and at a moderate cost, a basic bibliography could be supplied on any conceivable subject in American history.

To illustrate the possibilities of machine sorting and selecting on the substantive side of research, consider the history of the public lands in Kansas. Here is a fertile field for research. Fortunately, sufficient monographic literature exists to provide a point of departure and to indicate the enormous quantity of archival material at local, state, and federal levels that has never been used. Heretofore scholars such as James C. Malin, Paul Wallace Gates, Thomas Le Duc, Allen Bogue, Leslie Decker, Homer Socolofsky, and Lawrence Lee have resorted to sampling procedures or have studied particular fragments of the question. They have recognized the limitations of their studies and have not claimed more for them than their data warranted. But there is still the relevant question as to what the conclusions would be if very much larger segments of data were placed on punched cards and some fundamental questions devised for putting to the machines. Using both state and federal census data and land entry records and papers housed in the National Archives the historian could ask questions concerning the age of the first settlers in the separate regions of the state; their residence prior to coming to Kansas to discover if they came principally from contiguous or non-contiguous states, from New England, the South or states of the Ohio valley; their occupation prior to coming whether farming, clerking, or teaching; the size of their families; the length of time that they stayed on their claims; the land act that they utilized; and the number of different entries that a given settler made before proving up. Obviously the compilation and coding of the data would be a monumental task for human hands and intelligence, but once compiled it could be used effectively. Without commitment as to the validity of the procedure, it seems that questions of demography, settlement, and adjustment are particularly well adapted to machine processes of research.

Another field where it would appear that mechanical sorting and selecting procedures might be tried is that of banking history. For example, there is not in print a comprehensive history of the national banking system from 1863 to 1913. The prime source material in the records of the Office of the Comptroller of the Currency for live, operating banks and their successors is not open to researchers. Students of the question have often wondered if the printed quarterly reports of the banks would shed any satisfactory light on the operation of the system. Perhaps they would if somehow the statistical material relating to the banks could be brought into manageable form. Data could be compiled on capitalization, the accumulation of reserves, the relation of circulation to capitalization, the relation of deposits to capitalization and to circulation, the holdings of bonds, legal tenders, and specie, the due from other banks, and due to other banks, and the total resources of each bank. The banks that failed could be identified and made the subjects of special analysis as a control group because a great body of information is available on each one of them. It is obvious that once compiled and coded a wide range of significant questions could be answered and the answers could be made to rest on the use of all of the printed data. No scholar working alone could hope to live long enough to analyze, sort, select, and summarize his data in the conventional pattern. He is often tempted to conclude that one of the characteristics of a failed bank during its active career was an abnormally large "Due from other Banks and Bankers" item in its quarterly reports. He cannot prove that this was true of all of the failed banks and more significantly he cannot prove that other banks of similar capitalization in similar sized towns did not operate in the same manner. Machine sorting and selecting could at least reduce the statistical data to meaningful terms and make it available.

In spite of the apparent benefits to be derived from the application of mechanical aids to the processing of data a word of caution is needed. The characteristic of an historical event that is almost certain to be lost in the machine process is that of uniqueness. An individual human being, quarter-section of land, or bank inevitably becomes lost when sunk in an average or a median. The individual professor who receives two thousand dollars less than the median salary of all professors does not admit that the median figure reflects accurately the unique condition of his bank account. To him it reflects only the fact that he is seriously underpaid by contrast with his colleagues. The same is true of almost every historical fact that is susceptible of reduction to a punched card. The four quarters of a section of land may appear to be identical in all of the characteristics that can be placed on the cards such as kind of soil, degree of slope, depth to ground water, distance to railroad, date of settlement, land act utilized, and proportion of arable land. Likewise the characteristics of the settlers may appear to be identical as to age, size of family, origin in the same county in the same state, and their religious and educational backgrounds. All of this data can be punched into the cards and when sorted for the items indicated all four cards will fall in the same pocket. The card-punch historian upon seeing this result would be tempted to conclude that the history and development of the four quarters of land and of the people who entered them were essentially if not entirely the same.

But as students of land problems well know, the history of each quarter-section of land will be uniquely and significantly different. The breaking and planting of a larger acreage during a favorable year may have gotten one settler off to a better start and presently a larger home and better fences appear on the one tract. Perhaps in spite of coming from the same county in their former state of residence one family had lived in a town and had never farmed. Obviously a double adjustment is necessary, a slower start is made, severe droughts are encountered, and this farm becomes run down and weed-ridden.

These subtle and unique aspects of the separate units cannot be discerned by the machine yet it is the quality of uniqueness that the historian must seek to know and to understand. The machine can call attention to significant similarities and to sharp differences; it can produce meaningful summaries; it can provide the foundation for the discernment of general trends; but it cannot accurately capture the quality of uniqueness.

In a sense the use of the machine to sort and select data can scarcely become anything but a gigantic sampling process with all the strengths and weaknesses of sampling. In addition the coder must know almost as much about the subject as the research scholar and the latter must become adept in classifying his data so that the correct categories are established or else he cannot ask the right questions. It is conceivable that many historians will shortly become as proficient in placing data upon punched cards as they are in taking notes in longhand or in typing the first draft of their manuscript. There will be one basic difference; a mistake once made cannot easily be detected or corrected because it will be buried in a mass of similarly punched cards.

Because mechanical aids, and especially those concerned with the sorting of large quantities of data, are particularly adapted to the discernment of characteristics and trends, it is quite likely that they will appeal most strongly to those historians who view history as a social science. The historians who aspire to know enough so that they can venture predictions and those who have the kind of mind that revels in statistics will be fascinated by the possibilities of machine recording and sorting of data. They will be disposed to accept and act upon new concepts of the uses of source materials similar to those that seem to be developing in government agencies. Morris B. Ullman, Chief of the Statistical Reports Section of the Bureau of the Census, has commented upon the shift in emphasis in the use of census materials from use for historical study–the backward-looking process–to use in making current decisions and planning future operations. In elaborating on the procedures involved in the new uses of census materials Ullman said, "Experiments are designed, samples are selected, statistics are analyzed with reference to decisions that must be made, controls that must be exercised, judgments that entail action." The preoccupation of American historians with the twentieth century suggests that the shift away from history as a backward-looking process has begun. If because of their obvious adaptation to the handling of masses of data mechanical aids tempt historians to enter the arena as prophets and planners, history as a separate discipline will be well along the way toward extinction.

Moreover, historians as individual scholars may become the victims of the Frankensteins that have been devised to assist them. Depersonalization has been almost a universal concomitant of the application of machine techniques to a process of production. If machine sorting and selecting are utilized, trained research workers must still compile the data and provide the general framework for coding. Because the capacity of the machine to process data will far exceed the capacity of the individual searcher to produce it, there will be an almost inevitable stimulus to group research or resort to staffs of research assistants. In either case the status of the individual scholar may well become inferior to the machine.

The transcendent role of the individual scholar in utilizing mechanical aids in research is emphasized by J. W. Kuipers in his discussion of "Microcards and Documentation." After emphasizing the usefulness of mechanical aids in collection, he observes that the greatest usefulness is in freeing the individual to make new observations, arrive at new relationships and conclusions, and make new contributions to knowledge. It seems safe to conclude that the potential benefits of mechanical aids to individual historians is of such magnitude that possible misuses should not deter members of the profession from exploring a wide range of possible applications of machine techniques to historical research. Possibly someone with the vision and organizational ability of Herbert A. Kellar will develop a program of exploration and secure the support that is essential to its development.

BIBLIOGRAPHY

Binkley, Robert C. *Manual of Methods of Reproducing Research Materials.* Ann Arbor, 1936.
————. *Memorandum on Auxiliary Publications.* 1937.
Blum, John M. "Editor's Camera: The Letters of Theodore Roosevelt." *American Documentation,* 1: 181–184 (October, 1950).
Bornet, Vaughn Davis. "Oral History *Can* Be Worthwhile." *American Archivist,* 18: 241–253 (July, 1955).

Brown, W. Burlie. "Microfilm and the Historian." *Mississippi Valley Historical Review*, 40: 513–518 (December, 1953).

Ellsworth, R. S. "New Horizons with Microfilm." *American Documentation*, 2: 221–228 (October, 1951).

Erickson, Edgar L. "Microphotography at the American Historical Association." *Journal of Documentary Reproduction*, 5: 49–52 (March, 1942).

————. "A Program for Microcopying Historical Materials." *Journal of Documentary Reproduction*, 5: 3–29 (March, 1942).

————. "The Sessional Papers Project." *Journal of Documentary Reproduction*, 4: 83–93 (June, 1941).

————. "Microprint: A Revolution in Printing." *Journal of Documentary Reproduction*, 7: 184–187 (September, 1951).

————. "General Program on Documentary Reproduction of the American Historical Association." *College and Research Libraries*, 14: 303–306 (July, 1953).

Fisch, Max H., ed. *Selected Papers of Robert C. Binkley*. Cambridge, 1948.

Harper, Lawrence A. "Microphotography and History." *Pacific Historical Review*, 15: 427–434 (December, 1946).

Huntley, Francis C. "A Bibliographical Method for the Individual Scholar." *Historian*, 12: 182–188 (Spring, 1950).

Kellar, Herbert A. "The Historian and Life." *Mississippi Valley Historical Review*, 34: 3–36 (June, 1947).

————. "Report of the Committee on Historical Source Materials." *Annual Report of the American Historical Association for the Year 1939*, pp. 71–82. Washington, 1941.

————. *Memoranda on Library Cooperation*, No. 1, The Library of Congress. Washington, 1941.

Lawson, Murray G. "The Machine Age in Historical Research." *American Archivist*, 2: 141–149 (April, 1948).

McGaw, Howard F. *Marginal Punched Cards in College and Research Libraries*. Washington, 1952.

Parker, Ralph H. *Library Applications of Punched Cards: A Description of Mechanical Systems*. Chicago, 1952.

Ullman, Morris B. "Contemporary Trends in the Production and Use of Social Data." *American Documentation*, 4: 137–146 (October, 1953).

Wise, Carl S. and Perry, James W. "Multiple Coding and the Rapid Selector." *American Documentation*, 1: 76–83 (April, 1950).

FOUNDATIONS AND THE STUDY OF HISTORY

by Richard D. Younger

University of Houston

*T*HE philanthropic foundation as we know it today is largely a creature of the twentieth century. Industrial leaders created the first foundations under the impetus of the "Gospel of Wealth." Later their number multiplied rapidly under the pressure of income and inheritance taxes until by mid-century hundreds of foundations are in existence to carry out objectives of every possible description.

Of this multitude, only a handful give support and encouragement directly or indirectly to the study and writing of history or the preservation of historic sites. The story of foundation aid to history is almost entirely an account of support given by a few large organizations. Until the 1920's brought assistance from Rockefeller philanthropy, history drew what foundation help it received entirely from the Carnegie Institution of Washington.

Shortly after Andrew Carnegie sold his industrial empire to United States Steel for over $225,000,000 in 1901, the Scottish philanthropist created the Carnegie Institution of

Washington for the purpose of encouraging research. In 1903, trustees of the Institution followed the recommendation of a committee of historians and established a Department of Historical Research headed by Professor Andrew C. McLaughlin. Armed with a budget of $8,500 a year, the department concentrated its efforts upon projects that would make research materials more readily available to historical scholars. Within a year, it published two volumes: McLaughlin's *Writings on American History*, 1903; and Claude H. Van Tyne and Waldo G. Leland's *Guide to the Archives of the Government of the United States in Washington*. It also commissioned Charles M. Andrews to begin preparation of an inventory of American materials in British archives, as the first of a projected series of archival guides. It was, however, the guidance of J. Franklin Jameson that brought the Department of Historical Research of the Carnegie Institution through expansion to maturity. Jameson came to Washington from the University of Chicago to become director when McLaughlin resigned in October 1905. For the next twenty-three years he charted the course of the department and at the same time edited the *American Historical Review*.

The Carnegie Institution's most tangible contributions to historical scholarship took the form of bibliographical guides and volumes of printed documents. In this way it sought to facilitate the work of individual researchers. In 1906 William R. Shepherd went to Spain to comb the archives for American materials. In the next decade, the institution dispatched Luis M. Perez to Cuba, Herbert Bolton to Mexico, Waldo G. Leland to France, Carl Russell Fish to Italy, and Marion D. Learned to Germany on similar missions. Each of these assignments resulted in a guide to American materials in the various archives. World War I interrupted the program of surveying European records, but by 1928 Jameson could report the completion of guides to materials for American history in the archives of eleven foreign nations. In addition, the department had published an inventory of materials for American religious history and a calendar of territorial papers in Washington. Each of the volumes of guides and documents published by the Carnegie Institution testified to Jameson's careful planning and supervision. On periodic European visits his diplomacy paved the access to foreign archives. Occasionally, however, Jameson expressed a sense of frustration as when he wrote Henry Adams in October 1910, "I struggle on making bricks without much idea of how the architects will use them, but believing that the best architect that ever was cannot get along without bricks, and therefore trying to make good ones."

Textual publication of documents formed an important part of the historical program of the Carnegie Institution, and resulted in several series of major importance to historians. Leo F. Stock's *Proceedings and Debates of British Parliaments Concerning North America*, Edmund C. Burnett's *Letters of Members of the Continental Congress*, Frances Davenport's *European Treaties Bearing on the History of the United States*, and John Spencer Bassett's *Correspondence of Andrew Jackson* each received Carnegie Institution support during long years of preparation and in publication. Publications of other departments of the Carnegie Institution also benefited historians. Before its discontinuance in 1917, the Department of Economics and Sociology financed the publication of John R. Common's ten-volume *Documentary History of American Industrial Society* and published several important histories of transportation, labor, industry, and trade in the United States.

The Carnegie Institution also provided other forms of encouragement to historians. Until 1907, the department had available each year a small amount of money for grants to assist research. In addition, each year a prominent historian joined the staff of the department in Washington as special consultant; Frederick Jackson Turner, Alfred Thayer Mahan, Ulrich B. Phillips, Max Farrand, Frederic L. Paxson and others served as advisors at various times. During Jameson's tenure as director, his office virtually served as a clearing house for American historians and as national headquarters for the historical profession. As editor of the *American Historical Review*, Jameson answered hundreds of requests for information each year. His dual role was a significant financial contribution to the young American Historical Association. Its rent-free headquarters were in Jameson's offices and the Carnegie Institution paid all editorial expenses of the *American Historical Review*. By 1928 the Carnegie Institution of Washington was appropriating $44,200 a year for the Department of Historical Research.

In the decade of the 1920's several large foundations joined the Carnegie Institution in encouraging historical study. After 1922 the Laura Spelman Rockefeller Memorial aggressively entered the area of the social sciences with grants in the fields of economics, sociology, political science, psychology, anthropology, and history. However, the Memorial concentrated heavily upon social work and economic studies and very little went directly into support for historical research. The Carnegie Corporation of New York, founded in 1911, and the Commonwealth Fund, created in 1918 by Edward S.

Harkness, were the only other foundations making appreciable grants to the social sciences in the 1920's. The Rockefeller Foundation, largest of all philanthropies, had long since been captured by the medical profession and most of its funds went to public health and medicine. During the years 1921 to 1930, American foundations granted a total of $27,313,715 to the social sciences, but of this total only $1,173,000 went directly to the field of history.

Large foundations that entered the area of the social sciences after 1920 did not follow the pattern established by the Carnegie Institution of Washington. They soon discovered that it was no simple task to put huge sums of money to work in a constructive and creative manner. The administrative burden of directing historical projects or of making hundreds of small grants caused the foundations to shrink from direct contact with individual researchers and to seek an alternate method of dispensing their funds. They found a partial answer in large gifts to universities and central agencies such as the Social Science Research Council, the American Council of Learned Societies, the Brookings Institution, and the American Historical Association. The grantee organization could then allot funds to large projects or dole them out as individual grants-in-aid. As a result, such foundation assistance as did find its way to history was frequently filtered through some administrative agency.

The American Historical Association received foundation support for several large projects in the 1920's. Most ambitious of these was the commission established to review the teaching of the social sciences in the schools. Contributions of $342,000 from the Carnegie Corporation of New York and $10,000 from the Commonwealth Fund made possible this study. A group of prominent historians working over a five-year period, produced a sixteen-volume report. A grant of $25,000 from the Laura Spelman Rockefeller Memorial enabled the American Historical Association to participate in the International Committee of Historical Sciences and support preparation of an International Bibliography of Historical Literature. In 1927 the Association, in co-operation with nine other learned societies in the field of social science, began preparation of the *Encyclopedia of the Social Sciences*. Financial assistance to the extent of $700,000 from Rockefeller foundations, $275,000 from the Carnegie Corporation, and $25,000 from the Russell Sage Foundation made the fifteen-volume work possible.

One of the more rewarding grants to the American Historical Association, as far as individual scholars were concerned, came in 1926 from the Carnegie Corporation. It gave $25,000 to the Association to establish the Carnegie Revolving Fund for publication of historical monographs. Several important historical works followed within a few years, including: Ella Lonn, *Desertion During the Civil War;* Arthur P. Whitaker, *The Mississippi Question;* Samuel Flagg Bemis, *The Diplomacy of the American Revolution;* and Charles F. Sydnor, *Slavery in Mississippi.* By 1939, the Fund had underwritten nineteen volumes. After publication of its thirty-fifth book it is near exhaustion. However, the Carnegie Revolving Fund was to remain unique in the type of assistance offered individual scholars. The large foundations have followed a policy of refusing to grant funds for publication.

The Social Science Research Council, organized in 1923, has proved an attractive grantee to foundations willing to bestow their benefactions upon the social sciences. Such gifts relieved foundations of most administrative burdens and had the additional lure of promising expenditure of funds upon projects that would utilize the resources of more than one academic discipline. In the first ten years of its existence, the Council received most of its income from foundation sources, with the largest share, $3,916,000, coming from Rockefeller funds. The Carnegie Corporation, Commonwealth Fund, Russell Sage Foundation, and Rosenwald Fund contributed a total of $206,000. The Social Science Research Council concerned itself principally with research projects that cut across two or more fields, but several of its studies have been primarily of interest to historians. Studies by the Council's Committee on Historiography produced two volumes: *Bulletin #54, Theory and Practice in Historical Study*, published in 1946, and *Bulletin #56, The Social Sciences in Historical Study*, published in 1954. The Council also carries out a fellowship program for research in the social sciences. This program includes all grants-in-aid of social science research given by the Rockefeller Foundation. Preference in the selection of recipients of fellowships is given to scholars whose research is interdisciplinary in nature, but through 1951, a total of 180 grants went to individuals interested primarily in historical research.

Organization of the American Council of Learned Societies in 1920 has provided foundations with another agency through which they can administer research funds. The Carnegie Corporation, Laura Spelman Rockefeller Memorial, and the Rockefeller Foundation have all made large contributions for the general support and special projects of the Council. The most important of these to history has been the monumental *Dictionary of American Biography*, launched in

1926 with $620,500 in Rockefeller money and completed in 1936 with the assistance of a host of American historians. As a member of the American Council of Learned Societies, the American Historical Association has from time to time received from the Council small grants for specific projects, such as the award to compile a bibliography of American travel.

The pattern of foundation operations, set in the 1920's, of working through specialized agencies and of favoring co-operative research projects, continued in the decades that followed. Such a policy may have simplified the task of distributing large sums of money, but it worried those scholars interested in individual research. Harold J. Laski speaking from England in 1928, voiced the concern of many American scholars when he deplored the tendency to "mass production" in research, a trend that he traced to the endowment policies of foundations. Laski cautioned that co-operative scholarship could never replace the vision and insight of the individual scholar. The danger of which Laski warned was more clearly apparent in the fields of economics, psychology, and social work where foundations had lavished most of their social science funds, but even in history the lone researcher had the least possibility of getting foundation support. Of all large foundations, only the John Simon Guggenheim Memorial, established in 1925, has devoted itself to making grants to individual scholars to enable them to carry out research projects of their own choice.

The 1930's witnessed an increase in the percentage of foundation spending directed toward research in the social sciences. Depression and economic collapse focused foundation as well as governmental attention upon the search for solutions to the economic crisis. The Rockefeller Foundation in particular spent heavily in the vain pursuit of a formula that would promote recovery. History, however, benefited little from the new enthusiasm for the social sciences. Foundation trustees tended to concentrate their efforts and money in research in the areas of economic stabilization and public administration. With the rise of dictatorships abroad international relations joined the group of favored fields for foundation spending.

History not only failed to attract a proportionate share of foundation funds, but it began to lose the support of its oldest and best foundation friends. Termination of Carnegie Institution of Washington assistance to history came about suddenly. Late in 1927 J. Franklin Jameson learned that the executive committee of the Institution had decided to abandon historical research in favor of the exploration of Mayan civilization. Deeply shaken by the suddenness of this change, Jameson resigned as director in 1928, ending a quarter-century program of publishing bibliographic guides and documents. Research projects begun under the Jameson regime, some of them twenty or more years in preparation, came to completion, but no new ones were undertaken. Charles O. Paullin's *Atlas of the Historical Geography of the United States,* begun in 1911, came out in 1932. Elizabeth Donnan completed editing the final volumes of *Documents Illustrative of the History of the Slave Trade to America,* and Helen Catterall finished several volumes of *Judicial Cases Concerning American Slavery and the Negro.* Leo F. Stock, Edmund C. Burnett, and John Spencer Bassett each edited final volumes in the three documentary series that they had begun many years before. The principal interest of the Division of

History, however, turned in the direction of archaeology and anthropology. In 1933 the Carnegie Institution divided the Division of History into three sections: Aboriginal History, United States History, and History of Science. Throughout the 1930's and 1940's, archaeological research dominated the division and most funds went to finance expeditions to Mexico and Central America. In 1951 the trustees of the Carnegie Institution recognized what had long been a fact when they changed the name of the Division of Historical Research to the Department of Archaeology.

Shortly after the depression of the 1930's began, the American Historical Association found itself in financial difficulties. Its membership dropped sharply as salary reductions became the order of the day at colleges and universities across the nation. The Association's problem was more serious because it no longer enjoyed rent-free quarters in Washington. By 1932 the income of the Association had declined until it was not sufficient to maintain a full-time or even part-time executive officer. In the emergency, the Carnegie Corporation of New York rescued the Association by underwriting its administrative expenses to the extent of $3,000 in 1932, $9,000 in 1933, $3,500 in 1934, and $3,500 in 1935. These grants enabled the Association to carry on during a very critical period.

Rockefeller funds formed a significant portion of foundation support for areas outside the natural sciences during the 1930's and 1940's. In 1929 the Laura Spelman Rockefeller Memorial, which had concentrated its efforts in the social sciences, merged with the Rockefeller Foundation. During the next ten years the Foundation appropriated a total of $27,000,000 for the social sciences and humanities. Although the bulk of this money went for economic studies and investigations of social problems, the Foundation also financed several important historical projects. As in the past, the Rockefeller Foundation found it more expedient to work through established agencies rather than to direct projects itself. The Social Science Research Council and the American Council of Learned Societies continued to administer the Rockefeller fellowship programs. The Foundation encouraged universities to establish social science councils that would administer foundation grants. The Rockefeller Foundation had little desire itself to determine the actual direction of research but was content to make large grants to well-known organizations for the attainment of broad objectives. It looked with the greatest favor upon projects that were exploratory in nature or that promised to take new research paths and develop virgin areas. Once the way had been pointed out, the Foundation preferred to move on and let others take over. It was in accord with this policy that the Rockefeller Foundation granted $300,000 to the Social Science Research Council in 1940 for research in the economic history of the United States. The purpose of the project was to throw light upon the roles of the state and of entrepreneurship in American economic development. Over a ten-year period the grant resulted in publication of six volumes designed to serve as "pilot studies."

In 1942 in an effort to develop a better understanding of local cultures, the Rockefeller Foundation inaugurated a program of regional studies for the United States. A series of regional conferences of writers and scholars launched the project. The Foundation followed these with a succession of grants to subsidize interpretative studies of various sections. Funds went to the Texas State Historical Association for studies of the Southwest, to the University of Wisconsin for investigation of the state's historical development, to the University of Oklahoma for a series of regional studies, to the Huntington Library for studies on the culture of the Pacific Southwest, and to the University of Utah for a similar program for the Mormon area. The Rockefeller Foundation also created a system of grants-in-aid to scholars in the fields of biography, folklore, and historical interpretation, to be administered by the Library of Congress. Similar awards went to the Newberry Library and the University of Minnesota to create centers for the study of Midwestern culture. Canadian regional studies also benefited from the Rockefeller program. The University of Saskatchewan received funds for work in western Canadian history and the universities of Alberta and New Brunswick obtained support for interpretative studies of their areas. This vast program instituted by the Rockefeller Foundation produced a host of important regional studies. Among those most valuable to historians are: Edward Everett Dale, *The Indians of the Southwest;* Everett Dick, *Dixie Frontier;* R. Carlyle Buley, *The Old Northwest;* Robert E. Gard, *Wisconsin Is My Doorstep;* and Walter Johnson, *William Allen White's America.*

Numerous individual grants from the Rockefeller Foundation have made possible other historical projects. The Foundation gave assistance to Dumas Malone for his biography of Jefferson, made a large grant to the Abraham Lincoln Association for a definitive collection of Lincoln's works, and financed compilation of the *Virginia Historical Index.* Rockefeller contributions also enabled Princeton University to inaugurate an interdepartmental program for the study of American life and traditions.

Historical research has also benefited indirectly from efforts of the Rockefeller Foundation to develop better library facilities. The Foundation appropriated funds to place the complete card catalogs of the Library of Congress in the fifty leading libraries of the world. Grants to the British Museum, the Bibliotheque Nationale, and the Prussian State Library have made possible extensive cataloging projects. Rockefeller support has enabled the Library of Congress to undertake an extensive program of photographing materials in European archives. Over a twelve-year period the Foundation also assisted thirty-eight microfilm projects of libraries and other institutions in the United States and abroad. Grants to the New York Museum of Science and Industry, the Brooklyn Museum, and the Buffalo Museum of Science have made possible experimental programs in training museum personnel.

Throughout the years before World War II, the Carnegie and Rockefeller philanthropies continued to dominate the foundation picture, but at least two smaller foundations made contributions to historical research. Beginning in 1930 the Commonwealth Fund granted money to the Foundation for Legal Research of Columbia University. Four studies of early American law followed: Julius Goebel, *Felony and Misdemeanor: A Study in the History of English Criminal Procedure;* Armand B. DuBois, *The English Business Company after the Bubble Act;* Shaw Livermore, *Early American Land Companies;* and Goebel, *Law Enforcement in Colonial New York.* In 1938 the Andrew Mellon Trust gave $30,000 to the University of Pittsburgh Press to assist in the publication of a series of historical studies of western Pennsylvania.

World War II impaired many foundation activities, but

the impact of wartime and post-war taxation induced hundreds of Americans to establish foundations. These tax-impelled foundations have great variety in their aims and objectives, but few of them undertake to promote history or historical research. In the last ten years, the Rockefeller Foundation has continued as the major source of assistance to historical projects. In the years immediately following the war, it made several grants that reflected a war-born interest in foreign affairs. The Council on Foreign Relations received funds for a history of American foreign policy from 1939 to 1946, which is being written by William L. Langer and S. Everett Gleason. The Royal Institute of International Affairs of London obtained grants for a history of the League of Nations, and for a history of international relations after 1939, to be written by Arnold Toynbee. The Foundation gave $250,000 to establish a Russian Institute at Columbia University as a center for training and research in Russian history, political institutions, and culture. The Huntington Library received funds to continue its studies of the history and culture of the Southwest. Harvard University acquired a five-year grant for support of its research center in entrepreneurial history. The American University obtained funds for a history of Washington, D. C., and the Rockefeller Foundation awarded $1,500,000 to the Social Science Research Council to initiate a capital fund for that organization. In 1954 the General Education Board of the Rockefeller Foundation gave $3,000,000 to the Council of Southern Universities for a ten-year program of faculty fellowships. The Carnegie Corporation continued its support of historical research with a grant of $375,000 to Duke University in 1955 for British Commonwealth studies.

Entrance of the Ford millions into the foundation picture in 1951 was a most dramatic and spectacular event. The first few years of Ford Foundation activity removed any doubt that the trustees might be hesitant to dispense their vast funds. The specter of a foundation that would hand out as much as $67,000,000 in a single year, much of it to the previously neglected social sciences, set American scholars to making plans to capture Ford funds for their projects. Like their predecessors in the foundation field, the Ford trustees indicated a strong preference for large-scale projects that would cut down the work of giving away vast sums of money. "Joint integrated research projects" utilizing the talents of scholars from several disciplines became more than ever the order of the day. The new and the novel in research seemed to have a particular appeal. Most spectacular in the line of group research projects has been the Center for Advanced Study in the Behavioral Sciences at Stanford University. The Ford Foundation granted $3,500,000 for construction and support of the center for five years. Each year thirty-eight "behavioral scientists" including several historians, receive scholarships to work at the center on projects of their own choosing. The expectation is that these scholars from different fields will influence and teach one another and that they will then utilize their newly-acquired techniques in research.

The only direct Ford Foundation support to the field of history has been through the American Historical Association. A grant of $96,000 made in 1956 will enable the Association to undertake a program of preparing and revising bibliographies in British history. Plans call for a new edition of Charles Gross, *Bibliography of British Municipal History*, and revisions of the Conyers Read bibliography of the Tudor period and the Godfrey Davies bibliography of the Stuart period. In addition, the Association plans two new bibliographies to cover the years 1789 to 1900 as well as a volume, *Writings on British History, 1901–1933*. Ford funds of $69,-000 have enabled the Association to begin photoduplication of German war documents now in the United States. The Ford Foundation has also granted the Association $148,000 for a three-year experimental program in assisting high school teachers to broaden their professional knowledge through fellowships. The Association has established a Service Center in Washington for teachers of history. It plans to publish annotated bibliographies and a series of pamphlets summarizing recent research.

In recent years one of the smaller foundations has assisted a unique historical project. The William Volker Fund has financed two historical conferences at the University of Kansas. In 1955 and again in 1956 the University invited about thirty-five young historians to its campus for a ten-day period of lectures and intensive discussions. The first group took up the problem of the nature and writing of history and the second examined the generally accepted interpretations of the Progessive period. Several other small foundations have financed projects of interest to historians. The Buhl Foundation is supporting a program for research in western Pennsylvania history through the Western Pennsylvania Historical Society and the University of Pittsburgh.

In the field of historical restoration the major benefactions have come from private individuals rather than foundations. John D. Rockefeller, Jr. has financed the restoration of Colonial Williamsburg and Henry Ford the construction of the Greenfield Village. However, several small family foundations have given support to restoration projects. The Clark Foundation has made possible the Farmers' Museum and village crossroads at Cooperstown, New York. The New York Foundation has pledged $50,000 to the Staten Island Historical Society for assistance in restoring Colonial Richmond-town, New York.

A review of a half century of foundation assistance to history focuses attention upon several problems of vital importance to all historians. Foremost among these has been the predicament of the individual researcher, that forgotten man of the academic world, who hears of the millions given for large-scale co-operative projects, but is often unable to obtain a small grant for his own research.

What critics have variously referred to as "team thinking," "bureaucratization of research," and "projectitis" has seemed to characterize foundation support not only of history but of all social sciences. At present, over seventy-six percent of research money for the social sciences goes to team projects. Since these are the research programs that make the headlines and win public attention, it is only natural that foundations' trustees should favor them. Dealing in bigness, however, has other advantages. Catering to individual researchers is expensive and time consuming, and most foundations have neither the personnel nor the patience to sift the myriad of individual requests for funds. It is far simpler to make a few large grants to well-known institutions and to support co-operative research. Although such a procedure may cut down the administrative expenses of foundations, it is not accomplished without sacrificing the imagination and insight of individual scholars. Guggenheim grants are at present the only research awards given by a major foundation directly to individuals. Other foundations have dropped similar programs because of the high cost of selecting grantees. The Fund for Advancement of Education of the Ford Foundation has established a fellowship program for college teachers, but awards are not made for research purposes.

Mounting publishing costs in the last ten years have presented historians, as well as other scholars, with a serious dilemma. They must either resort to less expensive methods of printing books and monographs or confine their publishing to articles. This would seem to be an area in which the major foundations could be of assistance, but such aid has been slow in coming. In fact, the only foundation-sponsored history publication project is in danger of coming to an end. The Carnegie Revolving Fund, administered by the American Historical Association since 1926, has exhausted its resources and at last report has been unable to persuade a foundation to replenish its funds. Late in 1956 the Ford Foundation announced the appropriation of $1,727,000 for a five-year program of grants to university presses to stimulate scholarly publication in the humanities and social sciences. Historians should benefit from a project that represents a reversal in foundation policy, for until recently, large foundations have not been willing to subsidize publication.

The social sciences and the humanities have always received considerably less support from foundations than the natural sciences. This continues to be true despite heavy subsidies for scientific research from government and private industry. The greatest difficulty that history and the social sciences have in competing for support is that scientific research produces results that are more tangible and frequently more capable of commercial use. Foundation trustees like to be able to see the effect of their spending in immediate and measurable rewards. This is true within the social sciences as well, where history encounters strong competition for foundation funds. The fields that attract the greatest attention are those that can promise the possibility of immediate utilization of research. Foundations have given important assistance to historical research over the past fifty years, but economic and psychological studies have received by far the largest share of funds allocated to the social sciences. Competition for foundation funds is very keen. If historical research is to receive an increased share of the millions that foundations dispense each year, historians will have to convince foundation trustees of the intrinsic rather than utilitarian importance of their research projects. The trend towards basic research in the sciences should be a significant precedent.

BIBLIOGRAPHY

Annual Reports of the American Historical Association (1890–1955).
Annual Reports of the Ford Foundation (1951–1954).
Annual Reports of the Rockefeller Foundation (1902–1955).
A. W. Mellon Educational and Charitable Trust—A Report of Its Work to December 1945. Pittsburgh, 1946.
Bulletins of the American Council of Learned Societies (1922–1951).
Donnan, Elizabeth and Stock, Leo F., ed. *An Historian's World, Selections from the Correspondence of John Franklin Jameson*. Philadelphia, 1956.
Fellows of the Social Science Research Council, 1925–1951. New York, 1951.
Flexner, Abraham. *Funds and Foundations*. New York, 1952.
Fosdick, Raymond B. *The Story of the Rockefeller Foundation*. New York, 1952.

Gourley, James M. and Lester, Robert M. *The Diffusion of Knowledge.* New York, 1935.

Hollis, Ernest V. *Philanthropic Foundations and Higher Education.* New York, 1938.

Kiger, Joseph C. *Operating Principles of the Larger Foundations.* New York, 1954.

Laski, Harold J. "Foundations, Universities and Research." *Harper's,* 157: 295–303 (August, 1928).

Lester, Robert M. *Forty Years of Carnegie Giving.* New York, 1941.

————. *Thirty Year Catalogue of Grants of the Carnegie Corporation.* New York, 1941.

McDonald, Dwight. *The Ford Foundation, the Men and the Millions.* New York, 1956.

Ogg, Frederick A. *Research in the Humanities and Social Sciences.* New York, 1928.

Rich, Wilmer S. *American Foundations and Their Fields.* New York, 1955.

The Rockefeller Foundation Directory of Fellowship Awards. New York, 1951.

The Social Science Research Council Decennial Report, 1923–1933. New York, 1934.

HISTORICAL ORGANIZATIONS AS AIDS TO HISTORY

by DAVID D. VAN TASSEL

University of Texas

and JAMES A. TINSLEY

University of Houston

*T*HE objectives of the historian have not changed much since Thomas Prince's exhortation "to find out the truth and relate it in the clearest order," but the tools to achieve these objectives have become as complex and specialized as the rest of twentieth-century society. Prince, William Stith, and other colonial craftsmen built their own libraries, gathered their own manuscript materials, wrote, published, and peddled their history. But today each of these functions has become the job of a specialist. The modern historian depends upon an army of specialists, sundry machines, and a variety of organizations.

Surrounded by the maze of guides and aids, libraries and

societies, foundations and presses, is the modern historian as rich as his colonial predecessor? What, in fact, do those organizations professedly devoted to history do to aid and promote historical research and writing? To answer these questions raises another as to classification of historical agencies according to their field of operation. Thus divided, they fall into approximately eight major categories: national, regional, state, local, family, church, ethnic, and topical.

The first historical organizations to appear were the state and local societies, of which there are about eighteen hundred in existence today. These organizations, beginning with the Massachusetts Historical Society in 1791, were founded by individuals whose interests were usually limited to their state or locality. More often than not the founders were actively engaged in promoting the growth of their area, and they viewed history as another means of furthering local interests and emphasizing local importance. It is no coincidence that the first historical societies were formed after the War for Independence. The Revolution and Constitution made it possible for any state to have a large voice in the making of national policy, and thus to serve its own interests. This was an opportunity not easily obtained while under the sway of the British crown, but in the new environment hot competition developed between the seaboard states and between their urban centers for political, economic, and cultural supremacy in the nation. One means of demonstrating a locality's right to an important position in state or nation was through its history. Few, if any, colonial scholars were concerned over the condition of historical studies in their particular locale, but they were very much interested in the condition of its history. Local historians lamented "the paucity of materials, and the extreme difficulty of procuring such [materials] as relate to the first settlement and colonial transactions" of their area, or the fact that their great men and great events had not received their justly earned fame because of the lack of a written history. Thus, the state and local societies were seldom interested in aiding or promoting general historical studies. They were not interested in the history of Europe or Asia, or even the United States, despite the clause in many historical societies' constitutions which expressed their interest in the 'history of the United States in general.'

The collection policies of the early state and local groups were generally quite broad. Those established before the 1880's aimed to rescue and preserve evidences of the whole past of their area, the entire range of human activity. Thus, the Historical Society of Michigan was incorporated in 1828 in order "to discover, procure, and preserve, whatever may relate to the natural, civil, literary, ecclesiastical and aboriginal history of the Country of the Lakes, and of the Territory of Michigan in particular." As a result of this ambitious vision, many societies active during this period became repositories for some surprising items, such as the New York Historical Society's collection of Egyptian mummies and artifacts, the Kansas Historical Society's fine collection of stuffed birds, and Wisconsin's skeleton of a two-headed calf. Aside from these oddities, much of value was collected and even published in the various series of collections, papers, proceedings, and transactions. The early publications are mines, for instance, of archaeological, anthropological, and even geological data, especially for New England, the middle states, and the old Northwest. Most of the older societies also have fine collections of local newspapers, local literature, pamphlets, directories, almanacs, and ephemera for the area they served during the nineteenth century.

Such sweeping collection policies became obsolete during the 1880's as academic historians gained ascendancy in the historical world. Fresh from the seminars at Harvard, Columbia, and Johns Hopkins, these men were primarily interested in political and legal institutions and in great national events. Hence, as they worked their way into policy-making positions in the existing historical societies or founded new ones, they helped to narrow the scope of collecting to fit their limited interests; but at the same time they made the goals more practical and collecting more efficient.

The academic historian alone did not force the historical societies to sharpen their focus. Exigencies of space and economics were also partly responsible for the compromise of the original vision. The phenomenal multiplication of paper work, made possible by the advent of the typewriter and cheap printing, made it impossible for local societies with little space and less money to purchase or house even a substantial part of their area's output. The fragmentation of history as a study narrowed horizons still further. Early in the twentieth century economics, sociology, geology, and anthropology became fields unto themselves, and their materials largely dropped from the ken of the societies.

Recently there has been some evidence of a trend back to the breadth of coverage at which the early societies aimed. As historians have broadened the scope of their interests to include social, intellectual, economic, agricultural, and business history, some of the state and local societies have accordingly enlarged their programs. The State Historical Society of Wisconsin has recently plunged into the collection of materials for business, labor, and medical history. A county society in Arkansas is devoting some attention to local businesses; and the Texas Gulf Coast Historical Association, organized in 1955, has as one of its major aims the collection of business records. Another function of the early nineteenth century historical society, the collection of pioneer reminiscences, has reappeared in the form of oral history projects, started by Columbia University and taken up by the state historical societies of Wisconsin and North Carolina.

State and local societies were organized first in expanding centers of concentrated population that contained some source of wealth and a group of educated men, such as Boston, New York, Worcester, and Philadelphia. Partly because the southern states had fewer urban centers, they lagged in the organization of societies, with college towns often serving as the focal point around which the society grew. Western states often had historical societies before or shortly after they gained statehood. The western societies appeared either in the state capital or proposed capital, or in the largest urban center.

The early nineteenth century societies in the east were primarily supported by private funds, by necessity more than by choice. The Massachusetts Historical Society occasionally applied for state aid but was refused, and the New York and Virginia societies repeatedly failed to get the state assistance they desired. The few societies on the Atlantic coast that managed to struggle through the first lean years usually did so with endowments from deceased members. Exclusively dependent upon private support, the early societies were severely limited in their operations and collections. Much depended upon the zeal of the individual member in building his own collection which might be left to the society. Because of the paucity of such zealous and loyal members, some state societies–Connecticut, New Hampshire, and Vermont, for example–are weak even in their states' colonial history, and the historian must look to the collections of the Massachusetts Historical Society and the American Antiquarian Society. Another handicap to the eastern societies was that their members' interests lay only in the colonial and Revolutionary periods. Hence, they were erratic in their collection and publications for the nineteenth and twentieth centuries. Even today the major emphasis of these societies is upon the colonial period. Only recently have newer organizations arisen in the East to fill that hiatus. The Library of Congress was the most active, if not the only, eastern organization in the nineteenth century collecting contemporary material.

The western state societies, beginning with Wisconsin in 1854, were far more successful than their sisters in gaining state aid. Some historians have looked upon the democratic membership and state support of historical societies in the West as one more proof of the frontier thesis. Actually, few westerners knew or cared anything about history; only a small number were anxious to place their state on a cultural par with those of the East and to preserve the records of the founding, settling, and early years of the state. Because there were usually too few men interested enough to support a historical society, most of the early western societies either failed or languished soon after their founding. Those that did survive did so because of state aid. The Wisconsin and Iowa state historical societies are typical examples. In the case of Wisconsin, the society was organized privately in 1846, but languished because of the lack of interest. In 1853 a few members close to the seat of power reorganized the society, incorporated it, and began to receive state funds for its operation and expansion.

State support did not always assure a society of a long and vigorous life. The Tennessee Historical Society was organized in 1849, reorganized in 1857 with the blessings of the state, became embroiled in politics by 1860, and relapsed into a dormancy from which it has never fully awakened. Nor were all western societies blessed with state support. The Historical and Philosophical Society of Ohio, in spite of its original location in Columbus, did not obtain state aid, but it managed to survive by moving to the more populous Cincinnati in 1849, and later by attaching itself to the University of Cincinnati.

Nevertheless, state aid, however fitful or meager, made it possible for many western societies to build libraries especially strong in contemporary nineteenth-century materials. In cases where the state published the collection or annals of the society, an outlet was not only furnished for historical writing, but the society was also provided a medium of exchange with which to fill out its library.

The greatest concentration of effort of the western societies has most often been centered in the territorial and early statehood period or around those events and personalities that gained national fame. The Texas society, for instance, is strongest in the period from the Texas Revolution through the Civil War and Reconstruction, but the late nineteenth and twentieth centuries are sadly neglected. The Wisconsin society is just now beginning to fill out the populist and progressive periods. The Kansas Historical Society's strength is in the period of the Kansas-Nebraska Act and Civil War. Lincoln has absorbed a disproportionate amount of organizational and individual energy in Illinois, to the detriment of a thorough history of the state. The same preoccupation exists in Oklahoma with badmen and Indians, and in California with the gold rush days.

Some organizations have deliberately attempted to right the balance. In New York, Dixon Ryan Fox, the first trained historian to be president of the state association, promoted the writing and publication (1933–1937) of a ten-volume monographic history of the state. This work still stands as one of the best state histories, and it not only furnished New York with a good, comprehensive history but drew attention to periods other than the colonial and revolutionary times.

The American Historical Association, founded in 1884, was this country's first genuinely national historical organization. It was organized by the first crop of professional historians to come out of the graduate seminars at Berlin, Ann Arbor, Boston, New York, and Baltimore–men who at first scorned the existing state and local societies because of the latter's interest only in local history and romantic nostalgia for "the olden time." These men were nationalists, typical of the new national state created by the Civil War, Reconstruction, and galloping industrialism. They viewed history as a scientifically disciplined study through which man could learn more about himself and the reasons for his action. The new professors took positions in colleges and universities more often than not away from their native town or state. Here they quickly found that promotion depended upon scholarly publication and recognition, and that these two turned in direct ratio upon the national significance of the historian's work. The first efforts of the men who set up the American Historical Association then were to nationalize history in America.

In the formative years, the A. H. A. operated in much the

same manner as the state and local groups. But it went further. It helped to stiffen the backbone of individual Ph. D.'s who were reminded annually through its meetings and periodically through its publications that they were members of a profession with rising standards and with a mission to promote the new approach to history. The trained historians set out, as did the medical and legal professions, to eliminate quackery and malpractice and to work for the accumulation of more data and better methods and working facilities. The fruits of this missionary work began to appear in abundance after the turn of the century. They were manifest in the prolific growth of new and varied historical organizations that performed a bewildering variety of tasks and services in the "golden age" from 1900 to 1940.

Committees and activities started in the late 1890's began to bear fruit after the turn of the century. The Historical Manuscripts Commission was established in 1895, the first standing committee of the Association. It made a preliminary survey of the manuscripts in Washington, D. C., and after 1900 it began to publish surveys of state archives and important papers, such as the correspondence of Calhoun, Chase, and the French ministers during Washington's administration. The major objective of this committee was to promote the centralization of all the papers of all the bureaus and agencies of the federal government. The reports and propaganda emanating from this commission and the lobbying of John Franklin Jameson finally bore fruit in 1928 when Congress voted funds for a national archives building. Stimulated by the concern of the A. H. A. over the national archives, state legislatures became interested in the systematic preservation of their papers and began to form state historical commissions or departments of archives. Generally it was a trained historian who inspired the move or who first manned the new job. These state archival commissions have been very active in collecting manuscripts, publishing documents and historical journals, and stimulating research in state history. The A. H. A. has also extended historical knowledge by awarding research prizes and by recommending minimal secondary school history curricula.

The *American Historical Review,* established by a few historians as a private venture in 1895, gained the support of the A. H. A. in 1898. By 1900 it was on firm financial ground. It gained recognition as the organ of professional historians, was arbiter of professional standards through the quality of its articles and its book reviews, and served as the model for most of the historical journals that soon began to appear all over the country.

The greatest weakness in the Association's program was its reluctance to extend co-operation and leadership to the state and local societies. In 1890 Herbert B. Adams promised that the A. H. A. would cater to the needs of the local societies, but by 1900 it had done nothing beyond the annual publication of a list of historical societies in the United States and A. P. C. Griffin's very creditable bibliography of these societies. When state and local groups showed signs of setting up their own national organization, the A. H. A. moved to block the formation of a competing group. In 1904 the Conference of State and Local Historical Societies was created as a part of the program of the American Historical Association.

The creation of the Conference silenced some of the protests of the state and local men. It gave recognition to the importance of the local groups and also gave them a forum for the exchange of ideas. For years the Conference met in conjunction with the American Historical Association's annual meeting and held sessions devoted to the problems of historical societies. In 1915 the Conference inspired a group of Northwestern historical societies to co-operate in employing Newton D. Mereness to calendar all of the material relating to the history of each member state in the archives of the federal government. As the years passed, however, the Conference did little besides meet as one more paper-reading session of the A. H. A. convention, and its members grew restive.

In 1937 Herbert A. Kellar read a paper at the meeting of the Conference suggesting a plan for a strong national organization of state and local historical societies, and thus gave impetus to the movement which finally resulted in the establishment in 1940 of the Association for State and Local History. Kellar and his group felt that their interests and problems were so different from those of the A. H. A. that they decided upon complete separation, even to time and place of meetings. During the new Association's sixteen years of existence, it has had some notable success, but has yet a long way to go in realizing its original goal of bringing about closer co-operation of state societies. It has aided historical societies by publishing occasional pamphlets on various phases of society work, a service the Conference might have performed had it published even half of the good and informative papers that were read at its meetings. The Association also publishes a monthly newsletter, *History News*, which serves to keep societies abreast of each other's activities, but heavily emphasizes popularization programs and mechanics with only little attention to research projects, collection policies, or manuscript and library acquisitions. The magazine *American*

Heritage originated in 1947 as the organ of the Association and was designed to promote and broadcast work in local history. After two years the journal changed format and policy. Finally in 1954, under the joint sponsorship of the Association and the Society of American Historians, the magazine turned into a money-making proposition, and nothing remains of its original purpose. Now the *American Heritage*, in hard covers, has as its mission the popularization of national history among the *Fortune, Vogue,* and *Better Homes and Gardens* clientele. The Association has also issued from time to time some very useful "do-it-yourself" pamphlets, such as how to organize and run a local historical society, how to write local history, and how to write a town's war history.

While the national organization of local societies was being perfected, regional historical societies were formed by historians not entirely satisfied with the single yearly meeting of the American Historical Association. The A. H. A. meetings were inconvenient and expensive to attend and at best could devote only one session to specific areas of interest. In 1895 a group of southerners, led by Colyer Meriwether, a Johns Hopkins Ph. D., founded the Southern History Association in Washington, D. C. This organization died in 1907 from lack of funds, but it left eleven volumes of its publications on southern history and a solid precedent for the formation in 1934 of the more healthy Southern Historical Association. In 1904 Max Farrand, H. Morse Stephens, and other west coast historians organized the Pacific Coast Branch of the American Historical Association. In 1907 Clarence Paine, secretary of the Nebraska State Historical Society, began a movement among historical societies of the Midwest which led to the formation of the Mississippi Valley Historical Association. Some of the founders attempted to make this organization another branch of the A. H. A., but their idea was engulfed by the policy of promoting the study of regional history and co-operation between state societies. The constituent societies, however, rapidly lost control to the academic historians, who turned it into a second national organization for American historians.

The trend toward the formation of regional associations has continued to the present. There are now at least seven regional organizations which draw their membership almost solely from the history departments of colleges and universities. For this reason they are not wealthy, but all of their resources are devoted to furthering the interests of historical studies on a broad base.

In the decade of the twenties, topical, ethnic, and family organizations came into being. The topical organizations represented the trend toward specialization among historians, with the exception of such societies as the Marine Historical Society (1929), the Railway and Locomotive Historical Society, or the Steamship Historical Society of America, which were largely the product of a nostalgia for a passing era. The ethnic historical agencies, such as the American Swedish Historical Museum (1926), the Norwegian-American Historical Association (1926), and the Swiss-American Historical Society (1928), were formed at the time when immigration was being restricted, quotas being disputed, and the contribution of various immigrant groups to American history were being sought out and heralded in print. The American Jewish Historical Society was founded in 1892 at a time of heavy Jewish migration to the United States and a period of rising anti-Semitism in the country. The Association for the Study of Negro Life and History was founded in 1916 during a period of aggressive activity by Negroes to win equal civil rights for their race.

Family historical societies, trusts, or libraries, were primarily a development of the twentieth century. Few families in the United States have remained important enough or rich enough, or stayed in one place long enough to warrant a family archives any more elegant or institutional than an old trunk in the attic. Early in the twentieth century the Adams family set up a trust to maintain the John Quincy Adams house in Quincy, Massachusetts as an historic shrine, and to maintain the family library and papers on deposit in the Massachusetts Historical Society, but closed to the public until 1952. Fortunately for historians, other families have not followed the Adams example. The Fairbanks family organized a trust in 1910 to maintain their homestead, "the oldest frame house in the United States," in Dedham, Massachusetts, but their papers are in the Dedham Historical Society library and are open to scholars. The McCormick family of Chicago formed a family historical society and in 1915 hired a trained historian, Herbert A. Kellar, to run it. Kellar broadened the scope of the society beyond the immediate family and by the time of his death had developed the best collection of colonial and nineteenth-century agriculture materials in the country.

Since Herbert Hoover endowed the Hoover War Library at Stanford, it has become the fashion for Presidents of the United States or their friends to establish a private depository for their papers. These collections are handled by professional archivists, but historians have been called in for their advice upon policy matters. Quite often, therefore, these new organizations have followed the pattern established by Kellar by broadening the scope beyond those things immediately related to the particular person. The Hoover War Library is building a rich collection of materials on World War I and on war in general. The Roosevelt Library at Hyde Park takes in almost anything relating to the administration of Franklin D. Roosevelt, broadly defined. The administrators of the Truman Library have decided to concentrate upon building a collection of materials relating to foreign affairs.

As historical organizations have multiplied, their functions have become more sharply defined. In the nineteenth century the same personnel in an agency maintained a museum and an art gallery, built a research library, edited the publications, and raised funds. Some state organizations still carry on these omnibus programs but have tended to specialize within themselves, delegating the museum to curators, publications to editors, and separating the library and manuscripts divisions. Historical societies founded since 1890 have tended to specialize in collecting and publishing, leaving museum activities to a separate organization, as is the case in Texas. Even the American Historical Association was founded on an early pattern of the historical society and was authorized to build a museum and a library, but the close proximity of the Smithsonian and the Library of Congress soon obviated these functions. The elderly Massachusetts Historical Society has decided to devote its energies solely to its function as a research institution.

Along with the rise of specialized agencies and specialization within organizations, certain refinements and innovations in functions appeared. The history magazines, rare in the nineteenth century, were established by societies all over the country during the twentieth century. As trained historians worked their way into the ranks of the historical societies, magazines sprang into being as a means of spreading knowledge of the locality's history and as an outlet for scholarly articles. In 1906 the *Maryland Magazine of History* was founded and edited by William H. Browne of Johns Hopkins University. In 1915 Solon Buck, whisked from under the wing of Clarence Alvord at Illinois to rejuvenate the Minnesota Historical Society, established *Minnesota History*. Milo M. Quaife, fresh from the graduate school of the University of Chicago and the first trained historian to fill the office of Superintendent of the State Historical Society of Wisconsin, founded the *Wisconsin Magazine of History*. One organization after the other followed the trend, until by 1950 there were over one hundred and thirty quarterly or monthly magazines devoted entirely or largely to history. The embarrassingly rich number of outlets for historical research obviously demands a central abstracting system such as *Historical Abstracts*, a new periodical published in Germany.

During the great splurge of publication, historical agencies concentrated on documents and bibliographies. Local efforts, such as the *Historical Index of Virginia*, culminated nationally in the publication of the twenty-one volume *Dictionary of American Biography*. In more recent years several historical societies invaded the publishing field to become virtually university presses.

Due to the rising costs of printing, the publication programs of historical organizations now emphasize interpretation rather than documentation. The one-time goal of every historical society, the publication of manuscript collections, has all but lapsed. The ponderous volumes of proceedings, once packed with articles and source material, are now starved skeletons of their former selves or have disappeared entirely in favor of a skimpy account of meetings and finance hidden in the back pages of the organization's journal.

Despite the passing of some scholarly luxuries, historical societies managed to gain a small share of the new opulence based on the post-war boom and cold war spending. Memberships climbed, sometimes doubled over the previous decade. Money poured into the coffers, sometimes by appreciation of real estate and security values, but also by increased dues, donations, and legislative appropriations. Most of this new wealth, however, did not go into research projects or new aids to history. It was absorbed by higher maintenance and printing costs, long-needed face-liftings for the physical plants, and invested as capital funds.

New organizations did appear during the past decade, as may be seen in the swollen list in the 1956 *Directory of Historical Societies and Agencies in the United States and Canada*, but there was little novelty in the type of organization formed. Only three new organizations differed very greatly from the established patterns: The Civil War Round Table, started in 1948; the Forest History Foundation, established in 1946; and the National Trust for Historic Preservation, chartered by Congress in 1953. The Civil War Round Table evolved from the informal gatherings of Civil War experts and amateurs at the Abraham Lincoln Book Store in Chicago. Missionaries from this original center have planted local branches all over the land, the most active of which are the Round Tables in Chicago, New York, and Washington, D. C. The local organization usually sponsors monthly meetings for sipping cocktails, eating good food, listening to the latest expert on a facet of *The* War, and trading books. These organizations have been a boon to the second-hand book sellers dealing in Civil War materials. They have made the old *War of the Rebellion Official Records* worth its tonnage in gold, furnished a ready-made lecture trail for authors of Civil War histories, and inspired the establishment in 1954 of a new journal, *Civil War History*.

The Forest History Foundation, started as the Forest Products History Foundation, an adjunct to the Minnesota Historical Society, was established in 1946 by a grant from the lumbering families of Weyerhaeuser and Denckmann. In 1955 the Foundation severed its ties with the Minnesota Historical Society and set up independent housekeeping. Its main function has been the promotion of the study of the lumber industry, conservation, and the history of forests in the United States or Canada. The Director, Elwood R. Maunder, has traveled over the country persuading lumber companies to preserve their records in some permanent depository. The Foundation has given aid to scholars, has published two books, and will soon publish *Forest History Sources of the United States and Canada*.

The National Trust for Historic Preservation aims "to preserve and interpret structures and sites of historic and/or architectural merit on a nation-wide scale." Although the organization is privately supported, it manages to publish a quarterly, *Historic Preservations*, and pamphlets, and employs a full-time historian. The Trust is building a library of documents and material on historic sites throughout the nation. Its research and reports are valuable to historians of architecture and culture, and to biographers of those people whose homes have been preserved. If the Trust, in its efforts to supplement work of the National Park System, follows the latter's methods and promotes the careful and accurate footnoting of restorations throughout the country, it will be doing a great service to history.

Since 1946, historical societies have consciously departed from their traditions by popularizing history and by professionalizing their staffs. The effort and energy directed toward popularization, or public education, has so increased since World War II as to become one of the most time-consuming features of the work of historical agencies. The need for popular support and the demand for broad dissemination of historical knowledge is by no means new, even to the twentieth century. Even that staid old lady of history, the Massachusetts Historical Society, sponsored a popular lecture series in the 1830's to gain financial support and to spread historical knowledge. In 1897 Reuben G. Thwaites, director of the State Historical Society of Wisconsin, declared that a state society, in order to survive, had "to cultivate some of the arts of popularity." Many of the trained historians moving into historical society work realized that they must gain popular support in order to get the backing necessary to carry out expensive collecting and publication programs. Benjamin F. Shambaugh of Iowa, in the vanguard of the Progressive movement, attempted to prove the utility of the society by establishing an applied history project. He hired trained researchers to throw the light of history on current problems of the state in the belief that the historical perspective would aid state leaders to make wise decisions. Although the project gained wide acclaim and seven volumes were published, this was not the path of public service historical agencies were to follow. In 1918 Floyd C. Shoemaker expressed the line that historical societies would take when he asserted that "popularizing state history is profitable as well as educational. Any commonwealth which exploits well its own annals has an advantage in retaining its population and in attracting new citizens." The selling of local history for its economic benefits became far more prevalent than emphasizing the utility of history in the solution of current problems.

Historical societies have been sensitive to the intellectual climate of the years following World War II. The overflow of patriotic enthusiasm, the tensions of the Cold War, and the defections of Americans to Communism have brought loud demands for a re-emphasis upon Americanism. State legislatures required loyalty oaths of state employees and American history courses in schools and colleges. Popular magazines ran American heritage series; programs based on American history on radio and television were numerous. Americans were searching their past for guidance, for faith and for ammunition to fight an aggressive ideology. While much of the searching and selling of Americanism through history went on outside the usual historical circles, the historical societies benefited by, and took advantage of, the new boom in American history. Some astute directors of historical agencies saw the direction of the wind and chose the proper tack, as did S. K. Stevens in an article entitled "Local History–Foundation of Our Faith in Democracy."

The state historical societies led the way in popularizing history because of their need for increased appropriations. Museums, the traditional drawing card of historical societies, were refurbished, displays made more attractive, topical, and timely. The journals were sandwiched between slick colorful covers, journalistic columns were added, and pictures introduced. Monthly or bi-monthly bulletins were sent out to members to keep them abreast of the activities of the staff and of town and county societies. The radio and television were utilized in the effort to bring history to the people. The Texas State Historical Society inaugurated in 1941 a junior division with a magazine of its own to encourage school children to write history, and the movement spread over the country after the war. The State Historical Society of Wisconsin has started an annual history caravan of society staff members who stump the state booming history. The Wisconsin society also sends a privately-endowed "historymobile" with museum displays touring the state, visiting county fairs and other public functions. The North Carolina State Department of Archives and History has utilized movies.

The new spirit of the history promoters was best expressed by Christopher Crittenden, head of the North Carolina State Department of Archives and History, in a colloquium on "The Role of the Historical Society in Modern America." Crittenden declared, on behalf of his department, that "we believe in using every trick in the bag, in not pulling our punches, in bringing out every weapon in the arsenal, in order to sell our state's history to our people." The results of these efforts to popularize state, local and national history have thus far been beneficial to the study of history. Wisconsin, North Carolina, New York, and other states carrying on concerted efforts to "sell" their state's history are also doing much more than ever before in their original fields of collection and publication.

The second trend that began to take shape in this post-war decade was the professionalization of historical society staffs. Before the war the men who ran historical agencies generally had Ph. D.'s in history and served their apprenticeship in the teaching and writing of history. When they took on a historical society job, as often as not it was in conjunction with teaching duties. There were in the twenties and thirties only a small group of men, such as Herbert A. Kellar, Floyd C. Shoemaker, and Milo M. Quaife, who spent all or most of their professional lives as officers of historical agencies. After World War II, however, the number began to increase. The first wave of men granted Ph. D.'s after the war filled the backlog of teaching vacancies and jobs became scarce, especially at the time of the outbreak of the Korean War. Under these straitened conditions, graduate students who stuck to history began to hedge against the future by taking minors in education to get teachers' certificates, or in government in preparation for foreign service or the Central Intelligence Agency. Some found their way into historical society work, either immediately after acquiring their degrees or through part-time work in societies affiliated with the university which they attended. The increasing prosperity and expanding public services of historical agencies put a premium upon young men with some historical society experience. Today the economic future for the new history Ph. D. with historical society experience is far brighter in historical agency work than it is in teaching.

Not only are the new historical society officers coming directly from graduate schools to submerge themselves in organizational problems, but there is some indication that they soon will be trained for this work in graduate school. In 1952 the Library School of the University of Wisconsin inaugurated a course in the work of historical agencies which was initiated and taught by the staff of the State Historical Society. The course has been accepted as a minor for candidates for the

Ph. D. in history. This course has been widely acclaimed, though not as yet imitated.

Another step toward the professionalization of historical agency workers has been the organization of their own associations. The librarians and archivists have long had their own associations. Museum directors have their professional organization, and since 1940 the historical society officers have had their professional agency in the Association for State and Local History. Thus historical society staffs are receiving specialized training as librarians, archivists, museum directors, and society officials.

The two trends of popularization and professionalization, although well-established, have by no means swept the whole field of historical agencies. In those agencies affected, history as a whole has generally benefited. However, there are certain dangers to historical studies if these trends are over emphasized. The old liaison between the practicing historians and historical agencies established between 1900 and 1940 is being weakened as the contacts and the common interests decrease. The agency worker who is trained to his job, who is concerned with promotion and administrative problems, who goes to professional meetings only with men of his ilk, who receives professional bulletins filled with matter dealing only with organizational and promotional problems, is bound to lose touch with, not to speak of sympathy for, the needs of research historians.

The justification for spending time in promotional work and popularization has been that it is the duty of the historical society to educate the people in the state's or locality's history; that the research that goes into making a museum display, a popular book, a radio or television program, or a pageant is just as much historical research as the work that goes into a dry monograph, and that it pays off in more money and support for the collection, preservation, study, and publication of historical materials. These arguments are all quite valid and the new developments in historical society work will continue to benefit the study of history if the limitations of each justifying argument are kept clearly in mind.

The dissemination of historical knowledge was indeed one of the original purposes of most historical societies, but the founder usually spoke of this aim in terms of the publication of documents, original articles, and books, and not in the modern terms of "selling" or "bringing history to the people." Today, as always, in order to interest large numbers of people in history, it must be made palatable, either interesting as a form of entertainment or vital as a form of instruction. The objective of the popularizer or public instructor is mixed. His major aim is to get his message across to the largest possible audience and distort the truth as little as possible in the process. The goal of the historical scholar is to search out the truth about historical processes, not only to depict exactly what happened but to find out as nearly as possible why it happened, and thus add, change, or correct in some degree the body of knowledge of mankind. As a by-product, a historian's work may be popular if he happens to be a skilled writer or if his findings are sufficiently earth shaking, but his major objective as a student of history is discovering truth. As long as historical agencies recognize the distinction and the importance of their functions toward furthering basic knowledge, their efforts to bring history to the people will aid history.

The record of historical agencies substantiates their vital and varied services to history. However, there is much that could be done by these agencies that is not being done. Historical societies would do well to imitate one another's best projects instead of operating in a provincial vacuum and vying with each other for originality of ideas. Every agency should issue periodically lists of gaps or areas needing more study in their spheres of interest with some notation on the materials they possess or need for such studies. Rarely are the members of historical societies fully utilized in its work, nor are they as thoroughly canvassed for materials as for money. The need for co-operation among historical agencies still goes unfilled, although the number of national, regional, and state co-ordinating organizations continues to grow.

The Association for State and Local History could be a great force in suggesting and initiating co-operative research projects that would be supported or encouraged by local historical societies. The effect of this co-operation would be to broaden the contribution of historical agencies and enlarge their service to Clio. This is the proper function for all who wear her badge.

BIBLIOGRAPHY

Alexander, Edward P. "What Should Our Historical Societies Do?" *Bulletins* of the American Association for State and Local History, 1: 3–26 (1941).

Angle, Paul. *The Chicago Historical Society, 1856–1956, an Unconventional Chronicle.* Chicago, 1956.

Blegen, Theodore C. "State Historical Agencies and the Public." *Minnesota History*, 9: 123–134 (1928).

Bourne, Henry E. "Development and Work of American Historical Societies." American Historical Association *Annual Report* (1904).

Dunlap, Leslie W. *Amercian Historical Societies, 1790–1860.* Madison, 1944.

Fox, Dixon Ryan. "Local Historical Societies in the United States." *Canadian Historical Review,* 13: 263–267 (September, 1932).

Hesseltine, William B. *Pioneer's Mission.* Madison, 1954.

Malin, James. "Notes on the Writing of General Histories of Kansas." *The Kansas Historical Quarterly,* 21: 184–223, 264–287, 331–378, 407–444, 598–643 (1954–1955).

McCormick, Richard P. "The Future of Historical Activities in New Jersey." New Jersey Historical Society *Proceedings,* 69: 230–234 (July, 1951).

Sellers, James L. "Before We Were Members." *Mississippi Valley Historical Review,* 40: 3–24 (June, 1953).

Sioussat, St. George L. "After Fifty Years: A Review of the Beginnings." *Maryland History Magazine,* 50: 273–281 (December, 1955).

Stevens, S. K. "The Present Status of Organization and Aid for Local History in the United States." *Proceedings of the Conference of State and Local Historical Societies* (1939).

Thwaites, R. G. "State Supported Historical Societies and their Functions." American Historical Association *Annual Report* (1897).

————. "Bibliographical Activities of Historical Societies of the United States." Bibliographical Society of America *Papers,* I (1906–1907).

Ubbelohde, Carl. "The Threshold of Possibilities–The Society 1900–1955." *Wisconsin Magazine of History,* 39: 76–84 (Winter, 1955–1956).

Vail, R. G. *Knickerbocker Birthday, A Sesqui-Centennial History of the New York Historical Society, 1804–1954.* New York, 1954.

Van Tassel, David D. and Tinsley, James A. A Questionnaire Sent to 100 Historical Organizations in 1957.

Wesley, Charles H. "Racial Historical Societies and the American Heritage." *The Journal of Negro History,* 37: 11–35 (January, 1952).

THE GROWTH OF AGRI-
CULTURAL HISTORY

by WAYNE D. RASMUSSEN

United States Department of Agriculture

*A*GRICULTURAL history became an established field of scholarship about a generation ago with the publication by the Carnegie Institution of Washington of a *History of Agriculture in the Northern United States 1620–1860*, by P. W. Bidwell and J. I. Falconer and the *History of Agriculture in the Southern United States to 1860*, by L. C. Gray. These volumes resulted from an interest that had developed at the University of Wisconsin in agricultural history at a time when the Carnegie Institution of Washington had funds available for such work. Frederick Jackson Turner had injected agricultural economics into history in his paper on "The Significance of the Frontier in American History" in 1893. At about the same time Richard T. Ely had begun to emphasize the historical approach to economic questions. Together with their colleague, William A. Scott, they encouraged students at Wisconsin to write dissertations in the field of agricultural history. Among the important pioneering studies produced were "The Decline of Landowning Farmers in England," by H. C. Taylor, and "The History of Agriculture in Dane County, Wisconsin," by B. H. Hibbard. Although Hibbard was a student of economics rather than of history, his work is still used by historians and is often cited as a model descriptive study of dynamic economic forces operating in a limited area.

H. C. Taylor's interest in the historical approach to economic problems led to his being asked by K. L. Butterfield in 1906 to write a history of land tenure as part of a project of the Carnegie Institution of Washington in economic history. Later Taylor accepted responsibility for developing a history of agricultural production in the United States from 1840 to 1860, and in 1916 he took charge of the agricultural history section of the Carnegie project. He did some work himself on both projects, but his greatest contribution was in interesting a number of graduate students, including J. I. Falconer, L. C. Gray, O. E. Baker, and O. C. Stine, in agricultural history.

Falconer's foundation study on northern agriculture from 1840 to 1860 grew out of his doctoral dissertation in 1914. Carnegie funds secured P. W. Bidwell of Yale University as a collaborator in the United States Bureau of Agricultural Economics from 1921 to 1924 to write a history of northern agriculture prior to 1840. The works of Falconer and Bidwell were combined and published by the Carnegie Institution of Washington in 1925.

Meanwhile, in 1911 L. C. Gray had written a dissertation on the plantation system of the South during the colonial period. This study was expanded and revised and, with support from the Carnegie Institution and the Bureau of Agricultural Economics, was published in two volumes in 1933.

Taylor's influence extended beyond the publication of the pioneer studies into the inauguration of formal history work in the United States Department of Agriculture. On Taylor's recommendation, O. E. Baker was appointed in 1912 to carry out geographical work in the Office of Farm Management, where he was joined in 1916 by O. C. Stine. After producing a series of dot maps to summarize statistical data, they worked with H. C. Taylor and others on the series of historical articles on agricultural commodities in the *Yearbooks of Agriculture* for 1921 through 1925. Taylor, himself, became chief of the Office of Farm Management in 1919, and in 1922 organized and headed the Bureau of Agricultural Economics.

The history work in the new Bureau of Agricultural Economics was placed in the Division of Statistical and Historical Research, headed by O. C. Stine. Until his retirement in 1951, Stine was administratively responsible for the work, ensuring the continuity of historical research in the Department of Agriculture.

Before the inauguration of historical studies in the Department of Agriculture, several individuals had been carrying on historical investigations either as an approach to current research problems or as an avocation. Rodney H. True, a botanist in the Department from 1901 to 1920, published a number of historical articles which focused on the agricultural and botanical interests of Thomas Jefferson and the locale and persons associated with him. Lyman Carrier became interested in the history of forage crops and in 1923 published *The Beginnings of Agriculture in America*, a history of colonial agriculture. C. A. Browne, an agricultural chemist, published many historical books and articles during his long career with the Department. Alfred Charles True, a Department administrator concerned with state relations, made a major contribution to the history of agricultural institutions with his studies of agricultural extension work, agricultural education, and agricultural experimentation and research. Claribel R. Barnett, librarian of the Department from 1907 to 1940, developed the library as a research center, and was responsible for acquiring its invaluable collection of early farm journals. She also wrote a number of articles of historical interest, including twenty-five on agricultural leaders for the *Dictionary of American Biography*.

In the spring of 1939, M. L. Wilson, then Under Secretary of Agriculture, invited a number of agricultural historians to meet in Washington to appraise current research programs in the Department of Agriculture and to make suggestions for the future. The conferees included H. C. Taylor, Herbert A. Kellar, Harry J. Carman, O. E. Baker, C. A. Browne, E. E. Edwards, L. C. Gray, O. C. Stine, Carl C. Taylor, and A. G. Peterson. The conference made a number of sweeping recommendations, including: (1) The Department of Agriculture should actively encourage the collection, preservation, and the making available of source materials for research workers in agricultural history; (2) the Department should encourage the keeping of current records and the preservation of records which might be useful for research in the future; (3) the preparation and publication of bibliographies should be continued; (4) provision should be made to publish documents; (5) monographs relating to agricultural history should be published by the Department; (6) the Department should encourage state and local groups to carry out research in agricultural history; (7) the Department's history staff should conduct research in the field of agricultural history; and (8) the Department should assist in the establishment of a Museum of American Agriculture, which would be part of a larger concept, a Hall of Agriculture, which would serve as a center for presenting the various aspects of agriculture to the public.

A number of the conference recommendations have been adopted. The History Section of the Division of Statistical and Historical Research was strengthened by additional staff members over a period of two years. The Department established a series of publications entitled the Agricultural History Series and in 1941 established a Department of Agriculture Committee on Agricultural History to determine policy and standards for the Series. Mary G. Lacy, Assistant Librarian of the Department, was the first chairman of the committee. She was succeeded by Lois Olson in 1943. The committee was reconstituted in 1947 with O. C. Stine as chairman, with the additional duty of encouraging the keeping of appropriate historical records of the development of the Department's programs and administration.

The Agricultural History Series consisted of seven publications issued between 1941 and 1943. The most widely circulated of the studies was *Some Landmarks in the History of the Department of Agriculture*, by T. Swann Harding. *A History of Livestock Raising in the United States, 1607–1860*, by James Westfall Thompson, had a wide appeal to agricultural and economic historians. The impact of war upon research was reflected in studies by Arthur G. Peterson and Thomas J. Mayock on agricultural problems during World War I. The last number in the Series was *Jefferson and Agriculture: A Sourcebook*, compiled and edited by Everett E. Edwards, and published in 1943.

The sourcebook on Jefferson was one part of the work of

the National Agricultural Jefferson Bicentenary Committee established in 1943. The Secretary of Agriculture was appointed chairman of the committee; he, in turn, appointed E. E. Edwards secretary of the committee. The Bicentenary Committee was active, within the limitations imposed by the war, in encouraging research, publication, and public addresses upon Jefferson's contributions to agriculture. On April 13, 1944, the committee sponsored a pilgrimage to Monticello. Several addresses were presented upon that occasion, including one by Herbert A. Kellar entitled "Living Agricultural Museums."

The war hampered the work of the Jefferson committee, but it encouraged the development of current recording of policy and administration, and the study of major administrative problems and program developments of the Department of Agriculture. This work, encouraged throughout the government by the Bureau of the Budget, was assigned to the Department's Director of Information in 1941, transferred to the Bureau of Agricultural Economics in 1943, where it was placed under the direction of O. C. Stine. The Department obtained the services of John M. Gaus of Harvard University as consultant to the project and employed Gladys L. Baker to assume full-time responsibility for the project. This activity resulted in the collection of a highly selected group of documents relating to the Department of Agriculture's war and postwar activities, in the publication of *The Farmer in the Second World War* by W. W. Wilcox, in the preparation of several studies of administration that could not be published at the time, and in the preparation and publication of eleven monographs dealing with wartime changes in various sectors of agriculture. The work proved to be of considerable use in the Korean War, and the program was enlarged to cover that conflict and subsequent agricultural policies and programs.

The formal and informal interests in history within the Department found organized expression in the Agricultural History Society, which was established in 1919. The first steps toward organizing the society were taken by R. C. True, who became its first president. W. J. Trimble of North Dakota Agricultural College, largely responsible for the affiliation of the society with the American Historical Association, became vice-president. Lyman Carrier was elected secretary-treasurer, and R. W. Kelsey of Haverford College and O. C. Stine of the Office of Farm Management were elected members of the executive committee. The list of charter members also included O. E. Baker, C. R. Barnett, P. W. Bidwell, J. I. Falconer, and A. C. True, all of whom subscribed to the society's objectives of stimulating interest, promoting study, and facilitating research and publication in agricultural history.

Herbert A. Kellar, Director of the McCormick Historical Association, was among the growing band of agricultural historians who joined the new organization. Kellar's position alone made him an important addition to the society, but his interest and enthusiasm soon made him one of its moving spirits. He served as vice-president from 1921 to 1922, as president from 1922 to 1924, and as secretary-treasurer from 1924 to 1927.

The society has long urged the establishment of a national agricultural museum. As early as June 1919, Kellar prepared an extensive report on a proposed museum to portray the development of harvesting machinery, and in 1922 suggested that the society prepare and publish a guide for local, regional, and national agricultural museums. He continued to make other suggestions over the years. In May 1939, he presented "A Suggested Plan for a National Organization of Agriculture." This plan was an elaboration of an idea that had been proposed by the National Grange and further developed by M. L. Wilson, then Under Secretary of Agriculture and a charter member and past president of the society. Kellar's plan envisioned a museum of agriculture that would also provide housing for the major national farm organizations as well as for the society. The plan was presented to the Agricultural History Conference called by the Department of Agriculture in May 1939. World War II caused a suspension of the society's agitation for a museum, but in 1944 Kellar revived the idea in his Jefferson Bicentenary address at Monticello.

The collection of manuscripts, the establishment of museums, and similar enterprises are of great historical value, and encourage the writing of history. However, it is also essential that some means of publication be provided for the history after it is written. In carrying out one of its original purposes to facilitate the publication of research in the field, the Agricultural History Society reached an agreement in 1920 with the American Historical Association whereby the association would allot at least 300 pages of its annual report to the society. The society issued these pages separately, under the title of Agricultural History Society *Papers* in 1921, 1923, and 1925.

The arrangement with the association was of great assistance, but it was not a satisfactory substitute for a journal. A publications committee devoted much time to the problem beginning in 1922. In 1925, Herbert A. Kellar presented a report entitled "Suggestions Concerning the Proposed Journal of the Agricultural History Society." These efforts resulted in the establishment of *Agricultural History*, the first issue of which appeared in January 1927, with O. C. Stine as editor. Two issues appeared in 1927; since then the journal has been on a quarterly basis. Stine served as editor until 1931, followed by Everett E. Edwards, until his death in 1952. Edwards was succeeded by Wayne D. Rasmussen, acting editor until April 1953; Vernon Carstensen, 1953–1956; D. A. Brown, 1957; and C. Clyde Jones since 1958. An editorial board has served from 1928 until the present. Herbert A. Kellar was a member of the board from its inception until his death in 1955.

Shortly after O. C. Stine became editor of *Agricultural History* he appointed Everett E. Edwards to serve as a member of the staff of the Division of Statistical and Historical Research. While Stine had interests in the fields of economics and statistics as well as history, Edwards was a professional historian who devoted his life to agricultural history. During the twenty-five years that he served in the Division he made *Agricultural History* one of the most useful and highly respected historical journals; he did much to define the field of agricultural history. He prepared bibliographies and other research tools that encouraged historians to work in the field, and he prepared a number of definitive articles and monographic studies.

Prior to the appointment in Washington, E. E. Edwards had been associated at Harvard University with Frederick Merk, who had been trained at Wisconsin in Turner's thesis and approach to agricultural history. Edwards, in turn, spread the Turner thesis through the courses he gave at the Department of Agriculture Graduate School and the American University and informally, through the assistance he extended to young researchers in the National Archives and Library of Congress.

The first formal course of record in agricultural history which has continued to the present was announced at Iowa State College in 1913 and given in 1914. The course was taught for thirty-six years by Louis Bernard Schmidt; it was then given by Earle D. Ross from 1950 until his retirement in 1956. The course was another product of the fruitful Turner seminar at Wisconsin. The next course in agricultural history of which there is a definite record was offered in 1923 at North Caroline State College as a course in sociology by Carl C. Taylor. It was subsequently transferred from the Sociology to the History Department. Other courses have been given for considerable periods of time at a number of institutions and have contributed to arousing an interest in the subject.

Research and publication in agricultural history during the past fifty years has encouraged many historians and some editors to give greater attention to the subject. Some indication of this may be found in the plans made for the nine-volume *Economic History of the United States*, published by Farrar and Rinehart. Two of the nine volumes, bracketing the nineteenth century, were to be devoted to agriculture. The volume covering the period 1860–1897, by Fred A. Shannon, was published in 1945 under the title of *The Farmer's Last Frontier; Agriculture, 1860–1897*. The volume covering the period 1815–1860 is being written by Paul Wallace Gates of Cornell University.

In 1934, the Columbia University Press made an outstanding contribution to the field with the inauguration of the Columbia University Studies in Agricultural History. The series was edited by Harry J. Carman and Rexford G. Tugwell, then professors, respectively, of history and of economics at Columbia University. The series, which comprised thirteen volumes through 1956, has included reprints of early writings important to American agriculture, the publication of farm and plantation journals, and the publication of monographs upon special aspects of agricultural history.

The valuable research which has been done in agricultural history illuminates those areas in which more work is necessary. The results of research published prior to 1930 were classified and summarized in Everett E. Edwards' major contribution to bibliography, his *Bibliography of the History of Agriculture in the United States* of 1930. Edwards also prepared many historical bibliographies on particular aspects of agricultural history between 1930 and 1944. The comprehensive bibliographic index of the history of agriculture which Edwards instituted at the Department of Agriculture is currently maintained and is available for consultation by scholars. The Library of the Department of Agriculture has published a number of specialized bibliographies of interest to agricultural historians although none of them has been devoted primarily to historical research. Since 1953, E. M. Pittenger of the University of Wisconsin College of Agriculture has prepared a list of books on agricultural history published each year in the October issue of *Agricultural History*.

There is no comprehensive, chronological account of American agricultural history available to the general reader or the college teacher. The volumes previously mentioned by Bidwell and Falconer, Gray, and Shannon, as well as the forthcoming volume by Gates, are excellent for the periods that they cover. The more recent period will eventually be covered by James H. Shideler, who has projected a detailed history of American agriculture from 1900 to 1930. Many instructors rely upon N. S. B. Gras, *A History of Agriculture in Europe and Amer-*

ica (revised 1940) for a short history of rural life in America. The essay by Everett E. Edwards, "American Agriculture– The First 300 Years," summarizing developments to World War I, which appeared in the *Yearbook* of the Department of Agriculture in 1940, is generally considered to be the best general synthesis of the history of American agriculture yet available. Two or three scholars are considering undertaking a more detailed, one-volume history. Such a volume is particularly needed for courses in agricultural history.

The social history of agriculture has received some attention on both a nationwide and regional basis. Joseph Schafer made a substantial contribution to the field with his *Social History of American Agriculture* (1936). He discussed land, subsistence and other types of farming, and social and political trends in rural life. Clayton S. Ellsworth of the College of Wooster has a more detailed social history of agriculture in progress. Jared van Wagenen's *The Golden Age of Homespun* (1953) is social history concerned mainly with the Northeast. Everett Dick's *Sod House Frontier, 1854–1890* (1937) covers the northwestern plains.

Not all regional agricultural history has been social history. W. P. Webb, in his classic *The Great Plains* (1931), discusses the geography, social influences, and other factors surrounding the Plains, emphasizing the uniqueness of the region. The grasslands centering around Kansas and Nebraska have been given intensive study by James C. Malin. His concern with the integration of all factors as necessary to an understanding of the region is shown in such volumes as *Winter Wheat in the Golden Belt of Kansas; A Study in Adaption to Sub-humid Geographical Environment* (1944), *The Grassland of North America; Prolegomena to Its History* (1947), *Grass-*

land Historical Studies; Natural Resources Utilization in a Background of Science and Technology; Vol. 1, Geology and Geography (1950).

While a major need still exists for regional agricultural histories, considerable progress has been made in the publication of state agricultural histories. By 1956, volumes had appeared for California, Colorado, Georgia, Indiana, Iowa, Maine, Minnesota, New Jersey, New York, North Carolina, Ohio, Pennsylvania, and Wisconsin. The preparation of histories for the states not yet covered is one of the most useful tasks to which the agricultural historians could address themselves. State agricultural histories synthesize much useful but scattered material, permit generalizations for important areas, permit comparisons between developments in different states, and provide the bases for regional and national surveys.

The work of preparing state histories is facilitated where definitive agricultural histories of state regions, counties, and communities exist. N. A. McNall's *An Agricultural History of the Genesee Valley, 1790–1860* (1952) might well be used as a model for histories of areas within states. The author traces developments within the region in detail and relates them to the agricultural history of the northern United States.

Many regional and state agricultural histories have been written from the viewpoint of the production of a particular crop or agricultural commodity, while particular crops and commodities have also been analyzed on a nationwide basis. The histories of tobacco and of regional types of tobacco illustrate these trends. J. C. Robert, in *The Tobacco Kingdom* (1938), discusses the development of the industry from 1800 to 1860, while in *The Story of Tobacco in America* (1949) he surveys the entire picture. His works provide a clear, comprehensive picture for the student, yet are of use to the specialist. The thorough treatment on tobacco points up the need for similar work on cotton, rice, and other crops to complete the historical coverage of Southern agriculture. A comprehensive history of the Southern cane sugar industry has been written by J. C. Sitterson; a similar study is needed for beet sugar. The hemp industry has also received comprehensive treatment by J. F. Hopkins in his *History of the Hemp Industry in Kentucky* (1951), but Southern horticulture has received almost no attention from historians despite its importance. Corn has been treated primarily with respect to its origin and botanical development. Wheat growing has been discussed in a number of historical articles and economic analyses, but no major work has been devoted to the subject during the last twenty-five years.

Livestock raising has been the most fully discussed of the agricultural industries. Many able agricultural historians, among them E. N. Wentworth, J. O. Oliphant, and G. F. Lemmer, have written important articles, while books on the subject are numerous. The range and ranch cattle industry, which developed after the Civil War, has been the subject of more writing than any similar aspect of agricultural history. Three general accounts have become standard works: E. S. Osgood, *The Day of the Cattlemen* (1929); E. E. Dale, *The Range Cattle Industry* (1930); and Louis Pelzer, *The Cattlemen's Frontier* (1936). Recently some writers have turned their attention to the institutions that developed around the livestock industry; Maurice Frink's *Cow Country Cavalcade; Eighty Years of the Wyoming Stock Growers Association* (1954) is an example. While some of these works bring their subjects to the present, the evolution of the feeding and fattening industry and of the specialized breeds has not yet been fully told.

The dairy industry has been analyzed only in part. Some of the results have been published as articles. The project of Everett E. Edwards in this area was not completed although he published three major articles. Types of dairy cattle are discussed on a historical basis by E. P. Prentice in *American Dairy Cattle* (1942). J. B. Frantz' *Gail Borden: Dairymen to a Nation* (1951) is one of the very few full-length historical studies that has been published. A number of analyses dealing with particular regions or states are under way and may result in useful additions to the literature.

A unique historical study that appeared in 1941 had the distinction of influencing food policy during World War II. This volume, *The American and His Food; A History of Food Habits in the United States* (1940), by R. O. Cummings, is now regarded as a standard reference. The general area of food consumption, dietary preference, and food processing still offers many opportunities for the research historian. This area is a middle ground between agriculture and industry, and developments here were factors in the rise of commercialized farming. Developments in labor and machinery have even more profoundly influenced farming. Slavery has been the subject of many able studies since U. B. Phillips, yet the successor labor system, sharecropping, has not yet been subjected to comprehensive historical analysis. Economists and sociologists have published a number of useful works on the subject, but historians have produced only a few useful articles. The general history of farm labor in America, which would include slavery and sharecropping, has yet to be written. P. S. Taylor is engaged in such a project, valuable portions of which have been published as articles. Aside from histories of government programs affecting farm labor and economic and sociological analyses of the problem, few studies of particular aspects of non-slave labor have been published.

The development of farm machinery has been discussed in a number of articles and popular accounts, but few full-length scholarly studies have appeared. The most comprehensive of such studies are Leo Rogin, *The Introduction of Farm Machinery in Its Relation to the Productivity of Labor in the Agriculture of the United States during the Nineteenth Century* (1931) and R. M. Wik, *Steam Power on the American Farm* (1953). The influence of fertilizer upon American farming has received little attention from historians except for a valuable series of articles by R. H. Taylor.

The use of credit by farmers is another of the factors of production that deserves additional historical study. Two works of major importance, A. G. Bogue, *Money at Interest; The Farm Mortgage on the Middle Border* (1955), and L. A. Jones and David Durand, *Mortgage Lending Experience in Agriculture* (1954), have filled gaps in this field, but the opportunity for major research is still great. In general, agricultural historians have steered clear of such economic aspects of their subject as transportation and marketing.

The country store is discussed by L. E. Atherton in *The Southern Country Store, 1800–1860* (1949) and *The Pioneer Merchant in Mid America* (1939). He captures something of the flavor as well as the problems of the small town in its attempts to meet the marketing and credit needs of the surrounding rural population in *Main Street on the Middle Border* (1954). The development of futures trading in the great commercial centers, which is discussed by H. S. Irwin, *Evolution of Futures Trading* (1954), offers a considerable contrast to the activities in the small towns.

The path of the farmer's rise from near-subsistence to commercial operations is marked by his numerous organizations, institutions, and agencies to improve his lot. The history of these organizations has attracted many able historians, but there remain many profitable areas for work. C. C. Taylor has presented *The Farmers' Movement, 1620–1920* (1953), and he is completing the succeeding volume. The early farm societies have been discussed in the Philadelphia Society for Promoting Agriculture, *Memoirs 6* (1939) and in W. C. Neely's *The Agricultural Fair* (1935). The Grange, first of the national farm organizations to arise after the Civil War, and the related Granger movement, have been described and analyzed by S. J. Buck in works that are regarded as virtually definitive for the period covered. Succeeding organizations and the related Populist movement have been analyzed in J. D. Hicks' definitive *The Populist Revolt* (1931). The organizations that developed after 1900 are discussed by Theodore Saloutos and J. D. Hicks, *Agricultural Discontent in the Middle West, 1900–1939* (1951).

Many farm organizations received support from farm journals, which also gave almost universal support to the agricultural fairs. Agricultural periodicals, the first of which appeared in 1810, have been discussed in articles and books. The standard reference on the pre-Civil War period is A. L. Demaree, *The American Agricultural Press, 1819–1860* (1941). The past eighty years of farm periodical publication, however, have received little attention, although Southern periodicals published since 1900 have been studied by George C. Osborn. D. R. Murphy's history of *Wallaces' Farmer and*

Iowa Homestead was published as the September 1956 issue of *The Palimpsest*.

The farm journals and societies have been influential forces in promoting agricultural education. This point is made in the outstanding general history of agricultural education, A. C. True's *A History of Agricultural Education in the United States, 1785–1925* (1929). The early efforts to reach those farmers who did not come into contact with formal agricultural education has been told by J. C. Bailey, *Seaman A. Knapp; Schoolmaster of American Agriculture* (1945). The development of the federal-state co-operative extension service has been recounted a number of times, A. C. True's work and Gladys L. Baker's *The County Agent* (1939) being among the more useful accounts.

The governmental programs that have had the greatest long-time effect upon American agriculture are those dealing with the disposal of public land. Marshall Harris points out in his *Origin of the Land Tenure System in the United States* (1953) that problems in this area began with the first colonial governments. A number of historians, among them G. L. Anderson, T. P. Abernethy, D. H. Ellis, P. W. Gates, W. S. Greever, Thomas Le Duc, Irving Mark, and A. R. Reynolds have conducted research on particular phases of land policy. Many useful volumes have been published in this field. Because of the large number of studies published and the high quality research work which has been done, those interested in undertaking new projects will wish to begin by consulting one or more of the authorities.

Biography has been a particularly fruitful field for the agricultural historian. Biographies, memoirs, and collections of writings furnish some of the most comprehensive information available on particular phases of agricultural history. Many historians of political movements and parties have emphasized the part played by farmers. This is natural since farmers comprised the overwhelming proportion of the population in our early history and have been in a majority until recent years. Thus, much American history is basically agricultural history, even though it is not so labeled.

The review of agricultural history leads to the two basic conclusions of achievement and remaining opportunity. The achievements include the definition and recognition of agricultural history as a field of study, the establishment of historical research as an activity of the U. S. Department of Agriculture, the founding of the Agricultural History Society and its establishment of *Agricultural History*, the organization of courses in agricultural history in educational institutions, and the publication of many distinguished and useful studies. The list of remaining opportunity is even more impressive. Some areas, such as land policy, the western livestock industry, and agriculture in the ante bellum South have, for various reasons, received more attention than others, yet the research possibilities have not been exhausted even in those areas. Other areas, such as some of our major staple agricultural products and agricultural marketing, are virtually untouched. Still other areas have been explored by workers in other disciplines, but they still need the perspective and technique of the historian. Agriculture offers the historian many rich and virgin fields in which to plough.

BIBLIOGRAPHY

Agricultural History. 31 vols., 1927–1957.

Edwards, Everett E. "An Annotated Bibliography on the Materials, the Scope, and the Significance of American Agricultural History." *Agricultural History,* 6: 38–43 (January, 1932).

————. *A Bibliography of the History of Agriculture in the United States,* U. S. Department of Agriculture, Miscellaneous Publication 84. Washington, 1930.

————. "Middle Western Agricultural History as a Field of Research." *Mississippi Valley Historical Review,* 24: 315–328 (December, 1937).

————. "Objectives for the Agricultural History Society During Its Second Twenty-Five Years." *Agricultural History,* 18: 187–192 (October, 1944).

Kellar, Herbert A. "Living Agricultural Museums." *Agricultural History,* 19: 186–190 (July, 1945).

Peterson, Arthur G. "The Agricultural History Society's First Quarter Century." *Agricultural History,* 19: 192–203 (October, 1945).

Rasmussen, Wayne D. and Edwards, Helen H. "A Bibliography of the Writings of Everett Eugene Edwards." *Agricultural History,* 27: 26–37 (January, 1953).

United States Bureau of Agricultural Economics. *Agricultural History in Relation to Current Agricultural Problems; A Report of the Agricultural History Conference at the Department of Agriculture, Washington, D. C., May 22–24, 1939.* Washington, 1939.

THE HISTORIAN
AS EDITOR

by LESTER J. CAPPON

Institute of Early American History and Culture

SOME historians take a condescending attitude toward the historical editor, vaingloriously boasting that the historian does his own writing, the editor only edits the manuscripts of others. This half-truth suggests an arrogance and a self-sufficiency on the part of the historian which is unworthy of his profession. More grievous, however, is his failure to acknowledge the common bond of scholarship between the historical editor and himself. Since both are deeply concerned with problems of historical research, it is a dangerous assumption on the part of the historian that, by virtue of his task, he has a keener insight into the significance and meaning of the raw materials or that he must necessarily exercise more historical imagination. This assumption implies that the editor, whether of documents or monographs, is concerned only with accurate reproduction, on the one hand, or with commas and semi-colons on the other. In its own sphere, historical editing is as creative as historical writing; they are also mutually dependent.

173

A backward glance at early American editors of historical manuscripts suggests that the gateway to History has always been open as well to the editor as to the writer, regardless of his background or gainful occupation. One can only be impressed by the attainments of those men who, coming from widely divergent walks of life and of varying intellectual interests, turned editor on occasion and produced documentary volumes of superior quality: Postmaster Ebenezer Hazard, who during the Revolution conceived the first collection of state papers as a foundation of American history; his contemporary, lawyer William Waller Hening, whose *Statutes at Large* . . . *of Virginia* (1809–1823), inspired by Jefferson, became invaluable at once to his own profession and increasingly important to historians; and James Savage, antiquarian and genealogist, who produced meticulous compilations and accurate texts during almost three-quarters of a century. All these men were editors by avocation, a type which prevailed throughout the nineteenth century. Indeed the left-handed editor has survived to become an anachronism in a time when professional standards, though not necessarily the professionally-trained historian, have become increasingly recognized as essential for the task. Historical editing may never be the exclusive preserve of the professional, for excellent poachers are certain to appear whose work will be accorded due recognition, but they are the exceptions who prove the rule.

Editing will no doubt receive from time to time its accolade as an exacting profession rather than as the chance pastime of amateurs; but even the great editorial projects multiplying today have so much of the fortuitous about their inception that, in the opinion of one of our most distinguished editors, the historian's whole-hearted support on their behalf as an established function of the guild cannot be taken for granted. Julian P. Boyd has deplored the fact that "these enterprises, despite the labors of J. Franklin Jameson and others, arose on the edge of the profession, beyond it, or even on occasion, in spite of some obstacles thrown up from within it." Although they are providing authoritative editions of basic source material (in fact, among the most significant in American history), in the minds of some historians such editorial activity is carried on in another world, divorced from their own ideas of original research and without appeal to young scholars.

While the amateur has become less prevalent among editors of historical materials in the course of the present century, he has not been readily replaced. The historical profession has been consistently apathetic and indifferent to its own needs and equally so to the opportunities for apprentices. The growing demand for editors has outrun the supply of professionals. At all levels–local and state, regional and national–new projects during the past decade have brought about an increasing demand for the historical editor, until today he is much sought after in a kind of blindman's buff. We can point out notable contemporary historical editors, but where is the undiscovered genius or the promising apprentice to be found? None is listed in occupational directories. The classified "editor" is almost without exception a journalist; the classified scholar may be a historian or an archivist; but we look in vain for the classification of "historical editor." While the promising young historian can be found through the faculty of the graduate school, he is presumably a teacher, whether he has taught at all or has expressed an interest in teaching. It is not customary to evaluate him, and certainly not to train him, as a potential editor, even though he might evidence capacity and interest in that field during his graduate days. Our professional schools devote little time to editorial principles or problems, although every historian who engages in writing history gets involved in editing at one time or another. But more important is the fact that inspired editing, like inspired writing, cannot be taught in a formal sense. It rests upon the creative genius within the man. Editorial ability can only be polished, not established, by training and experience. The technique can be learned, but the inspiration must be inborn. It would seem, then, that the historical editor is born, not made by the process of formal training. And he is discovered largely by the happy accidents of time, place, and opportunity.

Some of the earmarks of the accomplished historical editor are his sense of form, his skill and artistry in presenting the material, and his consistency in maintaining unity throughout. To effect this unity of form and substance he must exercise scrupulous care at every stage. From assembling the documents to the final checking of front matter in the page proof of the printed volume, he takes nothing for granted without verification. Even if the editor is mistakenly considered as only a proofreader, careful proofreading demonstrates that editorial patience is productive of superior work. His plan of organization must do full justice to the documents, to his own sense of order, and to the needs of the user. The editor cannot afford to be hasty at any stage. Instead, he must develop a sense of leisure that will not be hurried at a critical juncture because time seems to have run out. And all these elements of form–unity, accuracy, organization, timing–cannot be imposed from without; they only emerge from a penetrating understanding of the nature and the detail of the materials he is editing. Thus, the editorial processes require a stricter intellectual discipline than many a historian ever applies to his writing. The historian may sometimes conceal his halfway measures in a passage of "fine writing" that escapes analysis for a season; but the editor can hardly afford to take the risk of skimming the surface, lest he be exposed by the scholars he aims to serve. Some historians are simply incapable of the historical editor's disciplined habits.

The personal approach to historical editing serves to explain the hit-and-miss inter-relationship of many of the sources that have appeared in printed form; and it also makes more understandable the gaps between them. Many a historian is moved to assume the temporary role of editor when, through his own use of a particular corpus of material, he appreciates its richness of content and potentiality for innumerable other historical studies and therefore decides to prepare the records for publication. Editorial projects planned in relation to large bodies of source material require careful preliminary surveys in terms of chronological period, geographical area, or correlated subject matter. Fortunately these large-scale projects during recent decades have usually been carried on by knowledgeable scholars who reflect current cultural trends and endeavor to project research interests of their own period into the future. Such was, in part at least, the viewpoint of the Carnegie Institution's Department of Historical Research, which J. Franklin Jameson directed during the first quarter of the present century; and under different circumstances, such is the objective of the National Historical Publications Commission today.

The close relationship between the collecting of source

material and historical editing is frequently overlooked. Collecting often stimulates editing. With well-established preliminary knowledge of the subject, the intelligent editor can project a tentative outline based upon the known extant records and upon others he may safely assume were created but must still be found. Thus Reuben Gold Thwaites enriched his edition of the *Original Journals of the Lewis and Clark Expedition;* thus L. H. Butterfield brought together an abundance of Benjamin Rush letters. But the continuous acquisition of newly-discovered material while the editorial program is in operation makes indispensable the various reference controls which the editor imposes on his files at the outset, before the more detailed work on the texts begins, and so continuously until the last document is printed.

An impressive example of the collector's zeal combined with the editor's objective was set by the first American editor engaged in a succession of comprehensive projects. Jared Sparks was an ambitious planner and indefatigable worker whose fruitful ideas spurred him on from one undertaking to another. The cultural resources of the young republic were as yet untouched and little appreciated. Few institutions had sought to collect and preserve them. In planning his edition of the *Writings of George Washington*, Sparks had to ferret out the manuscripts and secure copies before he could edit them. His extensive travels were typical of many nineteenth-century editors, before photography was adapted to the scholar's needs. Even with photography and other mechanical devices to serve them, our mid-twentieth-century editors—Boyd, Butterfield, Labaree, and others—are no less collectors, who augment the documentary stock pile and relate the parts properly to the whole.

With his manuscripts or copies of them in hand, the editor must decide how much he is obligated to elucidate them. It is conceivable, though improbable, that a person with sound editorial principles and little historical knowledge might provide a faithful transcript of the original text without getting involved in matters of judgment. Such was the position of the commissioners of Providence, Rhode Island, who prepared in the 1890's an accurate transcript of the early records of the town and did all the proofreading of the twenty-volume text. The commissioners did not attempt any editorial notes, doubtless a wise restriction among men of limited historical competence; yet the bare text seems to imply that no editorial problems of transliteration or meaning arose–a very dubious assumption. Forty years earlier the reputable scholar, Nathaniel B. Shurtleff, in editing the *Records of the Governor and Company of the Massachusetts Bay*, "studiously avoided making comments upon the subject matter of the records" and confined his notes to a description of the written volumes and identification of the various writers. There was a time when editors in general preferred to remain anonymous and eschew controversial questions considered to be beyond the proper limits of their professional responsibility. The newspaper printer purveyed the news and left opinion to his correspondents. Certain printers, however, who could not resist expressing their own opinion thus discovered they had an instrument of power for influencing men's minds. In the era of personal journalism the editor who made a name for himself was no longer a printer but rather a public figure in a new profession with expanding political influence.

The case of the historical editor is somewhat analogous. He has often been anonymous, reproducing the text without any indication that it had posed editorial questions of which the reader ought to be aware. If, however, we are to benefit fully from the standards of critical scholarship, the editor should be identified because his reputation is a factor in establishing the reliability of the text. He, too, wants his name associated with the work because he has contributed to the wider use of the documents; and we rather expect him to elucidate them with full editorial responsibility. The editor's responsibility is every bit as weighty and serious as the public duty of the journalist, for basically he is concerned no less with the truth of the matter.

In evaluating the editor, therefore, the reader scrutinizes his reputation as a historian, his mastery of editorial techniques, and his sense of historical values combined with critical judgment of the raw materials. In his preface the editor states his case and explains the mechanics of his work, so that the editorial devices used in the text will be clear and helpful. There has been a perennial argument between the purist and the revisionist over the rendering of manuscript texts into print. The undisciplined editor has taken liberties in transcribing and abridging to suit his own purposes, with scant respect for the original manuscript. During the reaction against such malpractices in the mid-nineteenth century, there came about the severely literal transcription, especially of early texts, with their peculiarities of calligraphy reproduced in print. Charles Francis Adams, Jr., in 1882 called such imitation "illogical, behind the times, and inconsistent," and maintained that the editor could be allowed some discretion in transcribing the text without emasculating it. If you think the editor is undependable, "bring in the camera, and trust him not at all," said Mr. Adams, thus anticipating by several decades the argument whether or not the photographic copy of the text is a satisfactory substitute for the printed and edited copy. The usefulness of modernizing the form was only grudgingly acknowledged by the purist, but the wider latitude allowed the twentieth-century editor is well exemplified in the alternatives set forth in the *Harvard Guide to American History*.

The clever devices which the skilful editor applies without unduly encumbering the text may, in the hands of the amateur, disfigure text and notes with the typographical pox. Assuming a fair measure of intelligence on the part of the reader, the editor will avoid excessive intrusion of the marks of pedantry by explaining in advance the peculiar nature of the original manuscript. Equally important, however, is the information he supplies on the provenance of the papers, pertinent data concerning their authorship, and the relationship of the present documents to others of similar subject matter. In historical research no body of records is sufficient unto itself. Besides, all these factors have a bearing on the internal evidence not yet revealed. It is the responsibility of the editor to make clear these relationships. He is the discoverer, charting the way for the historical writer who follows.

Having considered the elements of form, we should give no less thought to the substance of the text itself. Unlike the stenographic reporter who makes a verbatim record of the proceedings of a conference but cannot remember a word of it, the historical editor lives with his text, wrestles with it, and sheds new light upon its content and meaning. It was the content of the records which undoubtedly stirred the editorial enthusiasm of Justin Winsor, Worthington Chauncey Ford, and other distinguished scholars of their caliber. These men, by the very rigor of their editing, damned the frequent ano-

nymity of the editor of documents in nineteenth-century historical magazines and collections of historical societies.

Since editing is a creative process, its most uncertain and
hazardous element is the editor–that final dose of the human
element that makes history and frequently confounds the
writing of history. Clarence E. Carter, one of our leading
historical editors of today, asserts that "the editor must eschew
any and all forms of interpretation; he cannot deal with his
documents in a subjective manner." But it cannot be denied
that the editor stands between the reader and the text. Should
he then be unobtrusive, self-effacing, overly modest, leaving
the naked text to the user in utter privacy? Hardly so. The
fact is often overlooked that subjective judgment to some
degree enters inevitably into the editorial process. This evaluation may antedate the actual editing, for the decision to publish usually entails preliminary selection from the whole body
of manuscripts, to keep within the limits of the prescribed
volumes, or of the available funds. Thus even at the start, will-
ingly or unwillingly, the editor has withheld certain documents from the reader of the printed volume, and he may
subsequently omit passages from those printed, at the points
indicated, provided the meaning is not distorted. He has
stepped between the reader and the sources.

While the editorial notes are the most obvious part of his
work, whether partaking of fact or opinion, they represent
the editor communicating in his own terms with the readers.
If he sheds new light on the documents, it is, in part at least,
the light of his own generation; indeed, this may be the very
light that revealed the documents to him as worthy of editing. The historical editor is, therefore, in a strategic position
for good or evil. He might cast a shadow over the documents

rather than illuminate them–obscure rather than clarify them. On occasion the inept editor may even find himself dangerously near the province of the fabricator of documents whose evil genius converts him into an "editor" in the black art of forgery. If, however, the editor has evaluated the documents with historical perspective, that is, if he has fulfilled his function, his appraisal will be of prime importance for future research. He will perceive the implications of new facts for a modified view of the historical episode to which they contribute, and the contradictory elements they reveal.

The conscientious editor cannot feel satisfied to present a document or a series of documents isolated from the whole body of material with which he is concerned. If it is worthy of inclusion, its relation to the whole must be made clear. Inherent in the series may be internal problems peculiar to the historical nature of the subject of which the documents treat. How can they be used intelligently without proper organization, analysis, and interpretation? Confronted with a situation of this kind, the editors of the Jefferson *Papers* undertook a large-scale research project, comparable to the historian's preparation to write a monograph, in order to present in useful and meaningful form the Revisal of the Laws of Virginia. The material was not essentially "new" or unknown, but this significant episode, with which Jefferson was closely associated, had never been clarified by historians who wrote about it. Who should provide the last definitive word–the historian or the historical editor–is not the issue; but it is essential that the job be done authentically and intelligibly.

Given, then, the historian's capacity to distinguish between fact and fiction and to comprehend the relative merits of conflicting evidence, the editor has a critical role to play for the benefit of scholarship. His "unattainable goal," as Wilmarth S. Lewis has expressed it, is "to become so familiar with his material that he will be, as it were, inside the writer and recipient of the letters when they were written and read." He becomes more than a passive medium for conveying documentary information. Since he is a scholar himself, he is expected to exercise historical judgment in clarifying the text with supplementary facts and well-considered opinion. While it is not the editor's responsibility to resolve historical controversies, or appropriate to his function to act the partisan, he may call attention to the pros and cons of the argument and point out their relative merits as historical evidence. Within his knowledge of the subject it is part of his task to correlate such evidence with the immediate text. Can he be impartial in providing this editorial fare? Some critics will favor omission of opinion as the only safe course to follow. But that is the course of the timid editor, distrustful of his own enthusiasm or uncertain of his command of the issues.

If the value of the historical editor's labor is to be measured in terms of its usefulness, the following question must be answered: For whom is he editing? The answer is more easily oversimplified in theory than determined in practice. Although it may seem obvious that the historical editor edits for historians, this conception casts his work into a restricted mould. Documents of genuine historical value in the broad sense of that term will pertain to numerous subjects which in themselves represent separate fields of interest, in law or linguistics, government or technology, the graphic arts or bibliography. These examples suggest the wide variety of potential readers, if only the editor will recognize them and project his thinking beyond the traditional confines of history. He must not take too little for granted and thereby offend the intelligent user. If he will bear in mind, however, the universality of history, the well-edited text will attract readers from innumerable avenues of interest.

The old saying that "each generation rewrites history" may be applied to historical editing. The turn of the wheel is doubtless slower in the latter case because documents accurately rendered have a perennial value; nevertheless, the fact that historical editing is itself a historical process brings about the re-editing of certain bodies of source material, keyed to a new objective, assembled by means of a different criterion of selection, or offered to the elusive "general reader" rather than to the scholar. Each generation has witnessed its good editing and its bad. Although the good of one generation may be downgraded by its successor, it does not follow that a "law of progress," so to speak, has been in continuous operation. During the past fifty years the canons of historical editing have become both more exacting in terms of scholarship and more reasonable in terms of usefulness to a wider range of readers, with the result that the best editing of the twentieth century is on the whole superior to its counterpart of previous periods. However, throughout the nineteenth century one can find, in addition to earlier examples cited, numerous editors with high standards, like Peter Force, Edward B. O'Callaghan, and Paul Leicester Ford, whose work contributed substantially to historical research and writing, along with those of inferior quality who, no doubt, will always be with us in considerable number. A variety of quality must be expected because history is Everyman's province.

In turning to the functions of the historical editor of

secondary works, we are confronted with two forms of publication: The magazine and the book. Since each book has an individuality of its own and is physically more substantial and impressive, it is likely to achieve more recognition than an article, no matter how significant the latter may be. Yet, paradoxical as it may seem, the historian's essay written for periodical publication is likely to undergo far more careful editorial scrutiny of its historical content than the monograph submitted to a commercial publisher. The primary concern of the publisher must almost always be readability and saleability. He will rely on the author's judgment, largely, for the historical accuracy of the volume. And rightly so, for he cannot have specialists in every field on his editorial staff.

More sympathetic and detailed consideration of content is afforded by the university press or by the research organization whose purpose is to publish scholarly works without the immediate concern for profit-making, and to provide the author with constructive criticism, whether his work is acceptable or not. However, the willingness of the historical editor to go beyond the realm of "copy-editing" for the author's benefit is much more characteristic of editors of historical magazines, perhaps because they are usually teachers with firmly ingrained educational habits. We would be spared many a mediocre doctoral dissertation in print if there were more book editors who insisted upon extensive revision by the author before publication.

Let us restrict our attention to two aspects of the historical editor's concern with the historian's narrative: (1) As managing editor of a historical magazine; and (2) as the editor of a multi-volume historical project. The magazine warrants prior consideration, if only because of the multiplicity of such periodicals, and because of the medium they afford for historians to breathe and proliferate and become articulate from issue to issue. Despite the value placed upon these periodicals by teachers and researchers, historical societies, and other sponsoring agencies, only a very few have seen fit to employ a full-time editor. As a result, the typical historical magazine almost runs itself, with only occasional attention from the editor who publishes all he has on hand and cannot afford to be discriminating when he has no reserve supply. If he is faced with a continuous shortage of articles, the quality of the magazine almost inevitably declines. But it is more pertinent to consider the creative editor who can convert a dull publication into a scintillating one, rather than the pedestrian, unimaginative editor who shortly reduces his magazine to a reflection of his own poor self.

As the editing of primary documents is often associated with the collecting of such material for research purposes, so the magazine editor with fertile ideas projects his plans several issues in advance and solicits material from authors whose essays will fit into his scheme of operation. While the editor is tempted to obtain "big-name" authors for the prestige they lend to the magazine, he will seek to develop younger writers of excellence because of his sense of obligation to the profession and because of his natural bent as a teacher. There is a limited degree of competition among editors for pieces of superior merit, usually first read by their authors on some public occasion; but few historical journals pay their contributors. More important for the continuing growth of the magazine, however, is the editor's current knowledge of research in progress and his acquaintance with historians, both neophytes and veterans.

The historian as magazine editor is no less a teacher than the professor of history in the college classroom, if he will assume that responsibility in dealing with his contributors. He can be of great service to the young scholar by accepting a promising article conditionally, to be reconsidered on the second round in accordance with the editor's specifications. He can be of equal service by rejecting an unsatisfactory article and supplying the author with constructive criticism by which he may profit in his next attempt. The gratefulness of the neophyte, in retrospect, for the rejection which thus spared him embarassment may give the editor as much satisfaction as the word of thanks from another author assured of the birth of his first essay. How much rewriting the editor ought to do for his authors is a moot question. Every conscientious editor has rewritten many an article of genuine content which suffered only from the author's literary incapacity. Thus the author's brainchild is saved, thanks to the editor's service as midwife.

The author often fails to realize that the magazine editor must satisfy a variety of readers among his subscribers while he plays the diplomat with his individual contributors; that the conscientious editor seeks to improve as well as to indulge the taste of the readers; and that he must therefore season, if not spice, the ingredients supplied by the writers. When the historical editor is an able historian, he can edit with authority. He will have an unhappy time if he does not also edit with tact and forebearance; but as his magazine wins a distinguished reputation, he becomes *primus inter pares* in upholding historical scholarship.

The editing of monographs, whether independent single volumes or in a series, presents the same basic problems in relation to form and substance. The sustained labor required of one author to produce a multi-volume history was typical of past generations when history was literature written for select readers, not popularized for a widening cross-section of the population. Somehow the imposing works of Bancroft and Parkman, of Fiske and McMaster, are more in character with their times than anything on such a formidable scale in the twentieth century. Such extended histories are not in the mode or the mood of our own age any more than the comprehensive documentary projects of that same period. Nevertheless, what we accomplish in either category, source or secondary, depends basically upon the effectiveness of the editor, rather than the author, as the sustaining element. And the editor also provides the continuity throughout the series.

Co-operative history in many volumes may seem less difficult of attainment than the multi-volume work of the individual historian because it is not dependent upon the time and energy of a single scholar, but this assumption probably arises from a misconception of how well historians co-operate and from a lack of appreciation of the editor's indispensable role. The idea of such a project usually originates in an awareness of the need for a large-scale history to close a gap in the existing literature or to open new vistas for a reinterpretation. Accordingly, he enlists the specialized scholarship of the day to achieve his objective. First he must have a well-conceived plan covering the subject matter, the extent of the work in number and size of volumes, and a list of prospective authors. Secondly he must have a publisher who, in turn, will modify the editor's specifications for dealing with the authors. The financial risk of the publisher is well matched by the professional risk of the editor. He must be prepared

to bear the brunt of criticism as well as share the commenda-
tion for the completed publication.

In his unenviable position between publisher and authors,
the historical editor is more likely to suffer at the hands of
the latter than of the former. Having selected an interested
publisher and reached an agreement with him, the editor
knows the financial limits in relation to typographical format
and prescribed quantity of text. Having arrived at agreements
with selected authors, the editor hopes for delivery of each
manuscript without prolonged delay, but he must have the
courage and the wisdom to extend the deadline rather than
to bring undue pressure to bear at the expense of the quality
of research and writing. As in the case of articles for a magazine, his most important function is that of historical critic,
closely integrated with the role of editorial taskmaster and
stylist. Book editing is a bigger job in quantity and book publication has an aura of well-established authority that enlarges
the responsibility of the editor. Yet the principles of magazine and book editing are the same, and the editor must exert
the same prerogative to assure superior results throughout.
While each volume should bear the impress of its author and
reflect his individuality, the quality of the series as an entity
depends upon the editor.

Historical editing is concerned to a large degree with
human relationships, keyed of course to the indispensable
requirements of scholarly production. While the editor's own
scholarship is the basic factor, we must recognize that without respect and good will between editor and author, their
attainments fall short of what should be expected. Therefore,
the editor's selection of the authors in his series is his most
critical professional act. He may be inclined to favor able

young historians with reputations to make, who will grasp the opportunity to be associated with a distinguished editor in order to win their first recognition and enhance their budding reputation. There has been no finer editorial achievement of this kind than that of Albert Bushnell Hart at the beginning of the present century. His selection of able young scholars like Frederick Jackson Turner, Andrew C. McLaughlin, and Evarts B. Greene not only advanced them professionally through their individual volumes in *The American Nation*, but also prolonged the usefulness of the series a generation later through the established reputation of these historians, well maintained despite the rapid extension and restudy of American history. Indeed, Greene in his later years wrote one of the volumes in the *History of American Life,* which under the notable editorship of Arthur M. Schlesinger and Dixon Ryan Fox became the great landmark in the field of social history.

In some ambitious editorial undertakings the series as series has won a recognized place in historiography, so that the names of the editors and the titles of the series have become almost interchangeable. The name of Justin Winsor calls to mind his collaborative *Narrative and Critical History of America,* which demonstrated what a capable editor could accomplish at a time when professional historians were still seeking recognition in the United States. Winsor provided the inspiration for Hart, who got all twenty-eight volumes of *The American Nation* written and published within four years, an amazing and unequalled record. Allen Johnson's *Chronicles of America* with its more popular appeal was likewise a success, and during the past quarter-century we have been offered the rivers, the lakes, and the regions of America in historical series. The launching of several new series since World War II in the face of steadily rising manufacturing costs has required the prescription of short manuscripts, whether or not the subject can be adequately treated in condensed form. The author may suffer from this restriction, but the publisher must set the limit on length of text and notes; and it is the editor's responsibility to hold the author to account for the quality of his narrative.

The historian as editor has played a varied role in the preserving, writing, and interpretation of history. Whether amateur or professional, he often holds the key position by means of which valuable bodies of primary material become available to scholars. The historical writer is dependent to a larger degree than he may realize upon the historical editor who, at best, is his *alter ego*. The process of historical editing involves much more than observing the rules of the game which, though revised from generation to generation, do not alter the basic principles behind them. These intangibles pertain to history itself: to the historian's mastery of his materials and to the art of historical writing.

BIBLIOGRAPHY

Adams, Charles Francis, Jr. "The Printing of Old Manuscripts." Massachusetts Historical Society, *Proceedings*, 20: 175–182 (1882–1883).

Boyd, Julian P., ed. Editor's Preface in *The Papers of Thomas Jefferson*, I: xxv–xxxviii. Princeton, 1950.

Carter, Clarence E. *Historical Editing*, National Archives, *Bulletins*, No. 7 (August, 1952).

Ford, Worthington C. "The Editorial Function in United States History." *American Historical Review*, 23: 273–286 (January, 1918).
Handlin, Oscar, and others. *Harvard Guide to American History*, 95–104. Cambridge, 1954.
National Historical Publications Commission. *A National Program for the Publication of Historical Documents; a Report to the President.* Washington, 1954.
Whitehill, Walter M., ed. "Publishing the Papers of Great Men." *Daedalus: Proceedings of the American Academy of Arts and Sciences*, 86: 47–79 (1955).

HISTORICAL
RESTORATIONS

by EDWARD P. ALEXANDER

Colonial Williamsburg

*H*ISTORICAL perspective and inspiration are the reasons for studying history. Both of these purposes are served by historical restorations which, in increasing numbers, are contributing an unforgettable understanding and a moving inspiration of the American heritage. Restorations of historic places, old houses, villages, workshops and farms do more than bring history to life; they serve to create a historic mood through sensory perception.

Such mood may arise from seeing the flame of a candle flirting with its mirrored self in a crystal chandelier, smelling leaves smoldering in a cobblestone gutter, hearing the minor chord of the folk singer's guitar as he recites his sad ballad, tasting the horehound drops in the odoriferous country store, feeling the prickly aliveness of hemp in a rope walk, or sensing the exhilaration of the intricate steps of a country dance. These sensations take us back to our childhood, remind us of experiences buried deep in the subconscious, and foster a nostalgic feeling of having passed this way before.

This is the secret of the power of historical environment. Because Francis Parkman canoed or trudged on foot through the northern wilderness, actually lived for weeks in the smoky tepees of the western Indians, and spent several days in retreat at a monastery of Passionist Fathers, he could write with insight and vividness about the French in early America. In our own time Samuel Eliot Morison, having sailed a square-rigged, three-masted ketch over Columbus' route, transformed intimate understanding and feeling into a brilliant book on the Admiral of the Ocean Sea. This same quality explains the impact of the Roman glory of Pompeii, the Medieval fairy-land of Venice, and the Baroque magnificence of Versailles.

European observers are sometimes puzzled by American restorations. Since large sections of their cities have come down almost intact from the Middle Ages, they have difficulty understanding why such a young country needs to restore or reconstruct its past. The abundance of wealth, availability of materials, and the restless tendency to move with the frontier all explain why American buildings rise, and disappear, so rapidly. The need for restoration stems largely from the perils of wooden buildings: Hasty construction, fire, termites, rot, and ephemeral tastes in architecture. The sheer size of the United States and the diversity of its cultural regions are other justifications for moving buildings or even reconstructing them in order to obtain a more complete picture of a period and a region.

Yet, as Dr. Ronald F. Lee of the National Park Service has pointed out, the United States is fortunate in the amount of the physical record that has survived. Leaving out the Indian background and a few Norse explorations, civilization has resided in the New World for only about four centuries.

Each succeeding period of history has left an increasing number of sites, structures, artifacts, furniture, and furnishings. Careful restoration and reconstruction may be needed here and there, but the end result is that America possesses a far more complete three-dimensional panorama of its whole past than any country in the Old World can hope to have.

Restorations have had more than a century of development in the United States. In 1850 Washington's Headquarters at Newburgh, New York was purchased by the state and became the first historic house to open its doors to the public. Ten years later George Washington's plantation at Mount Vernon was placed on public display, thanks to the hardworking Mount Vernon Ladies' Association of the Union. Then in the great centennial year of 1876, Independence Hall in Philadelphia began to attract its millions of visitors.

By 1889 the federal government entered the movement, at first to protect Indian cliff dwellings and pueblos in the Southwest, and later the hallowed ground of Civil War battlefields. The establishment of the National Park Service as a branch of the Department of the Interior in 1916 was followed in 1935 by the Historic Sites Act which declared it "a national policy to preserve for public use historic sites, buildings and objects of national significance for the inspiration and benefit of the people of the United States." Even more recently, the ambitious state systems of historic buildings sponsored in New York, Ohio, Illinois, California, New Jersey, Pennsylvania, and elsewhere have come to maturity. In 1895 the English National Trust was organized by a private group of citizens to preserve and display historic sites and scenic places of importance, and to provide financial support for each property. Today, largely because of tax privileges, it holds more than one hundred houses and some 250,000 acres of unspoiled land. Success of the English National Trust led to similar organizations in the United States, including the National Trust for Historic Preservation, founded in 1949. Supported solely by memberships, gifts, and bequests, the National Trust enlists institutions and individuals behind the restoration movement, provides a staff of experts to furnish technical advice, and occasionally operates actual sites when it can assume their support. Strengthened by recent grants of $2,500,000 to endowment, it promises to furnish much needed additional leadership in the field.

Perhaps the earliest force behind the restoration movement in this country could be called antiquarianism and defined as a love for collecting and connoisseurship, a nostalgic feeling that the old things are in themselves good and beautiful and worthy of preservation. When a historic house has been placed on the market, or is in danger of being torn down for an automobile service station, an *ad hoc* committee often tries to save it. If it fails, it may organize to fight again on a broader base. Sometimes it manages to enlist private or public funds, and more recently the great force of tourism has increased the chances of making projects self supporting.

Perhaps a dozen of the most important American restorations have each been largely the work of a single patron. The motives involved appear to have been mixed—a desire to re-create an important part of the American past, a love for beauty and for planning and building, or the wish to provide an appropriate setting for a cherished collection of objects. These collections may run from the finest masterpieces of furniture, silver, or paintings, to simple wooden kitchen utensils, crude copper weathervanes, or naïvely carved cigar store Indians. In many cases federal estate and income taxes have certainly stimulated collectors to place their precious holdings in model museum villages designed for the public interest.

Of even more importance in the restoration movement has been the increasing fascination of Americans with their heritage. The United States from the time of the Declaration of Independence has been a proud nation, but for many years it was so challenged by the present and confident of the future that it took little interest in the past. Two world wars and an uneasy peace have jolted Americans into assuming the heavy responsibilities of world leadership; they have become more thoughtful about their traditions. They question the validity of the American dream and its pertinence in today's world. They doubt the ability of individuals to survive the onslaughts of the omnipotent state armed with frightful atomic weapons. These reflections have given Americans genuine concern about their roots and their background and have sent them to visit the places where American institutions were formed.

Social forces released by the industrial revolution and the machine also help account for the boom in restoration. As industry after industry shortens its work week, grants longer vacations, and pensions its older workers, more and more Americans have sufficient mobility to see their country. In 1895 there were only twenty historic houses and four registered automobiles in the United States. By 1955 there were about 1,000 historic restorations and some 61,301,000 cars. There were an estimated 47,953,902 visits to historic sites and buildings in the United States in 1954!

A less influential force in the restoration movement has

come from the open air or folk museum. In 1891 Dr. Artur Hazelius, a language teacher with a love for history, set up a new kind of museum in a seventy-acre tract on a bluff over-looking Stockholm, Sweden. This institution, called Skansen after a small fort which once stood there, included farmsteads of different regions and centuries, an iron-master's house, manor house, log church, windmills, stocks and whipping post, maypole, runestones, and a series of craft shops with printing office, grocer's shop, bookbinder's, goldsmith's, and an operating glassblowing workshop. There was even a cone-shaped turf hut of the nomadic Lapps, inhabited for a part of each year by a Lapp family with reindeer nearby. These structures were discovered in various parts of Sweden, taken down, transported, and re-erected with great care.

The outdoor museum movement spread throughout Europe, chiefly in Scandinavia, the Netherlands, and Germany. It came to include properly costumed interpreters in the buildings, strolling musicians, folk dancers, foods made from typical period recipes, and other colorful kinds of life on the scene. Though the European movement has not been too well known or influential in the United States, a somewhat parallel, largely independent development has taken place there.

The open air museum is not a true on-the-spot restoration, but its component parts include authentic structures care-fully re-erected in a typical setting and perhaps furnished authentically. American projects in the past have rather rarely moved buildings, and have tended to follow American restoration models, among which Mount Vernon and Williamsburg have been the most influential. In the last quarter-century, however, the open air museum is becoming more popular with the increasing influence of Greenfield Village at Dearborn, Michigan; Old Sturbridge Village, Massachusetts; Mystic Seaport, Connecticut; the Farmers' Museum at Cooperstown, New York; and Shelburne Museum in Vermont.

Today there are more than 1,000 historic houses and restoration villages in the United States. Together they present a great three-dimensional textbook of American history. Traces of the Spanish exist in the impressive Castillo de San Marcos (1672) in St. Augustine, the Palace of the Governors (1614) in Santa Fe, the Alamo (1754) in San Antonio, and dozens of picturesque missions in California and the Southwest. French remains are more numerous in Canada than in the United States, but their influence survives at old Fort Niagara (1726) in New York, the Porlier-Tank Cottage (1776) in Green Bay, Wisconsin, and occasional eighteenth- or nineteenth-century houses in the Mississippi Valley down to New Orleans with its Cabildo and Vieux Carré, representing a blend of the Spanish and French.

The Swedes have left Gloria Dei (Old Swedes') Church (1700) in Philadelphia, and the Dutch a handful of houses in the Hudson Valley including the Senate House (1676) at Kingston and Philipse Manor (1683) at Tarrytown. In New Castle, Delaware, almost an entire historic village has been preserved as a modern town; though settled by the Swedes and Dutch, it gives an over-all architectural impression of late eighteenth-century Georgian.

The period of English colonization is well represented. Fort Raleigh (1587), the small earthen work of the Lost Colony on Roanoke Island, North Carolina, has been discovered and restored. At Jamestown, Virginia, the first permanent English settlement, the earliest original construction is the brick

Church Tower (1639), but for the 350th Anniversary of the founding, the first timber Fort James (1607), the thatched Glass House, and the three ships which brought the first settlers have been carefully rebuilt. Plimoth Plantation (1620) in Massachusetts has had its fort and two small houses reconstructed; a replica of the "Mayflower" has crossed the Atlantic from England, and the rebuilding of the whole first town has begun on a nearby site. Another reconstructed Pilgrim Village (1630) is open at Salem, and Massachusetts possesses many seventeenth-century houses, concentrated most heavily at Ipswich.

The beautiful, shaded main street of Old Deerfield in Massachusetts is of eighteenth-century appearance, and Litchfield, Connecticut, and Newport, Rhode Island, have many remarkable buildings of that period, though engulfed by later styles. Fort Ticonderoga (1755) in New York is a restoration of an important military post. Colonial Williamsburg in Virginia is practically an entire eighteenth-century town built around eighty surviving original buildings and with structures ranging from simple outbuildings to an elegant Governor's Palace. Its sister capital of Annapolis, Maryland, has many fine eighteenth-century buildings set in the midst of later architecture. The Independence Hall project in Philadelphia displays one of the most sacred places of the American past, uncluttered and serene in the heart of a great city. The Henry Francis du Pont Winterthur Museum in Delaware, though not a restoration, has a series of colonial and early American rooms that display with superb taste the finest examples of American furniture and furnishings.

The profusion of nineteenth-century places includes typical re-created New England communities at Old Sturbridge Village and Storrowton (at West Springfield) in Massachusetts and an unusual folk museum at Shelburne, Vermont. Charleston, South Carolina, and Natchez, Mississippi, are examples of modern cities with many beautiful original houses. Communities that exhibit the economic life of other periods are Mystic Seaport, Connecticut, famed for its whalers; a typical New York State village crossroads with a Farmers' Museum at Cooperstown; ironworks at Hopewell Village near Reading, Pennsylvania and at Saugus, Massachusetts; and a milling community complete with the du Pont Powder Mill on the Brandywine in Delaware.

Three among dozens of early pioneer villages are found at the rebuilt Fort Harrod, Kentucky; restored Spring Mill Village, Indiana; and young Abe Lincoln's reconstructed home town at New Salem, Illinois. Frontier mining towns of the later West include Central City, Colorado; Virginia City, Montana; and Columbia, California. Closely akin to these are many individual buildings like Sutter's Fort in Sacramento, where the discovery of gold started the rush in 1849.

Chiefly of the later period is Greenfield Village at Dearborn, Michigan. With the huge Henry Ford Museum nearby, it gives a bird's-eye view of nearly the entire span of American industrial development. Newport, Rhode Island, is one of the best places to study the apogee of the Victorian style in America with its palaces of the industrial elite.

This broad outline of the American story includes only a few of the best known examples of restoration villages and historic houses. It can be embroidered almost endlessly with fascinating details. On the military side, for example, in addition to forts are the many battlefields and headquarters. Saratoga, Valley Forge, and Yorktown of the Revolution and

Gettysburg, Vicksburg, and Appomattox of the Civil War are only a small sample. Houses of famous men are well preserved–the White House itself in Washington; Washington's Mount Vernon, Jefferson's Monticello, and Lee's Arlington in Virginia; the Adams house in Quincy, Massachusetts; Jackson's Hermitage at Nashville; and for the more recent period, Theodore Roosevelt's home at Saginaw Hill at Oyster Bay and Franklin Roosevelt's Hyde Park. Numerous religious communities have left visible remains: Moravians at Old Salem in North Carolina or Schoenbrunn Village in Ohio; Rappites at Economy, and Seventh Day Baptists at Ephrata Cloister, Pennsylvania; Shakers at Chatham, New York; and Mormons in Nauvoo, Illinois, and Salt Lake City.

An example of both the problems and the processes of historical restoration was the work of Herbert A. Kellar in rebuilding the McCormick gristmill in the beautiful Valley of Virginia. Cyrus Hall McCormick was born at Walnut Grove, a small plantation which lay in Rockbridge County between Lexington and Staunton. There he invented the reaper and first publicly tested it near Steele's Tavern in the summer of 1831. Dr. Kellar, Director of the McCormick Historical Association of Chicago, visited Walnut Grove in 1936 and was intrigued with the opportunity to restore the farmhouse, barn, corncrib, springhouse, slave quarters, the workshop in which the reaper had been perfected, and the gristmill. The last two structures were of stone and log construction, and the mill, in bad condition, was rapidly crumbling away. Dr. Kellar envisioned re-creating an operating plantation of the early nineteenth century. This full-scale restoration, he thought, would effectively tell twentieth-century Americans about Cyrus McCormick, his times, and his significance.

With a sure touch, Dr. Kellar recognized the appeal of a mill, driven by a splashing stream, slowly grinding meal with its heavy, grooved stones. The project well exemplified the increasing belief of Americans in the labor-saving power of the machine and the sweet dream of the inventor. Harold McCormick, who owned Walnut Hill, caught this vision, and soon Dr. and Mrs. Kellar were in Virginia in the midst of a new and fascinating undertaking.

First came the research, the foundation of all good restoration. Books like Oliver Evans' *Young Millwright and Miller's Guide* (1795) were most useful, but equally important were the actual mills still standing along the Blue Ridge and the Great Smokies in Virginia and North Carolina. Their creaking wooden machinery was studied, measured, and photographed. Then there was the thrill of archaeology, digging below the smooth greensward that now covered the pit where once turned the great mill wheel at Walnut Grove. "With each foot of penetration we were uncovering conditions of approximately 20 years previous," wrote Dr. Kellar a few years later. "Five feet of digging took us a hundred years into the past."

With the research completed and the evidence marshaled, it was time to rebuild the past in three dimensions. Instead of the written word upon which the historian normally depends, Dr. Kellar followed the specifications and enlarged photographs of the mills he had examined. This was an unfamiliar but exciting process. There was, for example, the search for a white pine tree thirty-four inches in diameter sixteen feet above the butt and free from checks and knots; this huge timber would become the octagonal shaft of the water wheel. After it was found, came the cheerless day when it was trimmed down too far on one side and thus became out of balance and unfit for use. But by next day the workmen were laughing and chattering again, for one of them had almost miraculously discovered a new log in a lumber company millpond, had traded in the spoiled timber for lumber, and paid the difference of $11.93 from his own pocket. Dr. Kellar wrote that he "was much touched by this action and henceforth regarded the incident as marking the height of labor relations."

Certain building techniques had almost disappeared, and workers had to be found who remembered or who could learn the old ways. An aged mountaineer knew how to split shingles with the frow, and he taught three other workers, who in three weeks produced 7,500 properly rived shingles. Dr. Kellar with his book knowledge and surviving examples of ironwork inspired a blacksmith to learn how to pound out the right kind of nails, spikes and bolts, strap hinges, and locks and keys. By studying manuals and the old mills that still operated, Dr. Kellar came to understand the milling process itself, together with such skills as regrooving the upper and lower burrstones with steel picks. Learning to regulate the flow of water so that the stones would run from 104 to 106 revolutions a minute was no easy task.

After a year's work the mill was complete with operating machinery, millpond, dam, and race. The Kellars went back to Chicago in 1938 with a bushel of cornmeal, a bushel of white flour, and a bushel of bran and middlings, all ground in the Walnut Grove mill. They had also repaired the sturdy workshop where Cyrus McCormick gave substance to his dreams. They planned to restore and furnish the farmhouse itself, gathering furniture that had come from the home and purchasing other contemporary pieces in the vicinity. But Harold McCormick's death soon thereafter delayed the completion and opening of the restoration. Only recently, since Dr. Kellar's death, has Walnut Grove been given to the Virginia Polytechnic Institute as an experimental farm. The McCormick heirs have provided that the mill, the workshop, and some of the other buildings tell their story to the traveling public.

Dr. Kellar's pioneering work on the McCormick gristmill illustrated the fundamental problems that confront anyone who undertakes to reconstruct or restore the physical remains of the past. The two words which summarize these problems are "authenticity" and "interpretation." Each must become a major consideration of those who work in historical restoration.

Authenticity means re-creating accurately the environment of a historical period, telling the truth, being honest. The meaning differs somewhat from project to project depending on the purposes of each. In general most of them agree that preservation (scrupulous retention of surviving work by ordinary repair) is always to be preferred to restoration (recovery of the old form by replacing surviving work), which in turn, is preferable to reconstruction (securing a carefully justified form by entirely new work).

There are degrees of purism involved in preservation, restoration, and reconstruction. Some insist on leaving the remains of the past as they lie, with different periods of style existing side by side; they are reluctant to restore and will never reconstruct. Some think it unethical to remove a building from its original site. Others object to catering to the inalienable rights of twentieth-century visitors to hard surfaced streets or sidewalks, street lighting, restrooms, drinking fountains, or the like. There are also different philosophies about furnishing. Some perform miracles of research to secure inventories by which the project can be supplied with objects that were actually there or might have been there. Others tastefully assemble period rooms, not usually true to history but with furniture or furnishings of the finest workmanship. Still others confine their authenticity to the exteriors and use the interiors to display collections, for gift shops, or for some other adaptive purpose.

It is generally sufficient that the plan adopted be reasonably and honestly presented to the visitor, with its particular definition of authenticity closely adhered to. Despite the critics who delight in hurling the word "synthetic" at such undertakings, there is nothing educationally wrong in carefully reconstructing a building which has disappeared or in moving structures from their original foundations to a well-planned typical site. But it is all-important that historical restorations be created in the spirit of historical accuracy, especially since three-dimensional history is so believable. Visitors are accustomed to exercise scepticism toward the printed word, but they are not so ready to argue with brick and mortar or furniture and furnishings. History in the round has blandishments that can easily mislead all but the most expert.

Restoration villages do sometimes confuse their visitors. If they bring together buildings from widely separated regions and historical periods with no clear historical theme, the overall effect may be unconvincing and seem to be based only on personal whim. If modern business activities of such villages are not carefully separated from the restored area, the public may be uncertain what is old and what new. The restoration that loses its regard for authenticity is committing its own destruction. Experts will observe unreasonable lapses and uncorrected mistakes, and the word will spread to the public. Without a basic devotion to truth, a restoration can easily degenerate into a tourist trap.

Sound research is as essential in physical restoration as building materials. A common delusion of organizations planning such projects is a notion of false economy: Research is too expensive, visitors cannot see it, and therefore it does not pay. But it costs even more to correct errors built into projects because of faulty or inadequate research. The analytical and interpretative powers of archaeology, architecture, the decorative arts, and history must be harnessed in an integrated research program of broad range. There is no other way, no short cut, to the convincing historical mood that is the legitimate goal of restoration.

The use of archaeology has been relatively new in American restoration work. Archaeology has long been appreciated as an indispensable tool in tracing the ancient or classical cultures or that of the American Indian, but not until the last thirty years was it employed to locate colonial foundations and to sift the soil for fragments of stone, brick, tile, ceramics, glass, metalwork, and other artifacts that give clues on the form and furnishings of buildings. Today its usefulness has been proved, and any historic house or restoration of an authentic site should always conduct a careful archaeological search. Similarly when buildings are moved, their sites should be intensively explored by trained archaeologists.

Architects have their contributions to make to authenticity. Detailed study of the remaining buildings, their foundations, walls, brickwork, floors, partitions, ornamentation, stairs, mantels, windows, doors, and framing should be made with careful sketches and measurements. Layers of paint can be examined by scraping, and actual color samples obtained. Sometimes the process of stripping is employed, taking off a part of the facing of a structure down to the framing in order to observe changes made through the years. Other similar houses or details are examined, photographed, and perhaps located in the old builders' handbooks; here the architectural historian with his knowledge of styles of the period will be invaluable.

The landscape architect must also study the grounds, aided by the archaeologist and the student of horticulture who knows what plant materials were used in the period. The curator also will be busy, examining the artifacts sifted from the soil, poring over what documentary inventories he can find, and calling on his general knowledge of the decorative arts to work out a furnishings plan. Obviously, obtaining authenticity is a team operation demanding contributions from historian, archaeologist, architect, landscape designer, and curator.

During the last thirty years, American restorations have raised their standards of authenticity markedly. Their experience in using the research findings contributed by different disciplines has added to the convincing mood they seek, and the stimulation and cross-fertilization of this fuller research approach have led to more complete knowledge of the three-dimensional past. To take but a single example, it seems only yesterday that everyone was certain the interior trim of colonial houses was always painted white or pale gray. Careful study of historical records including shipping invoices to colonial merchants and the actual scraping of layers of paint in surviving buildings have proved the colonists used dozens of attractive and even gay shades of reds, blues, greens, yellows, and browns.

The stern discipline of historical truth is at times a chafing yoke on architects, landscape designers, and curators who are creative artists and sensitive to beauty. They may easily invent a picture of history that is too artistic. On the other hand, some restoration entrepreneurs are more interested in gate receipts or the sale of souvenirs than they are in securing the proper underlying research or adhering to standards of construction and maintenance much more expensive than unauthentic ones. Somewhere a good restoration must find supporters and workers to whom historical accuracy is important and worth maintaining.

If restoration authenticity has often been a subjective term, interpretation has been more given to license. It is the planned presentation of a restoration in the hope of invoking an appreciation for the past, a form of mass education without the usual classroom methods or mandates. Tourists do not constitute a captive audience; though in a relaxed and receptive frame of mind, they will receive instruction only as long as they enjoy it. There is ever the temptation to sacrifice accuracy to interest.

Historical research is as important for proper interpretation as it is for authentic physical restoration. If the visitor is to understand the significant contributions of an earlier period, he must not only see its houses, gardens, taverns, public buildings, schools, and churches but also know the political aspirations of its people, how they made a living, their educational, religious, and social customs, and insofar as possible, their very thoughts. This is a big order, so big that research must continue to pump new information into the interpretive program if it is to remain vital and persuasive.

Unfortunately, interpretation has lagged behind physical restoration. Too often houses or villages have been restored and furnished authentically only to stand idle. Advanced techniques of research, building, and furnishing may have been used, but the finished job has disregarded the needs of planned interpretation. Good interpretation methods are neither unknown nor mysterious. Long before the building starts, any restoration project should consider its purposes, the most efficient means of accomplishing them, and how to reach its chosen audience.

The future of historical restorations seems assured. As they improve in authenticity and interpretation they will attract a wider audience and better support. Some projects have already developed excellent techniques of research, restoration, furnishing, and maintenance. High quality interpretation is also understood and available. Historical restoration has achieved professional status.

History and historical restoration can give invaluable mutual assistance because they share basic purposes. As far as documentary research is concerned, it makes little difference whether it is presented in a book or a three-dimensional building, garden, or room. There is the same widespread search of source materials, the same careful determination of facts, the same conscientious weighing of the evidence. History will continue to furnish trained personnel for restorations and reap the reward in wider public knowledge and interest in the past. Restorations, in turn, frequently suggest new avenues and techniques of research to the elder discipline.

Out of the exchange of personnel and ideas a new kind of

profession is emerging with emphasis on historical entrepreneurship or administration of historical societies, museums, and restorations. This profession combines a concern for historical scholarship and an emphasis on communication with the public. If showmanship is allowed to run away with authenticity, if basic policies are controlled by chauvinists, advertising men, or commercial promoters, if the emphasis is put on method or technique at the expense of subject matter, restoration projects will suffer and so will the cause of history. The movement is growing so rapidly that there are available an insufficient number of trained historians interested and ready to help. Only if this type of talent can be found, nurtured, and used, can restorations carry forward their great purpose, "That the future may learn from the past."

BIBLIOGRAPHY

Allen, Douglas A. "Folk Museums at Home and Abroad." Scottish Anthropological & Folklore Society, *Proceedings*, 5: 91–120 (1957).
American Society of Architectural Historians, *Journal*, 1: nos. 3–4 (July–October, 1941).
Burns, Ned J. *Field Manual for Museums*. Washington, 1941.
Coleman, Lawrence Vail. *Historic House Museums*. Washington, 1933.
————. *The Museum in America; a Critical Study*. 3 vols., Washington, 1939.
Cummings, Abbot Lowell, ed. "Restoration Villages." *Art in America*, 43: no. 2 (May, 1955).
Fishwick, Marshall W. "Walnut Grove–Where Farm Mechanization Began." *The Iron Worker*, 20, no. 4: 1–12 (Autumn, 1956).
Huth, Hans. *Observations Concerning the Conservation of Monuments in Europe and America*. Washington, 1940.

Kellar, Herbert A. "An Early American Gristmill." *The Westerners Brand Book*, 6: 1–8 (March, 1949).

Lee, Ronald F. *United States: Historical and Architectural Monuments.* Mexico, D. F., 1951.

National Park Service. *Glimpses of Historical Areas East of the Mississippi.* Washington, 1937.

National Trust for Historic Preservation. *Primer for Preservation; a Handbook for Historic-House Keeping.* Washington, 1956.

Parker, Arthur Caswell. *A Manual for History Museums.* New York, 1935.

Tilden, Freeman. *Interpreting Our Heritage; Principles and Practices for Visitor Services in Parks, Museums, and Historic Places.* Chapel Hill, 1957.

A TYPOGRAPHICAL NOTE

The text of this volume was set in Linotype *Janson*, a modern recutting of a seventeenth-century face issued by Anton Janson of Leipzig. It is a favorite of readers and designers alike, combining classic grace and sparkle with functional sharpness and clarity. Display type was hand-set in *Caslon Old Style* with matching italics.

Typography and design by O. Lawrence Burnette, Jr.

Karl Höffkes / Uwe Sauermann

Albert Leo
Schlageter

Freiheit
du ruheloser Freund

ARNDT

Titelfoto: Dietmar Munier

CIP-Kurztitelaufnahme der Deutschen Bibliothek

Höffkes, Karl:
Albert Leo Schlageter : Freiheit, du ruheloser
Freund / Karl Höffkes ; Uwe Sauermann. – Kiel :
Arndt, 1983.
(Arndt-Taschenbuch ; 8)
ISBN 3-88741-008-4
NE: Sauermann, Uwe: ; GT

ISBN 3-88741-008-4

Rathaus-Buchhandlung GmbH, Abteilung ARNDT-Verlag
2300 Kiel, Postfach 3603
Druck und Bindearbeiten: Husum Druck- und Verlagsgesellschaft
Gedruckt in Deutschland

Baltikum, Spartakus, Oberschlesien, Ruhrkampf
von Karl Höffkes

November 1918. Durch die regennassen Straßen der Stadt drängen die aufgeputschten Menschenmassen. Unter der brodelnden Flut ihrer Körper ducken sich Obrigkeit, Bürgertum und Staatsgewalt. Kochender Menschenbrei, der sich stoßend und schiebend auf die großen Plätze der Stadt zubewegt, auf denen seit dem frühen Morgen die streikenden Matrosen die Massen aufputschen und die Revolution beschwören.

Rote Fahnen beherrschen das Bild, gespenstisch beleuchtet von den flackernden Fackeln der Matrosen. Vom Sturm gepeitscht ziehen dunkle Wolken über die Stadt, symbolisieren den Rhythmus der neuen Zeit.

Die meuternden Matrosen und streikenden Arbeiter schleudern immer wieder ihre Parolen in die brodelnden Massen. Die Menge hängt an ihren Lippen, antwortet mit Zwischenrufen. Vom Jubel begleitet unterbrechen sie immer wieder die Reden der Matrosen. "Alle Macht den Arbeiter- und Soldatenräte!n", "Nieder mit den Militaristen!". Die Forderungen breiten sich in Windeseile über die brodelnde Masse, pflanzen sich fort in den Straßen und Häusern, setzen sich in den Köpfen der drängenden Menschenknäuel fest.

"Stürmt die Gefängnisse der Bourgeoisie, befreit die Genossen!" ein Zwischenruf aus der Menge. Der Redner nimmt ihn auf, schleudert ihn zurück, peitscht die Massen voran, hämmert die Worte immer wieder in die wogende Menge.

Alles ist Bewegung und Lärm, tödliche Begeisterung, geballte Gefährlichkeit.

"Zu den Gefängnissen!" Gefesselt vom Rausch der eigenen Macht nimmt die Menge die Parole auf und wirft sie tausendstimmig zurück. Rote Fahnen, die sich in Bewegung setzen und den nachdrängenden Menschenmassen den Weg weisen. Masse formt sich zum Zug, folgt, schafft sich Bahn und wälzt sich tausendköpfig durch die Straßen der Stadt.

Und immer wieder fliegen die Parolen über die

Köpfe hinweg, peitschen die Menschen vorwärts.

Von irgendwo klingt die 'Internationale' auf, ergreift den ganzen Zug. Rote Fahnen zwischen grauen Häusern: Revolution im Reich. Das gleiche Bild auch in anderen Städten: Geballte Massen unter roten Fahnen, geführt von den putschenden Matrosen. Demonstrationen und Versammlungen. Parolen und Anschläge an den schmutzigen Backsteinwänden der Häuser fordern die Absetzung des Kaisers. Und während die Bürger, die Politiker und das Beamtentum schwerfällig beraten, ohne die Kraft zum entscheidenden Willen, jagen schwere Militärlastwagen über die Straßen der Städte, gefüllt mit bewaffneten und streikenden Matrosen, Soldaten und Zivilpersonen unter blutig-roten Fahnen.

Generalstreik ist ausgerufen, lähmt das Leben in den Zentren des Reiches.

Rathäuser werden besetzt, Waffenarsenale geplündert und ihr todbringender Inhalt an die streikenden Massen verteilt. Vor den wichtigen Gebäuden der Städte, an den Ausfallstraßen und Bahnhöfen beziehen bewaffnete Gruppen mit roten Armbinden Posten. Straßensperren und Maschinengewehre hinter eilig aufgestapelten Sandsäcken sollten von nun ab das Bild der Städte bestimmen.

Dazwischen das ziellose Treiben der Bürger und Politiker in seiner dünnen Wichtigkeit, eiteles Geschwätz, unfähig, einen raschen Entschluß zu fassen, gelähmt von der Wirkung der putschenden Truppenteile. Hexentanz und Auflösung mitten im Reich, während das deutsche Heer an der Front steht und sich verblutet.

Fünf Tage fällt Deutschland in fiebrige Hektik, hart und unerbittlich schlägt der Puls der Zeit.

Am 9. November dankt der Kaiser unter dem Druck der Verhältnisse ab und geht ins Exil. Innerhalb weniger Stunden ändert sich die politische Lage schlagartig. Der Sozialdemokrat Scheidemann ruft in Berlin die Republik aus: "Der Kaiser hat abgedankt ! Es lebe die Republik !"

Draußen steht das Heer, verteidigt die neubezogenen Stellungen gegen den wütend anrennenden Feind. Und während das Heer kämpft, verhandelt die neue Regierung mit den Alliierten.

Am 11.11. dringt die Meldung zu den Truppen, die noch tief in Frankreich stehen: Waffenstillstand. An allen Fronten schweigen die Waffen.

Auf der Grundlage der 14 Punkte Wilsons, die einen 'Frieden ohne Sieg' versprachen, hatte die neue Regierung den Alliierten ein Waffenstillstandsangebot unterbreitet.

Die Folgen treffen das kämpfende Heer wie Keulenschläge: Räumung der besetzten Gebiete und des linken Rheinufers. Aufhebung des Friedensschlußes von Brest-Litowsk, der den Verzicht Rußlands auf Livland, Kurland, Litauen, Estland und Polen und die Anerkennung Finnlands und der Ukraine als selbständigen Staaten beinhaltete und des Friedensschlußes von Bukarest, der den Deutschen die Nutzung der Ölquellen der Dobrudscha zugestand.

An der Front hatten die Truppen wenig von der wirklichen Lage im Reich gehört. Über die Gräben und Stellungen flogen in den letzten Tagen Wolken von Gerüchten, die von Meutereien und Gefechten zwischen Deserteuren und kaisertreuen Einheiten berichteten, aber genaues wußten die wenigsten.

Um so härter trifft sie der Befehl zum Rückzug. Unbesiegt und tief im feindlichen Land schlägt ihnen der Kurs der neuen Regierung die Waffen aus der Hand.

Und als ihre Offiziere den Rückzug befehlen, da erheben sich an allen Fronten die feldgrauen Heere aus den Gräben. Während die neuen Herren im Reich mit den jubelnden Siegern über die Bedingungen des Friedens verhandeln, ziehen sie in endlosen Kolonnen über Brügge und Lüttich zurück in ihre Garnisonstädte.

Kompanie um Kompanie, geführt von ihren Offizieren, eingehüllt in die lehmgrauen, zerschlissenen Röcke, verläßt das Heer das zerfurchte, blutgetränkte Land des Feindes.

Fronttruppen, mit scharfen, kantigen Gesichtern unter den Stahlhelmen, die Überlebenden der tosenden Materialschlachten in den Höllen von Bayonne und Scarpe, Artois, Arras und Verdun, Gestalten einer unbekannten Welt. Unbesiegt und bis an die Zähne bewaffnet strömen sie zu Hunderttausenden in das Reich zurück, dessen neue Herren ihren Rückzug befohlen hatten.

Als sich ihnen die Abgesandten der Soldaten- und Arbeiterräte mit ihren roten Armbinden entgegenstellen, um ihnen die Orden und Abzeichen von den grauen und abgewetzten Uniformen zu reißen, gleichsam als Zeichen dafür, daß sie nun alle Genossen seien, formieren sich die feldgrauen Gruppen zu steinernen Wällen, umgreifen ihre Hände die entsicherten Gewehre, verweigern sie den Räten und ihren Parolen den Gehorsam.

Unbehelligt rücken sie ein in ihre verlassenen Garnisonen, unfähig, die neue Welt in all ihren Formen zu begreifen, von vielen gefürchtet, von niemandem geliebt. Mißtrauisch und fremd, Verfemte und Ausgestoßene im eigenen Land. Soldaten Deutschlands, von der neuen Regierung verpflegt und besoldet, aber ungeliebt, vollzieht sich ihr Leben abseits der bürgerlichen Nichtigkeiten, abseits der neuen Politik und abseits der neuen Herren.

Dem Befehl zum Rückzug sind sie gefolgt, als ihnen nun befohlen wird, ihre Waffen abzuliefern, weigern sie sich. Ihr untrüglicher Instinkt sagt ihnen, daß der Krieg noch nicht zu Ende ist, daß die papierne Hülle des Friedens mit einem Schlag zu zerreißen droht.

* * *

Februar 1919. Sennelager im Teutoburger Wald. Garnisonstadt des 5. Badischen Feldartillerieregiments 76. Weitverstreut liegen die schmutziggrauen Kasernengebäude um den schneebedeckten Platz.

Eingehüllt in ihre grauen Wintermäntel stehen die Soldaten, die hier seit ihrem Rückzug vor wenigen Wochen aus Frankreich in ihren Quartieren liegen, in kleinen Gruppen zusammen und besprechen die Ereignisse der vergangenen Tage. Immer wieder treffen neue Nachrichten über die Lage im Reich ein. Die Soldaten sind bemüht, das undurchsichtige Bild der Geschehnisse zu entwirren, den ganzen Ereignissen einen Sinn zu geben.

Noch immer kontrollieren die Arbeiter- und Soldatenräte die Macht, auch wenn in der Zwischenzeit Friedrich Ebert, der neue Reichspräsident, regierungstreue Truppen gegen die Aufständischen marschieren ließ. In Berlin ist die Herrschaft der Räte bereits mit Waffenge-

walt gebrochen und an vielen Orten soll angeblich gekämpft werden. Teile der zurückgekehrten Truppen
kämpfen unter dem Befehl der neuen Regierung, die
große Masse der Soldaten aber liegt in den Garnisonen
und wartet. Wartet, ohne zu wissen worauf ...

Die Luft ist schneidend kalt. Die Soldaten stampfen
mit ihren schweren Stiefeln auf den gefrorenen Schnee,
um die Kälte aus dem Körper zu vertreiben.

"Hauptsache, der rote Spuk verschwindet ! In Berlin
haben wir doch schon mit dem Putschistengesindel auf-
geräumt. Wartet ab, noch ein paar Wochen und Ordnung
und Ruhe sind wieder hergestellt."

Das beifällige Murmeln der Umstehenden wird jäh
unterbrochen, als sich ein junger Leutnant einmischt
und seinen Vorredner scharf angreift: "Ruhe und Ordnung ! Putschistengesindel ! Was soll denn das heißen ?
So einfach ist die ganze Sache doch nicht abzutun. Natürlich ist vieles falschgelaufen, aber mit Ruhe und Ordnung kriegen wir die Sache doch nicht in den Griff.
Recht haben sie, die Kommunisten, wenn sie behaupten,
daß dieselbe Bourgeoisie wieder am Ruder sitzt, die
auch im Krieg schon auf unsere Knochen ihre drecki-
gen Geschäfte gemacht hat. Wir haben die Köpfe hingehalten und unsere Familien haben gehungert, aber die
feinen Herren hatten genug zu essen und vorne im Dreck,
da wo es wirklich drauf ankam, habe ich jedenfalls keinen von ihnen gesehen."

Die Schärfe der Worte läßt die Soldaten aufblicken.
Sie kennen den jungen Kriegsfreiwilligen aus dem
Schwarzwald, der mit seiner Batterie hier im Sennela-
ger liegt. Albert Leo Schlageter ist trotz seiner 24 Jahre
ein 'alter Hase', dessen Wort etwas gilt. Wer wie er vier
Jahre an der Front gestanden hat, weiß, wovon er redet.
Dafür, daß er sich nie gescheut hat, zu sagen, was er
denkt, ist Schlageter bei Freund und Feind bekannt.

"Ruhe und Ordnung", fährt Schlageter fort und seine Augen blitzen zornig auf, "wem nützen sie denn ?
Doch keinem anderen als dem dekadenten Bürgertum
und seinen politischen Marionetten im Reichstag. Die
Revolution der Roten, das war nur der Anfang des Ver-
suches, dem feisten Spießbürger und seinen verlogenen
Werten das Maul zu stopfen. Veränderung ist notwendig,

aber dies ist eine falsche Revolution, solange sie von falschen Inhalten bestimmt ist. Wir können unser Land nur vor dem Chaos bewahren" und selbstbewußt blickt er den jungen Soldaten um ihn in die Augen, "wenn *wir* ihr die richtigen Inhalte geben und wenn *wir* sie zu Ende führen."

Blunke, ein Feldwebel aus Berlin, und einer der Älteren im Regiment, der die ganze Zeit aufmerksam zugehört hatte, fährt dazwischen: "Du und Deine Inhalte, wie sehen die denn aus? Willst Du vielleicht mit den Roten zusammen gegen den Staat kämpfen?"

"Wenn es denn unbedingt sein müßte, ja! Aber hier geht es doch gar nicht um den Staat, begreift das doch endlich! Nicht der Staat ist das Unbedingte und Höchste, um das es geht, sondern unser Volk und unsere Nation! Der Staat ist nichts anderes als ein Mittel zu ihrer Verwirklichung!"

In den Augen der Soldaten liest er Zustimmung und tiefe Verbundenheit und er weiß, daß er für viele von ihnen spricht, die sich um ihn versammelt haben. Gedanken, die ihn schon lange bedrängen, formen sich zu Worten und seine Stimme läßt keinen Zweifel, wie ernst es ihm ist.

"Wenn die Politiker und Parlamente in einer Zeit wie der unseren, in der unsere Feinde an allen Grenzen stehen, um unser Land an sich zu reißen, nichts Wichtigeres zu tun haben, als zu reden und Sitzungsprotokolle anzuhäufen, dann sind *wir* der Staat, weil nur *in uns* noch der Glaube an Volk und Vaterland lebendig ist. Um die Parlamente brauchen wir uns nicht zu kümmern. Ihr werdet sehen, wie sie und die Sieger uns belügen, uns und das ganze Volk, und wie sie uns im Frieden um das bringen, was sie uns im Krieg nicht entreißen konnten. Ihr werdet erleben, wie sie unser Land verschachern, um ihre eigene erbärmliche Macht zu sichern.

Ihr wißt, daß viele unserer Kameraden sich den Freiwilligenverbänden angeschlossen haben und nach Osten ziehen, um die bolschewistischen Truppen zu stoppen, die sich Ostpreußen nähern und unser Land und Volk bedrohen. Ich habe genau wie ihr, verdammt noch mal keine Lust, mich wieder in den Dreck zu schmeißen und meine Knochen hinzuhalten, aber

Albert Leo Schlageter als Leutnant im 1. Weltkrieg

solange unsere Heimat und unser Volk bedroht sind, ist der Krieg noch nicht zu Ende. Wenn wir unser Land schützen wollen, dann dürfen wir nicht reden, sondern müssen die Freiheit verteidigen. Ich halte es hier nicht länger mit Warten aus, wer kommt mit nach Ostpreußen?"

* * *

Was war geschehen? Nach den letzten großen Frühjahrsoffensiven (im März bis Juli 1918) des deutschen Heeres an der Westfront, die zwar Geländegewinne einbrachten, aber keine entscheidende Wendung des Krieges bewirken konnten, erzwangen die alliierten Truppen, gestützt auf ihre ungeheure Materialüberlegenheit und die frischen Einheiten aus den Vereinigten Staaten, durch einen konzentrierten Tankangriff bei Amiens (am 8.8.1918) die Rückverlegung der deutschen Front in die sogenannte 'Siegfriedstellung', eine verkürzte, ausgebaute Verteidigungslinie von St.-Laurent (Arras) bis La Ferre Vailly.

Nach dem Zusammenbruch Bulgariens, bis dahin Verbündeter Deutschlands, verlangten deutsche Militärs ein Waffenstillstandsangebot an die Alliierten, das die deutsche Regierung auf der Grundlage der Wilsonschen 14 Punkte (Frieden ohne Sieg) im Oktober 1918 den Alliierten unterbreitete.

Angesichts der ungeheuren Übermacht des Gegners und des Hungers im Inneren des Reiches widersetzen sich im Oktober des Jahres 1918 die Matrosen der deutschen Hochseeflotte dem Befehl zum Auslaufen. Aus ihrer Weigerung heraus entwickelt sich ein revolutionärer Streik gegen die Kriegspolitik des Kaisers, der sich schlagartig auf viele deutsche Großstädte ausbreitet. Regierungstreue Truppen, die sich den putschenden Matrosen und Arbeitern entgegenstellen wollen, erhalten Schießverbot. In wenigen Tagen erfaßt die Revolution auch München und Berlin. Am 9. November dankt der Kaiser unter dem Druck der Ereignisse ab und geht nach Holland ins Exil. Die Regierung in Berlin wird ersetzt durch einen 'Rat der Volksbeauftragten', der am 9. November Friedrich Ebert zum Reichskanzler beruft.

Am 11. November unterzeichnet der Führer des linken Zentrums, Matthias Erzberger, den Waffenstillstand von Compiegne, der unter anderem die Räumung Belgiens, Frankreichs, Elsaß-Lothringens und Luxemburgs innerhalb von 15 Tagen, die Auslieferung der deutschen Flotte, die Ungültigkeit der im Osten geschlossenen Friedensverträge und den Fortbestand der englischen Hungerblockade um Deutschland beinhaltet. Währenddessen übernehmen überall in Deutschland Arbeiter- und Soldatenräte die Macht.

Nach Abschluß des Waffenstillstandsvertrages räumen die bis dahin unbesiegten deutschen Truppen unter Generalfeldmarschall von Hindenburg die besetzten Gebiete und ziehen sich in ihre Garnisonstädte zurück.

Die deutsche Kriegsflotte wird am 21.6.1919 bei ihrer Auslieferung an die Engländer auf Befehl ihres Admirals von Reuter im Hafen von Scapa Flow versenkt.

Im Innern des Reiches versuchen inzwischen unabhängige Sozialisten und Spartakisten aus dem Putsch der Matrosen und Arbeiter heraus eine rote Revolution nach russischem Vorbild. Als im Dezember 1919 der sozialdemokratische Politiker Gustav Noske den Oberbefehl über alle regierungstreuen Truppen übernimmt, wirft er den Aufstand der Spartakisten blutig nieder.

Während die deutsche Regierung mit den Alliierten um die genauen Friedensbedingungen verhandelt, stoßen bolschewistische Truppen in das Baltikum, das Küstengebiet zwischen Ostpreußen und Peipussee vor, besiegen die dort lebenden Litauer, Letten und Balten und bedrohen das waffenlose und ungeschützte Ostpreußen.

Als am 7.5.1919 der deutschen Delegation unter Leitung des deutschen Außenministers Graf Brockdorff-Rantzau die 'Friedensbedingungen' der Alliierten übergeben werden, sind die Forderungen unannehmbar. Der Ausruf des französischen Präsidenten Poincare an die deutsche Delegation "Die Stunde der Abrechnung ist gekommen!", zeigt den Geist dieser Verträge, die in Deutschland tiefe Erbitterung hervorrufen. Die deutsche Regierung und das Militär fühlen sich verraten und betrogen. Die Reichsregierung unter Scheidemann erklärt die alliierten Forderungen für unannehmbar und tritt zurück. Die neue Regierung aus Zentrum und SPD unterzeichnet schließlich unter dem Druck der Alliierten, die mit Gewaltmaßnahmen gegen das wehrlose Deutschland drohen, am 28. Juni 1919 im Spiegelsaal von Versailles das Friedensdiktat.

Mit dem in Wilsons 14 Punkten vertretenen 'Selbstbestimmungsrecht der Völker' haben die aufgezwungenen Verträge nicht das geringste mehr zu tun. Die Friedensbedingungen der Alliierten sprechen jeder Gerechtigkeit Hohn und tragen die Saat für neue Auseinandersetzungen in sich.

Deutschland verliert Grenzgebiete mit über 70.000 qkm Fläche und fast 7 Millionen Einwohnern. Elsaß-Lothringen fällt an Frankreich, Nordschleswig an Dänemark, große Teile von Posen, Schlesien, Ostpreußen und Westpreußen fallen an Polen. Ostpreußen ist vom Reich getrennt und Danzig wird 'Freie Stadt'. Das Hultschiner Ländchen fällt an die Tschechoslowakai, Eupen und Malmedy an Belgien, das Memelland und das Saargebiet an den Völkerbund.

Die Kolonien gehen verloren, und das Gebiet links des Rheines kommt für fünfzehn Jahre unter alliierte Besetzung, die Kohlengruben fallen an Frankreich.

Das deutsche Heer soll bis auf einen Rest von 100.000 Mann aufgelöst, schweres Kriegsmaterial und die Kriegsflotte müssen ausgeliefert werden.

Die Frage der Kriegsschuld wird per Dekret gelöst: Deutschland und seine Verbündeten tragen die Alleinkriegsschuld und haben dafür zu büßen. Die Reparationszahlungen Deutschlands an die Sieger werden auf 132 Milliarden Goldmark, zahlbar in 42 Jahresraten, festgelegt.

Ähnliches bestimmt der Vertrag von St. Germain für Österreich: Teile von Kärnten und der Steiermark fallen an das neugebildete Jugoslawien, das Sudetenland fällt an den neuen Staat Tschechoslowakai und Südtirol an Italien. Der bereits am 12.11.1918 von der österreichischen Nationalversammlung beschlossene Anschluß der deutschen Republik Österreich an das Deutsche Reich wird durch die Siegermächte verboten.

In dieser Situation bedrohen die bolschewistischen Truppen das ungeschützte Ostpreußen. Da das Deutsche Reich sich freiwillig entwaffnet hat und jede militärische Aktion scharf überwacht wird, bleibt der deutschen Regierung in diesem Moment nichts anderes übrig, als dem Drängen einzelner Offiziere nachzugeben, die Freiwilligenverbände — sogenannte 'Freikorps' — aufstellen wollen, um den bolschewistischen Truppen entgegenzutreten. Es sind also in der Regel reguläre Soldaten, die sich in den Freikorpsverbänden sammeln, verstärkt durch freiwillige Studenten und Arbeiter. Ihr Kampf gilt dem Schutz der deutschen Ostprovinzen gegen das Vordringen des sowjetischen Imperialismus. Die Alliierten ihrerseits greifen zunächst nicht ein, weil es in diesem Augenblick durchaus ihren Plänen entspricht, die vorrückenden russischen Truppen zu stoppen, um deren Macht nicht zu stark werden zu lassen. Die Freikorps sind also aus der Sicht der Alliierten zu dieser Stunde hilfreiche Verbündete im Kampf gegen einen erstarkenden möglichen Gegner. Aus dieser verworrenen Situation heraus bilden sich überall im Reich Freikorpsverbände, die nach Osten ziehen, um sich den plündernden bolschewistischen Heeren entgegenzustellen.

* * *

Seit Tagen zieht das Freikorps von Medem durch die endlosen Weiten des Baltikums. Eilmärsche treiben die Freiwilligen in ihren grauen Uniformen durch die hügellose, verlassene Landschaft.

Keine längeren Pausen gab es mehr, seit sie in Königsberg den Zug verließen. Die immer häufiger ankommenden Berichte vom blutigen Vormarsch der Bolschewisten erlauben kein Rasten.

Schweigend passiert das Freikorps die wenigen Höfe, die weit verstreut in der Landschaft liegen. Die Maisonne hat schon Kraft, und die verschwitzten Uniformen scheuern die Haut wund. Fluchend springt der Batterieführer Schlageter vom Wagen, um die müden Panjepferde anzutreiben, die die drei Geschütze des Freikorps über die sandigen Wege ziehen.

Flüchtlinge berichten den vorrückenden Soldaten von ungeheuren Greueltaten der Bolschewisten, die unter der deutschen Zivilbevölkerung in den Städten und Dörfern ein Blutbad anrichten. Gräßliche Nachrichten von Massenerschießungen deutscher Geiseln. Mord an über hundert deutschen Soldaten, die sich in Windau den roten Truppen ergeben hatten.

"Aufrücken! Aufrücken! Treibt die Pferde an! Nicht stehenbleiben!" Hauptmann von Medem, der Führer des Korps, ist überall; energisch treibt er die erschöpften Männer weiter. "Morgen sind wir in Riga! Denkt an unsere Landsleute in den Gefängnissen der Bolschewisten!"

Seit sich die Schreckensmeldungen häufen, ist jedes Lächeln aus seinem Gesicht verschwunden. Immer wieder treibt er seine Männer an und unermüdlich schleppt sich die Truppe vorwärts.

"Morgen sind wir in Riga! Morgen in Riga! Riga! Riga!" Monoton hämmern die Worte in den Köpfen der Soldaten, bestimmen die Stunden, zwingen sie, einen Fuß vor den anderen zu setzen.

Die Dämmerung ist schon hereingebrochen, als sie die vorgeschobenen Bauernhöfe von Mitau erreichen. Erschöpft und ausgepumpt werfen sie sich in ihre Quartiere. Ein trostloser Anblick: hier hatten die Bolschewisten schon gehaust. Spuren sinnloser Zerstörung an allem, was sie nicht mitschleppen konnten.

Die Männer fallen in einen bleiernen Schlaf: die letzte Nacht vor dem Sturm. In den Scheunen und Häusern der Umgebung liegen die Soldaten der verschiedensten Freikorps: Konzentration der Kräfte für den entscheidenden Sturm auf Mitau und Riga.

In den Scheunen stehen Pferde und Fahrzeuge. Geschützt hinter den festen Mauern der Häuser stapeln sich Waffen und Munition.

Starke Spannung lastet auf der ganzen Truppe. Melder hetzen von Gehöft zu Gehöft, in denen die Führer der Freikorps ihre provisorischen Quartiere bezogen haben. Nur wenige Kilometer vor ihnen liegt Mitau und dort stehen die vordersten bolschewistischen Truppen: lettische Schützenregimenter in den Diensten Rußlands, die Leibgarde Trotzkis. Ihre Grausamkeit gegen die Zivilbevölkerung und gegnerische Soldaten umgibt sie wie eine blutige Wolke: 'Gefangene werden nicht gemacht!'

Krachend fliegt die Tür auf und ein verschwitzter Melder stürzt auf Schlageter zu: "Leutnant Schlageter?" Ohne die Antwort abzuwarten sprudelt er seine Meldung heraus: "Alle Offiziere sofort zum Hauptmann! Lagebesprechung! Sturm auf Mitau noch heute Nacht!"

Über eine provisorische Karte gebeugt, entwickelt von Medem seinen Offizieren die Lage und gibt die Befehle für den Sturm. "Wir haben Befehl, direkt nach Mitau vorzustoßen. Schlageter, Sie tragen mit ihren Geschützen die Hauptlast und stoßen sofort zum Bahnhof vor. Die 'Eiserne Division' steht bereits im Rücken des Feindes, da kommt keiner mehr raus.

Wenn Mitau fällt, ist der Weg nach Riga frei und Sie wissen alle, was das bedeutet. Folgende Aufstellung: Infanteriespitze unter Oberleutnant Thöne, dann Sie, Schlageter, mit Ihren Geschützen! 200 Meter Abstand Stoßtruppschwadron unter Wolff. Munitionswagen mit Kavalleriebedeckung, MG-Abteilung, Rest der Truppe.

Wir müssen die Dunkelheit nutzen und die Bolschewisten überrumpeln. Schnelligkeit ist alles! Kein Mann darf nach Riga entkommen. Angriff um 1 Uhr 15. Noch irgendwelche Fragen?"

* * *

Tiefschwarz liegt die Nacht über dem Land. Leutnant Schlageter steht ruhig neben seinen Geschützen. Die Ziffern seiner Uhr zeigen 1 Uhr 10.

Noch fünf Minuten bis zum Sturm. Neben ihm stehen die Soldaten seiner Batterie: in der Regel junge Studenten und Arbeiter, bereit, sich den imperialistischen Truppen der Bolschewisten zum Schutz des Landes entgegenzuwerfen.

Unbeweglich und starr spähen sie in die Nacht, versuchen die Dunkelheit mit brennenden Augen zu durchdringen.

Die Sekunden verstreichen. Noch einmal prüfen die Hände die Granaten im Koppelriemen, entsichern die klammen Finger die geladenen Gewehre.

1 Uhr 15. Sturm auf Mitau.

Die letzten Nachrichten aus Riga verleihen den Männern Flügel: In den verschmutzten Gefängnissen der Stadt vegetieren Hunderte von deutschen Geiseln, von den Bolschewisten wahllos zusammengetrieben, und warten auf ihre Erschießung.

Sternklare Nacht. Kein Schuß zerrreißt die Stille, kein Postenruf weckt die ahnungslosen Bolschewisten.

Blitzartig stoßen die Spitzen der Freikorpsverbände vor, sickern in die Stadt, zerreißen das Gefüge der bolschewistischen Verteidigungslinien. Als der Gegner merkt, was mit ihm geschieht, stehen die Stoßtruppschützen schon tief in Mitau.

Deutsche Truppen auf dem Vormarsch! Nach den Demütigungen der letzten Monate, nach den unwürdigen Auflagen des Versailler Diktats ein erhebendes Gefühl.

Als sich der bolschewistische Widerstand organisiert, ist die Schlacht schon geschlagen. Gnadenlos schlägt das MG-Feuer der nachrückenden Infanterie in die Reihen der Russen. Dazwischen immer wieder die trockenen Schüsse der vorstürmenden Artillerie. "Nachsetzen! Dranbleiben!"

Abgeschnitten von der Rückzugsstraße nach Riga wenden sich die geschlagenen Bolschewisten nach Nordosten zum Babir-See; unfehlbare Ziele für die Scharfschützen der Eisernen Division. Die befreite Stadt bietet ein grauenvolles Bild, bestätigt die Schreckensnachrichten der Flüchtlinge. Überall finden die Befreier bestialisch ermordete Männer, Frauen und Kinder: die bolschewistische Soldateska kennt kein Erbarmen.

"Wir müssen durch nach Riga! Noch ein Stoß und wir werfen das ganze Pack aus der Stadt! Die Brücke über die Düna! Himmel noch mal, die Brücke! Der einzige Weg nach Riga! Wir müssen sie nehmen, sonst sind die Geiseln verloren."

Rasender Galopp treibt die Geschütze vorwärts. Da liegt die Brücke! Unversehrt spannt sie sich über den breiten Fluß. Schlageter reißt sein Geschütz herum, treibt seine Männer zum Äußersten. Fauchend verläßt die erste Granate das Rohr, schlägt in die Verteidigungsstellungen am anderen Ufer.

"Ein Geschütz auf die Brücke!" Unter dem Feuerhagel der Bolschewisten schieben die Männer ein Geschütz vor. Drüben beginnt die Panik! Rote Fahnen, zu Fetzen zerschossen, fliegen in den Dreck. Auseinanderlaufende Infanteriehorden.

Als die Infanterie nachrückt, ist die Brücke genommen: der Weg nach Riga ist frei!

In der Stadt treffen die Freikorps auf die gut ausgebauten Widerstandsnester der Bolschewisten. Überall Barrikaden, Straßenschlachten, Kampf Mann gegen Mann. "Zu den Gefängnissen!" Stoßtrupps kämpfen sich durch die Straßen vor.

Durch das schwere Tor des Gefängnisses dringen die Hilfeschreie der verzweifelten Geiseln zu den anstürmenden Soldaten, immer wieder begleitet von den Schüssen der bolschewistischen Bewacher, die wahllos in die wehrlosen Deutschen schießen.

"Sprengen!" Splitternd reißt das schwere Tor unter der Wucht der Granate. Jetzt gibt es kein Halten mehr. Von heiliger Wut getrieben, stürzen sich die Freikorpssoldaten auf die mordenden Bestien.

Die Geiseln sind frei! Den ganzen Tag über wird in der Stadt erbittert gekämpft, Straße für Straße gesäubert und die letzten Widerstandsnester werden vernichtet.

Als sich der Abend über das Land senkt, weht vom Turm der Petrikirche die deutsche Fahne. Riga ist frei!

* * *

Als die Rote Armee Ende des Jahres 1918 das Baltikum überfiel, besetzte sie uraltes deutsches Ordensland. Schon 1201 segelte Bischof Adalbert, Domherr zu Bremen und seit 1199 Bischof von Livland, mit einer großen Flotte ins Baltikum und gründete noch im selben Jahr mit Aussiedlern aus Bremen und Hamburg Stadt und Bistum Riga. Wenige Jahre später, 1219, folgte die Gründung von Reval, 1223 Narwa und 1225 Dorpat mit seiner Universität.

Im Kampf mit den sich immer wieder wehrenden Pruzzen beginnt der deutsche Ritterorden um 1230 die Kolonisierung des Baltikums. Von Danzig über Riga bis Reval schafft er in den folgenden Jahrzehnten neuen Siedlungsraum für nachrückende deutsche Bauern, Handwerker und Kaufleute, die in das weithin unbesiedelte Land vordringen und es in mühsamer Arbeit kultivieren.

Die deutsche Landbevölkerung, die Kaufleute, die vor allem an den Küsten seßhaft wurden, die geistlichen Stiftungen, der Deutsche Orden und die blühenden deutschen Städte gaben dem Baltikum sein eigenes Gepräge.

1252 wurde Memel gegründet und 1254/55 eroberte ein mächtiges Kreuzritterheer unter König Ottokar II. von Böhmen aus das Samland und sicherte es durch die Gründung Königsbergs. Es entstand so ein geschlossener deutscher Siedlungsraum, den der deutsche Ritterorden durch Gründung von 93 deutschen Städten und über 1400 deutschen Dörfern in den Jahren von 1230 bis 1410 allein im Baltikum festigte.

Einen entscheidenden Beitrag zur Erschließung und kulturellen Prägung des Baltikums leistete auch die deutsche Hanse, eine Vereinigung deutscher Kaufleute zur gegenseitigen Unterstützung, die seit dem 13. Jahrhundert den wirtschaftlichen Aufbau des Baltikums entscheidend beeinflußte.

Riga, Reval und Dorpat, die bedeutendsten Städte des Baltikums wurden Hansestädte und auch in Wilna bestand seit 1400 eine Niederlassung der deutschen Hanse. Jahrhunderte hindurch prägten die deutschen Handwerker und Kaufleute das Bild der baltischen Städte; die deutschen Bauern kultivierten das ungenutzte Land und begründen eine leistungsstarke Landwirtschaft.

In den Jahrhunderten nach der Blütezeit des Deutschen Ritterordens stellten die Nachkommen die Meister der Gilden und Zünfte und die Ratsherren und Bürgermeister der reichen Städte. Immer wieder versuchten die östlichen Nachbarvölker das fruchtbar gemachte, blühende Land in ihre Gewalt zu bringen. Die deutsche Bevölkerung widersetzte sich allen Angriffen und verteidigte deutsches Land gegen jeden östlichen Angreifer. Die jetzt einfallenden imperialistischen Truppen des Bolschewismus begnügten sich nicht mit der militärischen Besetzung des Baltikums, ihr Plan ist es vielmehr, durch die systematische Ausrottung der deutschen Bevölkerung den deutschen Charakter des Baltikums vollständig zu vernichten.

Die schlecht bewaffnete deutsch-baltische Landeswehr wirft sich von Anfang an den bolschewistischen Okkupationstruppen entgegen; der vielfachen Übermacht der Bolschewisten und ihrer Materialüberlegenheit aber kann sie allein nicht standhalten. Hilfesuchend wendet sie sich an die deutsche Regierung und bittet um Unterstützung.

In dieser Situation bilden sich mit Zustimmung der neuen Reichsregierung, die angesichts der von den Siegern diktierten Abrüstung keine andere Möglichkeit sieht, das bedrohte Ostpreußen vor den Bolschewisten zu schützen, und mit Duldung Englands, das durch den Vorstoß bolschewistischer Truppen in das Baltikum und den drohenden Einmarsch nach Ostpreußen um seine gerade erst durch den Krieg errungene Vormachtstellung in Europa fürchtet, überall in Deutschland militärische Freiwilligenorganisationen zum Schutz des deutschen Ostens, die sogenannten Freikorps.

Diese Verbände, deren Stärke oft nur wenige Dutzend Mitglieder umfaßte, die teilweise aber auch mehrere tausend Mann zählten, benannten sich entweder nach ihren Gründern und Führern oder den Landstrichen und Städten, in denen sie sich sammelten. So entstanden das Freikorps Roßbach, die Brigade von Loewenfeld, das Freikorps Medem — dem Schlageter als Batterieführer angehörte — die Baltische Landeswehr, das Freikorps Wesel und viele andere. Jedes Korps trug zudem sein eigenes Abzeichen: häufig das Wappen der Heimatstadt, ein Eichenblatt oder ein besonderes Ärmelabzeichen. Neben Offizieren und Unteroffizieren der deutschen Armee waren es vor allem Studenten, Gymnasiasten und junge Arbeiter, die als Zeitfreiwillige in die Freikorps eintraten.

Die Gesamtzahl der Freikorpsmitglieder dürfte in ihrer Blütezeit, im Mai 1919, bei etwa 200.000 gelegen haben, von denen aber nur ein Teil im Osten zum Einsatz kam.

Der notwendige finanzielle Rückhalt zur Bezahlung der Freiwilligen stammte in der Regel aus den Kassen der Regierung und der Reichswehr. Zu erklären ist diese finanzielle Unterstützung von staatlicher Seite vor allem damit, daß die neuen Politiker in den Freikorps auch ein Instrument zu ihrer eigenen Sicherung gegen die immer noch agierenden Arbeiter- und Soldatenräte und örtlich bestehenden kommunistischen Aufständischen sahen.

Die Bewaffnung der Freikorps stammte aus alten Heeresbeständen und bestand in der Regel aus einfachen Waffen bis hin zum Maschinengewehr. Geschütze waren die Ausnahme und stammten mit fortschreitender Dauer der Kämpfe im Osten in ihrer überwiegenden Mehrheit aus erbeuteten russischen Beständen.

Der Einsatz der Freikorps im Baltikum änderte die militärische Lage innerhalb weniger Wochen schlagartig. Die Einnahme der strategisch wichtigen Stadt Riga am 22.5.1919 durch die deutschen Freikorps brach die Vorherrschaft der bolschewistischen Truppen und zwang sie zur Rückverlegung ihrer Armeen. Die deutschen Freikorps und die baltische Landeswehr wollten nun ihrerseits diesen Sieg nutzen, um die angeschlagenen bolschewistischen Verbände zu verfolgen und vollständig zu schlagen. Der von ihnen angestrebte umfassende Schlag würde nicht nur die Sicherung Ostpreußens zur Folge haben, sondern darüber hinaus die Befreiung des gesamten Baltikums von den bolschewistischen Besatzungstruppen.

In dieser Situation offenbarte sich die hinterhältige Politik Englands. Jetzt, nachdem das bolschewistische Heer, das die alleinige Vormachtstellung Englands bedrohte, mit dem Blut der deutschen Freikorpssoldaten so weit zurückgeschlagen worden war, daß Englands Interessen gesichert und die Bolschewisten zu Verhandlungen mit der englischen Regierung bereit waren, wendete sich diese an die deutsche Reichsregierung und drohte mit militärischen Zwangsmaßnahmen, falls die deutschen Freikorps nicht unverzüglich das gesamte Baltikum räumen, die Waffen ablegen und sich auflösen würden. Die deutschen Freiwilligen hatten in dem schmutzigen Spiel, das England mit ihnen trieb, ihre Schuldigkeit getan: sie hatten den Vorstoß des Bolschewismus gestoppt, Moskau für England verhandlungsbereit gemacht und Englands Vormachtstellung gesichert.

Nach dem 'altbewährten' englischen System der 'balance of power', das ja in Wirklichkeit nichts anderes bedeutet, als jedes Land, das die militärische oder wirtschaftliche Vorherrschaft Englands bedroht, mit allen nur erdenklichen Mitteln in einen Krieg mit seinen Nachbarn zu treiben, wandte sich England nun gegen die deutschen Freikorps.

Nun waren sie es, in denen England neue Gefahren für seine Vormachtstellung witterte. Vorrückende, siegreiche deutsche Truppen stärkten das Selbstwertgefühl des gerade erst in die Knie gezwungenen deutschen Reiches und gefährdeten die bedingungslose Annahme und Erfüllung des aufgezwungenen Versailler Diktates.

Als sich der englische Druck auf die deutsche Regierung verstärkte und mit Sanktionen gegen die Zivilbevölkerung gedroht wurde, sah sich die Regierung gezwungen, die Räumung des Baltikums zu befehlen. Die Freikorps durchschauten das schmutzige Spiel, das die Engländer mit ihnen getrieben hatten, und viele von ihnen weigerten sich, das freigekämpfte Land zu verlassen.

Als sich die Freikorps weigerten, dem Druck der Engländer nachzugeben, schloß die deutsche Regierung die Grenze, sperrte den notwendigen Nachschub an Waffen, Munition, Lebensmitteln und Medizin und stellte die Zahlung des Soldes ein.

Plakate verkündeten, daß jeder, der die Meuterer — so nannte die Regierung jetzt die Freikorps — im Baltikum unterstütze, für sie werbe, oder versuche, ihnen Geldmittel oder Ausrüstung zu verschaffen, mit hohen Gefängnisstrafen belegt werde.

Die Freikorps, von nun ab völlig auf sich selbst gestellt, brachen ihrerseits mit der deutschen Regierung, von der sie sich nach getaner Arbeit verraten und im Stich gelassen fühlten.

Zur gleichen Zeit bemühte sich ein russischer Oberst, Fürst Awaloff-Bermondt, eine weißgardistische russische Armee aufzustellen, um gegen die Bolschewisten zu kämpfen.

Die im Baltikum verbliebenen Freikorps waren für ihn wichtige Verbündete, mit denen er unverzüglich über eine mögliche Zusammenarbeit verhandelte.

Das Ergebnis war die Bildung einer west-russischen Regierung mit der Basis Kurland und die Aufstellung einer west-russischen Armee, in die die Freikorps eintraten.

Unter russischen Abzeichen und unter dem Oberbefehl des Fürsten Awaloff kämpften rund 10.000 Freikorpssoldaten unter Führung ihrer Offiziere weiter gegen den Bolschewismus.

Als Löhnung ließ Awaloff eigenes Papiergeld drucken, dessen Deckung das Kriegsmaterial war, das erbeutet werden würde. Da Awaloff und die mit ihm verbündeten Freikorps nicht bereit waren, sich den englischen Plänen unterzuordnen, nach denen das Baltikum unter britische Gewalt gelangen sollte, stellten sich die Engländer auf die Seite ihrer Gegner und führten einen erbarmungslosen Krieg gegen Awaloff und die Freikorps.

Englische Offiziere landeten im Baltikum und hetzten die Litauer, Letten und Esten gegen die west-russische Armee auf, unterstützten die wieder vorrückende bolschewistische Armee mit Waffen, Munition, Lebensmitteln und Geldern und griffen, wenn trotz aller Übermacht die deutschen Freikorps vorrückten, direkt mit ihrer vor Riga liegenden Kriegsflotte in die Kämpfe ein.

Als der Winter 1919 einsetzte, war die militärische Lage der westrussischen Armee hoffnungslos. Ohne Geld- und Waffennachschub war sie den pausenlosen Angriffen der Gegner nicht gewachsen; der harte baltische Winter schlug tiefe Wunden in die Reihen der Freikorps: Stadt um Stadt mußte geräumt werden.

In dieser verzweifelten Lage kündigte Oberleutnant Gerhardt Roßbach der deutschen Regierung den Gehorsam und brach mit seinem Reichswehr-Jäger-Bataillon 37, einer gut ausgerüsteten Truppe mit einer Gesamtstärke von etwa 1000 Mann, von Ostpreußen aus ins Baltikum auf, um den bedrängten Freikorps zu Hilfe zu kommen und ihren Rückweg nach Ostpreußen zu sichern.

In Gewaltmärschen führte er seine Truppe ins Baltikum, warf die überrumpelten Letten und Bolschewisten zurück und sicherte den Rückzug der damit geretteten Freikorpssoldaten.

Am 13.12.1919 überschritt Albert Leo Schlageter mit den letzten deutschen Truppen bei Memel die Reichsgrenze.

England hatte sich wieder einmal durchgesetzt: die deutschen Truppen hatten das Land verlassen, das Baltikum war für Deutschland verloren.

Die Situation im Reich bestand aus einer Zusammenballung ungelöster alter und stetig hinzukommender neuer Probleme.

Hunderttausende ehemaliger Soldaten warteten auf ihre durch das Versailler Diktat erzwungene Entlassung.

Oberst Fürst Awaloff-Bermondt, Führer der Freiwilligen Westarmee.

Heinz Hauenstein, Führer der Selbstschutz-Abteilung Heinz.

Die 2. Kompanie des III. Bataillons Oberland auf dem Marsch in Oberschlesien. Auffällig ist die unzureichende Ausrüstung an Kleidung und Waffen.

Ihre Zukunftsaussichten waren niederschmetternd: Überall herrschten Arbeitslosigkeit, Hunger und steigende Inflation. Die politische Situation war ungefestigt: auf der einen Seite die Militärs und Freikorps, auf der anderen Seite immer wieder aufflackernde kommunistische Aufstände.

Die Politik der Reichsregierung stand unter einem ungeheuren Druck von innen und außen. Die unnachgiebige Haltung der Alliierten zwang die deutsche Regierung zu unerfüllbaren Reparationszahlungen, während die eigene Bevölkerung hungerte. Der Haß gegen die Versailler Verträge und die alliierten Sieger wuchs.

Die Militärs fühlten sich von den eigenen Politikern verraten, kritisierten deren Zustimmung zum Versailler Diktat als Erfüllungspolitik. Das im Feld unbesiegte Heer bildete unter seinen Offizieren einen Staat im Staate; ein offenes Pulverfaß, das jederzeit explodieren konnte. In dieser Atmosphäre der Unsicherheit und Not, des gegenseitigen Mißtrauens und der Enttäuschung putschen am 13.3.1920 Einheiten der Reichswehrtruppen und Teile der Freikorps unter der Führung des ostpreußischen Generallandschaftsdirektors Wolfgang Kapp und des Generals Freiherr von Lüttwitz gegen die Politik der sozialdemokratischen Reichsregierung, erklären sie für abgesetzt und rufen Kapp zum Kanzler aus.

Als die Reichsregierung ihrerseits General von Lüttwitz absetzt und gegen Kapp und die übrigen Putschisten Haftbefehle erläßt, marschiert Korvettenkapitän Ehrhardt mit 6000 Freiwilligen in Berlin ein und zwingt die Regierung zur Flucht. Zur gleichen Zeit besetzt das Freikorps Oberland mit 5000 Mann München.

Der Regierung, die von der Reichswehrführung die Niederwerfung des Putsches fordert, verweigert General von Seeckt, seit 1920 Chef der Heeresleitung, mit dem Hinweis "Reichswehr schießt nicht auf Reichswehr" den Gehorsam.

Die Regierung, die Sozialdemokraten und die Gewerkschaften rufen daraufhin zum Generalstreik auf, der das wirtschaftliche Leben im Reich stillegt. Regierungstreue Truppenteile stellen sich den putschenden Truppen entgegen. Kommunistische Gruppen überfallen kleinere Einheiten der Freikorps und ermorden Hunderte. In Magdeburg, Halle, Kiel, Frankfurt, München und Berlin wird gekämpft.

Doch das Bürgertum und breite Teile der Bevölkerung versagen Kapp ihre Unterstützung, der Versuch schlägt fehl. Am 17. März treten Kapp und Lüttwitz zurück: der Putsch ist gescheitert.

Während noch die Freikorps ihre eigene Situation zu klären suchen und die Regierung bemüht ist, Ordnung in das undurchsichtige Bild der einander bekämpfenden Gruppen zu bringen, nutzen die Spartakisten die Gunst der Stunde und entfachen einen kommunistischen Aufstand mit dem Ziel, die Macht in Deutschland an sich zu reißen. Ihre Propaganda heizt die Erregung der Arbeiter weiter an, malt die Gefahr einer neuen Militarisierung und fordert zum organisierten Streik aller Werktätigen. Die kommunistischen Aufrufe zur Bildung von Arbeiterbataillonen und zur Gründung einer Räterepublik nach dem Vorbild der russischen Bolschewiki finden vor allem bei den hungernden und arbeitslosen Massen im Ruhrgebiet Anhänger. Innerhalb weniger Tage bildet sich dort eine sogenannte 'Rote Armee', die die Arsenale der Reichswehr stürmt und sich mit Waffen und Munition versorgt. Düsseldorf, Duisburg und Mülheim müssen von der Reichswehr geräumt werden; Dortmund, Wetter und Essen fallen in die Hände der Roten Armee. Gleichzeitig tobt auch in Sachsen-Thüringen der Bürgerkrieg. Unter der Führung des Kommunisten Max Hölz errichten die Spartakisten ein Terrorregime, erschlagen die Angehörigen der Bürgerwehren und der Polizei und rufen die Diktatur des Proletariats aus. Sie erklären die Reichsregierung für abgesetzt und drohen für den Fall eines militärischen Gegenzuges der Reichswehr, die besetzten Städte anzuzünden und die Bourgeoisie abzuschlachten.

Die Reichsregierung versucht zunächst zu verhandeln, um einen Bürgerkrieg zu vermeiden. Als die Gespräche aber keine Ergebnisse bringen und der Terror der Roten Armee gegen die Bevölkerung wächst, wendet die Regierung sich hilfesuchend an die gerade noch verfemten Freikorps. Mit ihrer Hilfe soll die Reichswehr den Spartakistenaufstand niederschlagen.

Die Alliierten ihrerseits erheben dagegen zu diesem

Zeitpunkt keine Einwände: denn nichts kommt ihren Plänen zur vollständigen Zerschlagung Deutschlands gelegener, als ein innerdeutscher Bürgerkrieg, der die letzten Reserven verbrauchen und Deutschland nur um so leichter unter ihre Gewalt bringen soll.

* * *

"Menschenskind, Schlageter, hast Du schon gehört ! Im Ruhrgebiet putscht eine 'Rote Armee'. Die Spartakisten haben die Zechen und Rathäuser gestürmt und die Reichswehrtruppen vertrieben. Wart's ab, noch ein paar Tage und wir werden wieder gebraucht. Ohne uns geht' s der Regierung an den Kragen, diesmal machen die Roten ernst !" Der kleine Veit ist ganz aufgeregt.

"Eine Regierung, die unser Volk verraten und uns alle um unseren Lohn geprellt hat, was geht die uns an ?" Mißmutig winkt Schlageter ab und starrt aus dem schmutzigen Fenster seiner Mansarde. "Hast Du schon vergessen, wie sie uns im Stich gelassen hat, als wir in Riga standen ? Wenn die Politiker einmal Rückgrat gezeigt hätten, wieviele von uns könnten noch leben !" Schlageters Augen funkeln wütend auf.

"Rausgeschmissen haben uns die feinen Herren, für die wir unsere Knochen hingehalten haben. Ein paar lumpige Geldscheine als Abfindung und schon standen wir auf der Straße.

Mensch, Veit, bis jetzt sind doch immer *wir* die Verlierer gewesen ! Wir verachten das Bürgertum und retteten es doch mit unserem Blut ! Wir sind angetreten, um die Freiheit der Nation zu sichern, und schützten eine Regierung, die die Nation und das Volk verraten hat ! Wir sind gegen Englands schmutzige Politik, und doch waren wir seine besten Soldaten ! Und jetzt, wo es der Regierung, die uns allen in den Rücken gefallen ist, an den Kragen geht, da sollen wir wieder unseren Kopf riskieren ? Veit, denk doch mal nach !"

Der junge Soldat in der abgewetzten Jacke schweigt betreten. So hatte er seinen Leutnant noch nie erlebt.

Schlageter steht noch immer am Fenster, sein Gesicht ist unbewegt. Dann wendet er sich an Veit und nickt ihm zu: "Das Schlimme ist nur, daß Du recht hast.

Wir müssen marschieren, ob wir wollen oder nicht. Wir wissen alle, was es heißt, wenn wir ins Ruhrgebiet ziehen. Bürgerkrieg ist der schmutzigste aller Kriege. Wir wissen, daß wir den englischen Interessen dienen und dennoch müssen wir marschieren. Wir retten die Regierung, die uns bei nächster Gelegenheit wieder verfolgen wird; wir schützen die Bourgeoisie, deren Hohlheit und satte Selbstgenügsamkeit wir immer ablehnten. Und doch müssen wir kämpfen. Denn wenn wir jetzt nicht kämpfen, dann war alles umsonst: Riga, die gefallenen Kameraden, unser Einsatz, alles. Unsere Gegner sind überall, aber der gefährlichste Gegner ist der Spartakist.

Wir alle wissen, was passiert, wenn die Roten die Macht erringen. Da geht es nicht nur den Schiebern und Bonzen an den Kragen, da nehmen die es nicht so genau.

Ergreifen sie die Macht, dann regieren Chaos und Ziellosigkeit. In der kritischen Situation, in der wir uns befinden, ist das eine gefährliche Position, da sie uns im Inneren noch schwächer macht, als wir es ohnehin schon sind. Unsere Gegner hätten nichts eiligeres zu tun, als diese Schwäche auszunutzen und weitere Gebiete zu besetzen.

Wir müssen sie niederkämpfen, auch wenn sich unsere Feinde vor Freude ihre schmutzigen Hände reiben, denn sie sind im Augenblick gefährlicher als alle Bürger und Politiker zusammen.

In diesen Tagen werden die Weichen gestellt, die über das Schicksal unseres Volkes entscheiden. Neues und Gerechtes entsteht nur, wenn in uns der Wille zur Nation lebt. Und der siegt nur dann, wenn wir ihn in unseren Taten und Werken verwirklichen. Du hast recht, wir sind gezwungen zu handeln, wenn Deutschland noch eine Zukunft haben soll."

* * *

Endlos rattert der Zug durch die Nacht nach Westen, er zieht seine Wagen durch das niedergedrückte, hoffnungslose Deutschland. Eintöniges Grau zu beiden Seiten der Gleise, selten nur durchbrochen durch die hellen Fenster vereinzelter Bauernhöfe.

In den Abteilen und Gängen sitzen die feldgrauen

Freikorpssoldaten der Batterie Schlageter. Halblaute Gespräche, unruhiger Schlaf, gesammelte Spannung. Der eintönige Rhythmus der Lokomotive zieht alles in seinen Bann.

In einem der Abteile sitzt Leutnant Schlageter zusammen mit seinen Unteroffizieren und erklärt im Schein einer Taschenlampe auf einer grobskizzierten Karte die Lage: "Hier etwa steht die Rote Armee." Sein rechter Zeigefinger umkreist dabei das gesamte Ruhrrevier von Wesel über Dortmund, Hagen und zurück bis Düsseldorf und Duisburg.

"Über 40.000 Mann, teilweise gut bewaffnet aus den geplünderten Arsenalen der Reichswehr. In einzelnen Städten fanatische Führer, die ihre Leute gut im Griff haben. Aber auch kleinere Gruppen und Heckenschützen. Das wird kein Spaziergang. Hier links des Rheins stehen die alliierten Besatzungstruppen und so etwa verläuft der englische Brückenkopf." Sein Finger zieht dabei den Verlauf des Rheins auf der Karte nach und umschreibt zuletzt einen Halbkreis um Köln.

"Und hier stehen wir, rund um den ganzen Schlamassel! Hier im Osten die Division Has, daneben die Division Epp mit den Oberländern. Ganz im Westen, etwa hier, das Freikorps Wesel. Vor Münster stehen die Westfälischen Jäger und hier", und dabei tippt er auf eine Lücke, die zwischen Wesel und Münster klafft, "hier ist unser Platz!"

Er faltet die Karte sorgfältig zusammen und steckt sie in die Seitentasche seines Uniformrockes. "Gemeinsam mit den Roßbachern und der III. Marine-Brigade von Loewenfeld sollen wir über Haltern direkt nach Gladbeck und Bottrop ins Herz der Roten Armee vorstoßen. In zwei Stunden etwa sind wir in Borken; nutzen wir die Zeit für eine Mütze voll Schlaf."

* * *

Quietschend und zischend stemmt sich die schwere Lokomotive gegen die nachrückenden Wagen, verschwindet für Sekunden in ungeheuren Wolken von Wasserdampf.

Überall auf dem kleinen Bahnhof von Borken sta-

peln sich die Ausrüstungsstücke der wartenden Freikorpssoldaten, die in kleinen Gruppen zusammenstehen und
jeden Neuangekommenen freudig begrüßen.

Noch bevor Schlageter aus seinem Abteil treten
kann, meldet sich ein junger Soldat bei ihm und übergibt
eine kurze Meldung: 'Sofort nach Eintreffen im Gasthof
zur Linde melden. Kapitän von Loewenfeld'. Bekannte
Gesichter unter den Wartenden, Berge von Gepäck und
die zu Pyramiden zusammengestellten Gewehre auf dem
Bahnhofsvorplatz.

Schlageter kämpft sich durch die Enge des Bahnhofs,
verläßt ihn und schreitet zielstrebig durch die kleine,
noch schlafende Stadt. Die frische Morgenluft erfrischt
nach der langen Bahnfahrt. Über den taunassen Pflaster-
steinstraßen stehen die breiten Bürgerhäuser mit ihren
roten Klinkern und ihren kleinen Vorgärten. Eines der
wenigen Schaufenster schmückt spärliche Osterdekora-
tion. Buntbemalte Eier in kleinen Strohnestern, um-
rahmt vom Gelb der ersten Ginsterzweige. Ein handge-
maltes Schild wünscht 'frohe Feiertage' — vergessene
Bilder einer Zeit, die ihnen allen fast fremd geworden ist.

Der Gasthof zur Linde gleicht einem Taubenschlag.
Ständig verlassen kleine Gruppen von debattierenden
Offizieren das Haus durch die breite Eingangstür; andere wieder verschwinden in das Halbdunkel des großen
westfälischen Baues. Einer der breiten Türflügel ist weit
aufgestoßen, bewacht von einem feldgrauen Loewen-
felder, der alle Ankommenden kontrolliert. Ein Plakat
an der Tür weist auf das Hauptquartier der III. Marine-
brigade. "Sie wünschen?" Schlageter betrachtet aufmerksam das junge Gesicht und zeigt seine Meldung.
"Ah, Leutnant Schlageter! Der Kapitän wartet schon
auf Sie. Bitte gleich hier rechts in den großen Saal."

Als Schlageter den hellerleuchteten Raum betritt,
glaubt er in eine andere Welt zu kommen. Eben noch die
ruhige Beschaulichkeit der schlafenden Stadt, hier die
hektische Betriebsamkeit einer militärischen Komman-
dozentrale. Zwei Gesichter einer verworrenen Zeit.
Überall auf den schweren dunklen Eichentischen liegen
ausgebreitete Landkarten, kleine Fähnchen markieren
auf ihnen die militärische Lage. Gruppen von Offizieren
erörtern die Situation. Dazwischen immer wieder Melder

von den umliegenden Einheiten, die Informationen bringen und neue Befehle in Empfang nehmen.

"Meine Herren, darf ich vorstellen, Leutnant Schlageter!" Kapitän von Loewenfeld, der Bruder des letzten Führers der Deutschen Legion, ein großer, hagerer Mann mit einem entschlossenen Gesicht, begrüßt den Eintretenden herzlich.

"Schön, daß Sie da sind, wir haben schon auf Sie gewartet. Schauen Sie sich die Sache gleich mal an. Die Großwetterlage ist Ihnen ja bekannt. Seit gestern morgen steht Epp vor Dortmund und läßt keinen mehr raus aus der Stadt. Hatte böse Verluste beim Vormarsch, aber jetzt rückt er den Roten auf die Pelle.

Um Hagen und Remscheid steht General von Gellhausen mit dem Freikorps Hacketau unter Major von Falkenstein. Kampferprobte Einheiten, alles in allem rund zwölfhundert Mann.

Die Spartakisten sind gut bewaffnet. Teilweise sogar Artillerie. Weiß der Teufel, wo sie das ganze Zeug herhaben. Allerdings ist ihr Netz zerrissen, letztendlich fehlt doch die Disziplin. Zentrale Kommandostellen sind nicht mehr auszumachen, die Einheiten operieren zum Teil nach eigenem Gutdünken."

"Das riecht verdammt nach Häuserkampf", unterbricht ihn Schlageter, der den Ausführungen des Kapitäns aufmerksam zugehört hat. "Leider", fährt der Kapitän fort, "unnötiges Blutvergießen in diesem verdammten Bürgerkrieg."

"Nach Epps Vorstoß haben wir eine neue Marschrichtung: über Dorsten nach Duisburg und Bottrop. Entweder wir schneiden dem roten Gesindel den Fluchtweg zu den alliierten Besatzungszonen ab oder wir haben bei nächster Gelegenheit wieder den gleichen Ärger.

Schlageter, Sie übernehmen die zur Verfügung stehenden Geschütze und unterstützen die Freikorps Kühne und Roßbach bei ihrem Vorstoß.

Lassen Sie sich von Hauptmann Umber einweisen und versorgen Sie ihre Leute mit dem Notwendigen. Viel Zeit bleibt Ihnen nicht: Abmarsch heute Mittag gegen 14 Uhr. Sie wissen, worauf es ankommt. Schnelligkeit ist das Gebot der Stunde. Viel Glück!"

Der Kapitän schüttelt Schlageters Hand und ruft

Hauptmann Umber, um ihm die notwendigen Einzelheiten mitzuteilen.

* * *

Wenige Tage später. In den frühen Morgenstunden des 6. April treten zwei Bataillone des Reichswehrregimentes 61, verstärkt durch Freikorps und einen Zug Feldkanonen der Batterie Schlageter, den Vormarsch auf Bottrop an. Seit Tagen dringen die Freikorps an zerschossenen Fabriken und ausgebrannten Höfen weiter vor, legen den Ring um die eingeschlossene Rote Armee immer enger. In blutigen Kämpfen haben sie Stadt um Stadt befreit, jetzt treiben sie die fliehenden Verbände vor sich her.

Aber dies ist kein Krieg, wie sie ihn aus früheren Jahren kennen. Der Gegner stellt sich zu keiner Schlacht, ist nirgendwo greifbar. Es sind Heckenschützen, die hinter jeder Bodenwelle, jedem Eisenbahndamm, jedem Schotterhaufen lauern und blutig zuschlagen; Schatten, die in den Schachtanlagen und Tunnels, in den Kanalisationsschächten der Städte verschwinden, um wenig später an anderer Stelle wieder aufzutauchen; blutiger Terror an Gegnern und Zivilisten, der alles bisher Erlebte an Grausamkeit übertrifft.

"Das Ganze halt !" augenblicklich verharren die ausgepumpten Soldaten, um die kurze Verschnaufpause zu nutzen. "Offiziere zu mir !" ruft Schlageter über die Köpfe der schwer atmenden Soldaten hinweg. Melder eilen durch die Kolonnen und tragen den Befehl weiter.

Vor ihnen liegt Bottrop. Ein Gewirr von schäbigen Häuserblocks und grauen Backsteinsiedlungen. Schmutzige Zechenanlagen mit hochaufragenden Fördertürmen und rauchenden Schloten. Dampfende Schachtanlagen und feurig glühende Hochöfen. Qualm, Rauch und Feuer, Hämmern und Lärmen und inmitten der trostlosen Steinwüste die geballte Kraft der Roten Armee: zusammengetrieben und gestellt. Ihrem Schattendasein entrissen, haben sie keine andere Wahl, als sich zu ergeben oder zu kämpfen. Ein angeschossenes Tier und darum doppelt gefährlich.

Die entscheidende Schlacht. Schlageter weist die Offiziere ein und gibt letzte Befehle. In wenigen Minuten entwickeln die feldgrauen Kolonnen langgezogene Schützenlinien. "Seitengewehre aufpflanzen! Kontakt zum Vordermann halten und immer an den Häuserwänden entlang!" Vormarsch!

"Die Noskes kommen! Achtung die Noskes kommen!" ertönt eine schrille Stimme.

"Verdammtes Pack!" flucht Schlageter. "Was geht uns Noske an! Weiter, weiter, nicht stehenbleiben!" Die Unteroffiziere treiben die Männer nach vorne. "Straße frei! Macht die Fenster zu!" Drohend richten sich die Gewehre auf die offenen Fenster.

Immer tiefer dringen die Soldaten in die Stadt. Noch immer herrscht unheimliche Ruhe. "Verdammt, irgendwo müssen sie doch stecken!"

Gegenfeuer! Die vordersten Soldaten reißen die Arme hoch und sacken in sich zusammen. "Deckung!" Ohrenbetäubender Lärm, krachendes Splittern der roten Granaten. Jaulend heulen die Splitter über das Kopfsteinpflaster. Die Luft explodiert vom harten Knall der Minenwerfer. "Achtung, Flankenfeuer!" Aus einem der grauen Backsteinbauten hämmert ein Maschinengewehr auf die Freikorpssoldaten.

"Alles weg von der Straße!"

Rasendes Gewehrfeuer aus den umliegenden Häusern verwandelt die Straße in eine blutige Hölle. Auf dem nassen Kopfsteinpflaster liegen die Toten, zerfetzt von den Garben der Maschinengewehre.

Am Abend ist Bottrop genommen, die Freikorps kontrollieren die Stadt. Die Rote Armee ist geschlagen.

* * *

Nach der Einnahme von Bottrop rückten die Truppen der Reichswehr und die Freikorps südöstlich von Duisburg vor, um die nun überall fliehenden Einheiten der geschlagenen Roten Armee von ihrem Rückzugsweg zu den Alliierten abzuschneiden. Am gleichen Tag, an dem die III. Marine-Brigade und die Batterie Schlageter Bottrop befreit hatten, zog das Freikorps Epp in Dortmund ein, jubelnd von der Bevölkerung begrüßt.

Einen Tag später, mit der Wiedereroberung von Essen, der letzten wichtigen Stellung der Spartakisten, war die Niederlage der Roten Armee besiegelt.

Ihre Niederlage war aber nicht nur eine militärische, sondern vor allem auch eine moralische. Viele der selbsternannten Führer der Roten Armee verrieten ihre Untergebenen und ließen sie bei den letzten Gefechten im Stich. Wieder andere waren mit den geraubten Geldern aus Banken und Rathäusern untergetaucht oder zu den Alliierten geflohen.

Der Spartakistenaufstand im Ruhrgebiet war zugleich das letzte militärische Ereignis, in dem die deutschen Freikorps in großem Umfang zum Einsatz kamen.

Insgesamt verloren sie in den Kämpfen im Ruhrgebiet 208 Tote und hatten über 600 Verwundete. Dazu kamen über 123 Vermißte, die irgendwo im Gewirr der Häuserkämpfe den Heckenschützen der Spartakisten zum Opfer gefallen oder in irgendeinem Keller brutal zu Tode geprügelt worden waren. Über die Verluste der Roten Armee liegen keine genauen Angaben vor. Die Zahl ihrer Toten lag aber weit über 1000.

Am meisten aber war die Zivilbevölkerung betroffen, die unter dem blutigen Terror der Roten Armee ebenso zu leiden hatte, wie die Polizei. Über 2000 Tote, viele von ihnen von sogenannten 'roten Revolutionsgerichten' ohne Verhandlung ermordet, und eine unbekannte Zahl von Verwundeten waren zu beklagen.

Jetzt, als das 'Gespenst des Bolschewismus' gebannt und die deutschen Freikorps mit ihrem Blut die drohende Gefahr besiegt hatten, griffen wieder die Alliierten ein, die bisher dem Bürgerkrieg stillschweigend zugeschaut hatten, und zwangen die Deutsche Reichsregierung zur Auflösung der Freikorps.

Die deutsche Regierung ihrerseits tat alles, um diesem Wunsch der Sieger nachzukommen. Zu tief saßen bei den Politikern der Schreck des Kapp-Putsches und die Angst um die eigenen Pfründe, als daß sie ihre Kraft auf die wirklich entscheidenden Fragen der Zeit richten wollten. Die Auflösung der Freikorps begann.

Ein geringer Teil der Freiwilligen wurde in die Reichswehr übernommen, der Rest innerhalb weniger Tage entlassen.

Die Freikorpsführer ihrerseits waren nicht bereit, ihre Organisationen vollkommen auflösen zu lassen. Um die Möglichkeit der Remobilisierung zu wahren, aber auch, um den nun Arbeitslosen den notwendigen Unterhalt zu sichern, richteten einige von ihnen eigene Fürsorgebüros ein, die mit Hilfe privater Spender die ehemaligen Freiwilligen so gut zu versorgen suchten, wie es eben möglich war. Die große Zahl von Waffen und Munition, über die die verschiedenen Freikorps verfügten, verschwand in Scheunen und Kellern, unter dunkle Giebel und in eigens geschaffenen Erdhöhlen — 'für alle Fälle', wie es einer der bekanntesten Freikorpsführer formulierte. Andere Freikorpsführer begegneten der Auflösung ihrer Einheiten und der schlechten sozialen Lage ihrer Leute durch die Gründung von Firmen oder landwirtschaftlichen Genossenschaften.

Der militärische Druck der alliierten Sieger war zu stark und der Wille zur nationalen Wiedererstarkung bei der Regierung zu schwach, als daß sich die Freikorps dem Auflösungsbefehl hätten widersetzen können, obwohl es durchaus an verschiedenen Stellen zu Kämpfen zwischen Freikorpseinheiten und Reichswehrtruppen kam. Trotz aller Rettungsversuche der Freikorpsführer mußten viele Freiwillige ihre alten Formationen verlassen, kehrten zu ihren Familien zurück oder ließen sich immatrikulieren.

Schlageter selbst verknüpfte auch in dieser Zeit sein eigenes soziales Schicksal mit dem seiner Kameraden, arbeitete zusammen mit den Leuten seiner Batterie als Erntehelfer in Ostpreußen und Pommern und schaufelte mit ihnen im Winter 1920/21 in Königsberg den Schnee von Bürgersteigen und Straßen.

Die Freikorpsverbände befanden sich in einer Art von oberflächlicher Auflösung, jederzeit bereit, wieder anzutreten, sobald die Freiheit der Nation bedroht würde. Die alliierten Sieger nutzten ihrerseits sofort den erneuten Schwächezustand des Reiches und die Unentschlossenheit der deutschen Regierung, um ihre eigenen imperialistischen Pläne zu verwirklichen. Als die Reste der geschlagenen Roten Armee in die von den alliierten Truppen besetzten deutschen Gebiete flohen, sah Frankreich seine Stunde gekommen.

General Degoutte, Oberkommandierender der alliierten Besatzungstruppen verkündete: "Die Berliner Regierung hat eine plötzliche Offensive der Reichswehr gegen die Arbeiterschaft angeordnet. Sie hat dadurch eine der wesentlichen und feierlichsten Bestimmungen des Friedensvertrages verletzt. (...) Die Regierung der französischen Republik sieht sich daher gezwungen, sich zu sichern. Deshalb habe ich den Befehl erhalten, die Städte Frankfurt, Homberg, Darmstadt und Duisburg zu besetzen."

Angesichts der totalen militärischen Demobilisierung der deutschen Armee und eines Deutschlands, das an den ungeheuerlichen Reparationsforderungen des Versailler Diktats mehr und mehr zugrundeging, von einer notwendigen 'Sicherung' des waffenstarrenden Frankreichs zu sprechen, beweist, daß der französischen Regierung und ihren Militärs jedes Mittel recht war, um ihre imperialistischen Pläne zu verwirklichen.

Deutschland erlebte bittere Zeiten. Vertrauend auf Wilsons Friedensvorschläge, war es durch List hintergangen worden, nach dem Kriege niedergerungen, zerstückelt, seiner Armee beraubt und durch die skrupellosen Bedingungen des Versailler Diktats wirtschaftlich am Ende seiner Kraft.

Die englische Hungerblockade kostete noch 1919, ein Jahr nach der Kapitulation also, fast eine Million Menschen, vorwiegend Frauen und Kindern das Leben.

Das wenige, das die deutsche Wirtschaft und Landwirtschaft unter diesen Umständen produzieren konnte, wurde als Reparationsleistung nach Frankreich und England ausgeführt.

Auf den ohnehin völlig überlasteten Arbeitsmarkt drängten nun noch Hunderttausende von ehemaligen Soldaten und Millionen von Flüchtlingen aus den abgetrennten und geraubten deutschen Provinzen. Die Kassen der Regierung waren leer, das soziale Netz wirkungslos: das Elend war unbeschreiblich.

Jetzt sah auch Polen seine Stunde gekommen. Aufgrund des Versailler Diktates waren ihm schon Westpreußen und Posen zugefallen: Landgewinne ungeheuren Ausmaßes, die aber seinen imperialistischen Landhunger nicht befriedigen konnten.

Die polnischen Wortführer beanspruchten immer wieder das an Bodenschätzen reiche und hochindustrialisierte Oberschlesien. Dies war ihnen, aufgrund eines Einspruches der Deutschen Reichsregierung, nicht durch das Versailler Diktat zugefallen. Die alliierten Sieger beschlossen vielmehr, durch eine Volksabstimmung klären zu lassen, ob Oberschlesien Deutschland oder Polen zufallen sollte.

Bis zu dieser Abstimmung ging die Regierungsgewalt in Oberschlesien an eine interalliierte Kommission, die sich aus Vertretern Englands, Frankreichs und Italiens zusammensetzte.

Diese übernahm unter der Führung des französischen Generals Le Rond am 11. Februar 1920 die Amtsgeschäfte.

Le Rond stand eindeutig auf seiten der Polen. Die von ihm durchgeführte Ausweisung der noch vorhandenen Reste der Reichswehr und der deutschen Verwaltungsbeamten und ihre Ersetzung durch die interalliierte Kommission, und vor allem die Ausweisung der deutschen Post- und Eisenbahnbeamten und ihre Ersetzung durch polnische Beamte, schuf innerhalb weniger Monate ein starkes Übergewicht der polnischen Kräfte.

Im Sommer des Jahres 1920 brach der russisch-polnische Krieg aus. Der russische General Budjonny schlug mit seiner Reiterarmee die Polen und drang weit in den polnischen Korridor in das ehemalige deutsche Gebiet vor. Frankreich organisierte daraufhin seinerseits die Neuaufstellung der polnischen Armee, rüstete sie mit modernsten französischen Waffen aus und stellte an die Spitze der polnischen Verbände französische Offiziere.

Mit dieser massiven Hilfe Frankreichs gelang es der polnischen Armee im August des Jahres 1920 die weit auseinandergezogenen russischen Truppen vom Nachschub abzuschneiden und zurückzuwerfen.

Aus diesem erfolgreichen militärischen Vorstoß entwickelte sich in Oberschlesien ein polnischer Aufstand mit dem Ziel, unter Umgehung der beschlossenen Volksabstimmung, Oberschlesien gewaltsam an Polen anzuschließen.

Diese Absicht vereitelten die Verbände der deutschen Schutzpolizei in Oberschlesien. Daraufhin wandelte sich der polnische Aufstand in einen gnadenlosen Kleinkrieg gegen alles Deutsche mit dem Ziel, die abstimmungsberechtigte Mehrheitsbevölkerung der Deutschen in Oberschlesien einzuschüchtern und die Abstimmung für Polen zu entscheiden.

England, das seinerseits durch die Angliederung der oberschlesischen Industrie und Kohlengruben an Polen eine zu große Stärkung des polnischen Imperialismus befürchtete, hinderte zusammen mit Italien die Franzosen an einer allzu starken und massiven Unterstützung der polnischen Aufständischen.

Führer und Kopf der polnischen Aufständischen war Wojciech Korfanty, ein ehemaliger Abgeordneter im Preußischen Landtag und im Deutschen Reichstag und dort zeitweilig Führer der Polenfraktion, deren politisches Ziel schon immer ein großpolnischer Staat war.

Von seinem Hauptquartier im Hotel Lomnitz in Beuthen aus, überzog er, gestützt auf die im Stillen gewährte finanzielle Unterstützung durch den polnischen Staat, mit Hilfe seiner 'Polska Organizacja Wojenna', einer in der Art von Kommandotrupps aufgebauten Terrororganisation, ganz Oberschlesien mit Gewalt und Schrecken.

Und während die englischen und italienischen Truppen der interalliierten Aufsichtsbehörde den polnischen Terror wenigstens einzudämmen suchten, blieben die französischen Truppen in ihren Kasernen, erklärten sich für 'neutral' und verstießen damit eklatant gegen ihre Aufgabe, deretwegen sie überhaupt in Oberschlesien standen: die Vorbereitung der Volksabstimmung und der Sicherung der Deutschen.

Im Gegenteil: General Le Rond seinerseits half den Polen, wo immer er nur konnte. Mehrfach sprach er sich für die völlige Öffnung der Grenze von Oberschlesien nach Polen hin aus und votierte immer wieder für eine weitere Hinauszögerung des Abstimmungstermins.

Die unter seinem Oberbefehl stehenden französischen Truppen halfen den Polen in allen Belangen. In verschiedenen Gebieten entwaffneten und verhafteten sie die örtlichen deutschen Polizeiposten, übergaben die beschlagnahmten Waffen den Polen und verboten der deutschen Regierung die Entsendung weiterer deutscher

Polizeikräfte zur Sicherung der Zivilbevölkerung.

Nur unter dem Druck der übrigen Mitglieder der interalliierten Abstimmungs-Kommission stimmte Le Rond schließlich dem 20.3.1921 als Volksabstimmungstermin zu.

Jeder spätere Termin wäre ihm lieber gewesen, hätte er doch die Festigung des polnischen Einflußes in Oberschlesien weiter vorangetrieben.

Während die Deutsche Reichsregierung, gebunden an die Bestimmungen des Versailler Diktats, keine Möglichkeit hatte, die deutsche Zivilbevölkerung in Oberschlesien vor den Übergriffen der polnischen Banden zu schützen, steigerte sich der Terror der polnischen Kommandos zunehmend.

Bestialische Morde an der deutschen Bevölkerung häuften sich, je näher der Abstimmungstermin heranrückte. Immer wieder wurden Deutsche, die sich für deutsche Interessen einsetzten, aus ihren Wohnungen entführt und von den polnischen Terrorkommandos zu Tode geprügelt, die unter dem heimlichen Schutz der Franzosen immer dreister operieren konnten.

Gegen diesen Terror der Polen organisierten die Deutschen in Oberschlesien einen freiwilligen Selbstschutz, zumal die deutsche Reichsregierung ihnen aus Furcht vor möglichen Sanktionen der Franzosen im Ruhrgebiet keinerlei Unterstützung leistete.

Sie wandten sich darum an die verbotenen Freikorps, die ihrerseits in der Haltung der Reichsregierung nur einen neuerlichen Verrat an Deutschlands Einheit sahen und bereit waren, die Freiheit der Nation zu verteidigen.

Um die oberschlesische Zivilbevölkerung wirksam schützen zu können, organisierten Mitglieder der ehemaligen III. Marinebrigade unter dem Kommando des jungen Fähnrichs Heinz Hauenstein, eine Art von Spezialpolizei.

Finanziert durch private Spenden, entstanden so kleine Kommandoeinheiten, die die Deutschen vor dem Zugriff der Polen schützten, Waffen in das Abstimmungsgebiet schmuggelten und den polnischen Terror mit entschlossenem Widerstand beantworteten.

Unter diesen Freiwilligen war auch Albert Leo Schlageter, der zusammen mit ehemaligen Kameraden

seiner Batterie aus Königsberg, wo sie zuletzt als Arbeitsbrigade ihr Geld verdienten, nach Oberschlesien kam.

Diese relativ kleine deutsche Einheit, alles in allem nicht mehr als 500 Mann, brach den polnischen Terror und gab den Deutschen das Gefühl, nicht mehr nur allein auf sich selbst gestellt zu sein.

Am 20. März 1921 schließlich fand unter Beobachtung der Interalliierten-Abstimmungs-Kommission — und bis zum Schluß begleitet vom Terror der polnischen Korfantybanden — die Volksabstimmung statt.

Von insgesamt 1.186.356 abgegebenen gültigen Stimmen wurden 478.802 für Polen und 707.554 für das Verbleiben Oberschlesiens bei Deutschland abgegeben.

Die deutsche Zivilbevölkerung und die Freiheitskämpfer jubelten. Allem Terror zum Trotz hatten sie die Einheit des Reiches gerettet.

Vertrauend darauf, daß die Interalliierte Kommission nach dieser eindeutigen Abstimmung den Wiederanschluß Oberschlesiens unverzüglich durchführen und die polnischen Terroristen in die Schranken weisen würde, verließen die deutschen Freiwilligen das Land.

Innerhalb der Interalliierten Kommission aber kam es trotz des klaren Abstimmungsergebnisses zu Streitigkeiten.

Vor allem der französische General Le Rond versuchte immer wieder durch geschickt manipulierte Interpretationen der Abstimmung zumindest einen Teil Oberschlesiens den Polen zuzusprechen.

Trotz der klaren Mehrheit bestanden Korfanty und die polnische Regierung auf die östlichen und südwestlichen Gebiete Oberschlesiens, die Deutsche Regierung ihrerseits pochte auf das klare Abstimmungsergebnis und forderte ganz Oberschlesien.

So war die Situation, als am frühen Morgen des 3. Mai 1921 an der östlichen Grenze des oberschlesischen Industrierreviers und in den Kreisen Pless und Rybnik gleichzeitig der dritte polnische Aufstand ausbrach.

Wieder war es Korfanty, der mit seinen gut organisierten und bestens ausgerüsteten Truppen, alles in allem mehr als 35.000 Mann, zwar öffentlich von der polnischen Regierung verurteilt, aber heimlich in jeder Hinsicht von ihr unterstützt, den Aufstand anführte. In wenigen Stunden befanden sich weite Teile der Gebiete um Beuthen, Pless und Rybnik in den Händen der Aufständischen.

Lebenswichtige Eisenbahnverbindungen zwischen Oberschlesien und dem Mutterland wurden gesprengt, die Zivilbevölkerung verfolgt und die schwachen deutschen Polizeieinheiten entwaffnet und gefangengenommen. Die italienischen Verbände der Interalliierten Kommission waren zu schwach, um den Aufstand niederzuschlagen. Die Franzosen unter ihrem General Le Rond unterstützten sogar, wie schon zuvor, die polnischen Aufständischen, und die englischen Verbände, die vielleicht aus Gründen der eigenen Machtsicherung in Europa den Aufruhr hätten niederschlagen können, standen zu diesem Zeitpunkt nicht mehr in Oberschlesien.

Denn kurze Zeit nach der Abstimmung in Oberschlesien war in England ein Bergarbeiterstreik ausgebrochen, von dem die englische Regierung befürchtete, daß er sich auf die Transportarbeiter und Eisenbahner ausdehnen könnte. Zur Niederschlagung der Streikenden hatte sie die vier in Oberschlesien stationierten englischen Bataillone abgezogen und nach England zurückbeordert.

Unter diesen Vorzeichen blieb zur Sicherung Oberschlesiens und seiner Zivilbevölkerung keine andere Möglichkeit, als der erneute Einsatz von Freiwilligen.

Wieder ist es Heinz Hauenstein, der aus dem ganzen Reich die Freiwilligen zusammenruft. Sein Telegramm an Schlageter ist erhalten: 'Zurück nach OS. — Der Pole greift an. — Meldung in Neiße. Heinz Hauenstein. Freikorpsführer.'

* * *

"Diese verdammte Schraube ist total verrostet, wie festgewachsen !" Scheppernd fliegt der rostige Eisenbügel auf den Boden. "Langsam, langsam, nur nicht nervös werden. Hol' Dir von Michael die große Zange und versuch's noch mal. Das Ding muß raus, da hilft gar nichts."

"Du hast gut reden !" Fluchend klettert der kleine

Veit über die verrosteten Schrotthaufen und sucht Michael, den blondschöpfigen Norddeutschen, der erst vor wenigen Tagen zu ihrer Batterie gestoßen ist.

"Schaffen Sie es, Schlageter?" fragt Heinz Hauenstein besorgt. Der ölverschmierte Monteur im schmutziggrauen Arbeitskittel blickt von seiner Arbeit auf und lacht über sein ganzes Gesicht. "Was wir nicht schaffen, das muß erst noch erfunden werden. Schauen Sie sich doch um! Soweit das Auge reicht, alles was das Herz begehrt: verrostete Bleche, zerschlagene Rohre, verbogene Träger. Da müßte es doch mit dem Teufel zugehen, wenn wir daraus nicht wenigstens *ein* Geschütz zusammenbauen können."

"Ja, der Engländer hat ganze Arbeit geleistet." Hauenstein überblickt mit finsterer Miene den riesigen Platz der Neißer Reichstreuhandgesellschaft, auf dem sich die Reste der auf Befehl der Sieger aus deutschen Heeresbeständen abgelieferten und total zerschlagenen Kriegswaffen in wilden Haufen türmen.

"Immerhin haben sie uns das ganze Zeug hiergelassen. Sie werden sehen, in ein, zwei Tagen steht das Geschütz blitzblank vor uns. Hauptsache, Sie sorgen für die notwendige Munition."

"Keine Bange, dafür sorgen die Oberländer", antwortet Hauenstein und klopft dabei auf das schmutzige Rohr, an dem Schlageter arbeitet.

"Übrigens, da hinten kommen ihre Hilfsmonteure zurück." Schlageter steht auf und lacht über den kleinen Veit, der wie ein Rohrspatz schimpft und pausenlos auf Michael einredet. Dann wischt er sich mit dem Ärmel über das ölverschmierte Gesicht und wendet sich wieder seiner Arbeit zu.

* * *

"Deckung!" Die feldgrauen Gestalten werfen sich in die aufgewühlte schwarze Erde. Jaulend fliegt das Geschoß über sie hinweg, bohrt sich krachend in den Boden und schleudert feuchte, dunkle Erdklumpen auf die schutzsuchenden Soldaten. "Alles auf! Nach rechts hinter den Hügel!" Die Männer springen auf, reißen die schweren Munitionskisten hoch und stürmen über das Feld.

Wettlauf mit dem Tod ! Dicht hinter ihnen wühlen die Einschläge der polnischen Artillerie mit höllischem Lärm tiefe Trichter in die dunkle Erde. Der kleine Hügel gibt spärlich Deckung. "Munition zu mir !" Zitternd schiebt Winkler die ersten Gurte in das Maschinengewehr.

Nun brechen die Deutschen auf der ganzen Linie siegreich vor. Bei den Polen ist der Teufel los. Panik ergreift die wenigen Überlebenden: In wilder Flucht verlassen sie ihre Stellungen, geben das strategisch wichtige Vorwerk Strebinow auf und flüchten nach Osten.

Der Weg nach Zyrowa ist frei ! Ein blutiger Sieg, den viele Freikorpssoldaten mit ihrem Leben bezahlt haben.

Heinz Hauenstein tritt an die vergilbte, fleckige Karte, die an der Wand seines Quartieres hängt und fährt mit hastigen Bewegungen über die bunt schraffierten Flächen. Um ihn herum sitzen die Führer der benachbarten Freikorps: Hauptmann Ritter von Finsterlin, Major Siebringhaus, Hauptmann Östreicher, Leutnant Schlageter, Major Horadam und einige andere.

Im Nebenzimmer aufgerissene Schränke und Kommoden, ein umgestürzter Waschtisch; zerschlagene Bilder und zerschossene Spiegel an den Wänden. Kleider, Wäsche und Photographien liegen wild verstreut auf dem Boden. Zerfetzte Tapeten, ausgerissene Türen: noch wenige Tage vorher hatten die polnischen Terrorgruppen hier gehaust. Hauenstein entwickelt die Lage: "Unser Vorstoß auf Strebinow hat die Flanke der Polen aufgerissen. Eicken hat mit seinem Korps Sprentschütz und Niewke genommen. Wir haben also hier einen breiten Abschnitt erobert, von dem aus wir unsere weiteren Vorstöße entwickeln können.

Hier in Karlshof sitzt Lensch und hier", und sein heller Zeigestock umkreist immer wieder einen braun umrandeten Fleck auf der Landkarte, "hier sitzt der Pole. — Annaberg !"

"Also Sturm", sagt einer der Offiziere und erhebt sich, "wer den Annaberg hat, hat Oberschlesien, das wissen wir doch alle." "Das weiß aber auch der Pole." "Um so wichtiger, daß wir schnell stürmen, sonst führt er noch mehr Truppen heran."

"Langsam, langsam, meine Herren", unterbricht

Hauptmann Echterbruch, der Führer der freiwilligen deutschen Heimatwehr aus Krappitz. "Bevor Sie entscheiden, hören Sie mir bitte einen Augenblick zu. Wir haben Besuch aus Berlin bekommen, irgendein Abgesandter der Regierung, der uns eine Note zu überbringen hat. Ich lasse ihn hereinbitten."

Die anwesenden Freikorpsführer stutzen und schweigen verblüfft. "Ein Abgesandter der Reichsregierung? Das kann nichts Gutes bedeuten."

Einer der Unteroffiziere verläßt für einen Augenblick den Raum und führt wenig später einen blassen, kleinen Mann herein, der den Offizieren mit kalter Unverbindlichkeit begegnet.

Welch ein Unterschied! Hier die Männer, die nur ihrem Gewissen verpflichtet ihr Leben freiwillig einsetzen, um die Freiheit der Nation und ihres Volkes zu verteidigen. Da der blasse Vertreter der Regierung. Aalglatt, geschniegelt, unverbindlich. Leere Hülle ohne eigene Inhalte, stets bereit, die Wünsche der bourgeoisen Pfründedenker weiterzutragen.

"Meine Herren. Als Vertreter der Deutschen Regierung habe ich Ihnen folgendes mitzuteilen. Die Verhandlungen, die die Deutsche Regierung im Interesse des deutschen Volkes mit der Interalliierten Kommission führte, haben endlich den erwünschten Erfolg erbracht. Die Interalliierte Kommission ist bereit, einem Waffenstillstand zwischen den kämpfenden Parteien zuzustimmen. Der Grenzverlauf findet in Übereinkunft zwischen der Deutschen Reichsregierung und der Interalliierten Kommission auf der Basis der derzeitigen Stellungen statt, zwischen die eine neutrale Zone geschoben wird. Gleichzeitig befiehlt die Reichsregierung die Auflösung der Freikorps und ihre unverzügliche Rückkehr ins Reichsgebiet."

"Himmel nochmal!" fällt ihm Schlageter ins Wort. "Damit erklären Sie doch die ganze Volksabstimmung für ungültig. Ganz Oberschlesien gehört zum Reich." Von hinten schreit Major Siebringhaus erregt: "Das ist Verrat! Sie überlassen den polnischen Banden halb Oberschlesien und den Annaberg. Wofür kämpfen unsere Leute denn hier wie die Teufel? Waffenstillstand, daß ich nicht lache. Jetzt, wo der Pole rennt, da wollen die hohen Herren plötzlich einen Waffenstillstand. Nicht mit uns. Sagen Sie das Ihren sauberen Auftraggebern."

Die Offiziere stehen wie ein Mann gegen den Regierungsvertreter. "Wenn Sie und die Politiker in Berlin den Ausverkauf Oberschlesiens als einen erwünschten Erfolg der deutschen Seite bezeichnen, dann pfeifen wir auf Sie !"

Schlageter steht auf und stellt sich ganz dicht vor ihn: "Und sagen Sie denen in Berlin, daß wir nicht hier sind, weil es uns Spaß macht, andere Menschen zu töten, sondern weil es um den Erhalt der Freiheit geht. Sagen Sie Ihnen, daß wir keine Moradeure oder hirnlose Schlagetots sind, aber sagen Sie Ihnen auch, daß wir die Sache hier mit unseren Mitteln zu Ende führen werden.

Hier muß man nämlich nicht nur Recht haben, sondern auch die Kraft, das Recht durchzusetzen. Und diese Kraft sind wir !

Und nun entschuldigen Sie uns bitte, wir haben Wichtigeres zu tun !" "Ordonnanz, begleiten Sie den Gesandten bitte hinaus."

"Deutsche Regierung", spöttelt einer der Offiziere und wendet sich verächtlich ab, "verschachern unsere Landsleute an den Polen und zucken mit keiner Wimper."

"Also bleibt es beim Sturm auf den Annaberg ?" fragt der junge Leutnant, der vorher durch das Erscheinen des Regierungsvertreters unterbrochen worden war. "Vergeßt nicht, daß der Pole gutausgebaute Stellungen ausgehoben hat; der ganze Annaberg ist eine Festung. Ein Sturm kostet viel Blut. Zudem stehen dort auch französische Truppen: das kann Komplikationen geben."

"Der Pole hatte schon viele gute Stellungen und wir haben ihn immer geworfen", meldet sich ein anderer. "Wenn wir den Annaberg haben, ist der Pole gebrochen, nicht nur militärisch. Der Verlust des Berges wäre für ihn auch eine moralische Niederlage. Ich stimme auch für Sturm !" "Und die Franzosen ?"

"Das ist halb so schlimm", mischt sich Schlageter ein. "Da können wir ganz auf den Engländer vertrauen. Der Franzose unterstützt die Polen, England ist gegen sie, weil sie ihm zu stark werden, in diesem Fall also auch gegen die Franzosen. Wenn wir gegen den Polen marschieren, wird der Franzose sich hüten, einzugreifen, sonst hat er den Engländer am Hals: und der läßt bekanntlich nicht mit sich spaßen. Also Sturm !" "Hört, hört, der Schlageter, ein richtig ausgefuchster Diplomat." "Wenn es nützt, warum nicht ?" gibt Schlageter zurück. "Meine Herren !" Heinz Hauenstein bittet sie alle zur Karte und entwickelt den Angriffsplan zum Sturm auf den Annaberg.

"Südwestlich der Bahnlinie Gogolin-Kandrzin tritt die Kolonne Chappuis mit den Bataillonen Bergerhoff, Lensch und Winkler, und als Reserve das Bataillon Watzdorf an.

Nördlich und nordostwärts formiert sich die Angriffskolonne Horadam mit dem Freikorps Oberland, der Batterie Schlageter und meinem eigenen Korps.

Die Sicherung der linken Flanke gegen den Großsteiner Forst übernimmt das Detachement Strachwitz mit dem Angriffsziel Großstein. Die Einnahme der Ausgangsstellungen muß bis morgen abend abgeschlossen sein. Angriff übermorgen früh, 2 Uhr 30. Wünschen wir uns alle viel Glück, wir werden's brauchen. Der Pole weiß auch, worum es geht."

21. Mai 1921. Langsam rückt der Zeiger der Uhr vor. Zehn Minuten vor 2 Uhr.

Schlageter prüft noch einmal die strohumwickelten Räder seines Geschützes, tätschelt beruhigend den Hals der Pferde, die unruhig im Geschirr stehen.

"Nervös ?"

"Na ja, es wird sicher kein Zuckerschlecken. Der Pole ist bis an die Zähne bewaffnet und mehr als dreimal so stark wie wir." "Zigarette ?" Hauenstein ist die Ruhe selbst. Tief bläst er den Rauch in die Nacht. "Es sind nicht nur die Waffen. Gestern informierte uns Hauptmann Finsterlin, daß auch fünf Kompanien der polnischen Infanterieregimenter 27 und 16 und das 15. polnische Ulanenregiment in Oberschlesien stehen. Die lautstarke Verurteilung der Korfantybanden durch die polnische Regierung ist nichts als hohles Geschwätz."

"Wenn unsere Regierung nur halb so viel für uns täte." "Wieviel Uhr ?" "Noch zwanzig Minuten."

Hauenstein zieht ruhig an seiner Zigarette. Die Männer schauen wortlos hinaus in die Nacht. "Was machst Du, wenn hier alles vorbei ist ?" "Ich bin froh, wenn alles vorbei ist und wir unsere Aufgabe erfüllt haben. Die Jahre laufen uns davon. Ich werde studieren — Nationalökonomie oder Wirtschaftswissenschaften, genau weiß ich es noch nicht. Irgendwo im Schwarzwald, vielleicht in Freiburg."

Die Männer schweigen. "Und was machst Du?"

Hauenstein starrt lange in die Nacht. "Ich weiß es nicht. Ob wir überhaupt wieder Ruhe finden?" sagt er dann leise. "Vielleicht bleibe ich hier. Ein wunderbares Land mit seinen weiten Feldern und Wäldern und mit seinem sonderbar herben Geruch der schwarzen Erde."

"2 Uhr 30", Schlageters Stimme wird ernst.

"Dann also los! Holen wir uns unser Land!" Befehle huschen von Mann zu Mann, lautlos bewegen sich die grauen Gestalten durch die aufkommende Dämmerung vorwärts. "Tempo, Tempo, Anschluß halten", flüstert Heinz immer wieder. "Wir müssen vor Dollna stehen, bevor der Pole merkt, was sich über ihm zusammenbraut. Jede Minute zählt."

Schweigend marschieren die Männer in dichten Gruppen auf der schmalen Straße.

Eine Stunde später, als die Dämmerung bleiern über dem Land liegt, erreichen sie Kalinow.

Kurze Besprechung der Offiziere. "Bis jetzt hatten wir Glück, der Pole hat keine Vorposten aufgestellt, mit einem Angriff scheint er nicht zu rechnen. In einer halben Stunde sind wir in Dollna, dort liegen mit Sicherheit polnische Verbände. Ziehen sie die Männer weiter auseinander und schicken sie Beobachter nach vorne."

Wenig später lösen sich drei oder vier graue Schatten aus der Marschreihe und huschen geräuschlos nach vorne.

"Weiter!" Die Räder des Geschützes knarren leise, als sie von der Straße abbiegen und den sandigen Waldweg einschlagen.

Die Ruhe zerrt an den angespannten Nerven der Männer. Kurz vor dem Ort kommen ihnen die Kundschafter entgegen. "Polnische Infanterie mit vier schweren Maschinengewehren in Dollna. Zwei leichte Geschütze in ausgebauter Feldstellung am Ortsausgang Richtung Olschowa. Alles in allem etwa 150 Mann."

Im ersten Dämmerschein des aufgehenden Morgen weist Heinz die Gruppen ein. "Schlageter, Du mußt die polnischen Geschütze ausschalten und Dollna von Südosten her aufrollen. Unteroffizier Günter unterstützt den Vorstoß mit einem Maschinengewehr und zwanzig Mann Bedeckung. Der Rest geht mit mir, wir stoßen direkt in den Ort und packen den Polen, wo wir ihn kriegen!"

Das ist Heinz: ruhig und unbeirrbar, wie ein gewaltiger Klotz in der Brandung. In seiner Rechten den abgewetzten Karabiner, schwer behängt mit Munition, gibt er seine Befehle.

Langsam organisiert sich die Sturmreihe. Dicht gedrängt kauern die Männer in der Dunkelheit. Das Dorf liegt wie verlassen.

"Also los!" Wie ein Blitz springen die Männer auf und stürmen in das leblose Dorf.

Als der Lärm abflaut, sammeln sich die erschöpften Männer auf dem kleinen Platz zwischen den brennenden Häusern.

"Verluste?"

"Acht Tote, drei Schwerverletzte!" Der rauchgeschwärzte Melder atmet schwer. Sein Gesicht ist blutverkrustet. Die erbeuteten Waffen ersetzen die Ausfälle: zwei leichte polnische Geschütze, Granaten, vier Maschinengewehre und jede Menge Munition. "Die Verwundeten bleiben zurück. Günter, sie übernehmen mit ihren Leuten die Bedeckung und sichern das Dorf. Lassen sie sich von den Bewohnern Verbandstoff geben. Ich schicke sofort nach einem Arzt." Aus der Ferne dringt Kampflärm zu ihnen.

Ein Melder stürzt heran und steht keuchend vor Heinz: "Neue Meldung von Major Horadam. Sie sollen sofort nach Poremba, um die Zange zu schließen!"

"Zange? Welche Zange, Mann?"

"Ja wissen sie denn nicht, daß Bergerhoff schon in Zyrowa steht und die Oberländer den Annaberg von Wyssoka aus stürmen? Der Pole flieht auf breiter Front. Sie sollen mit ihrem Geschütz den letzten Sturm sichern."

"Oberland stürmt den Annaberg? Vorwärts Leute, wir werden gebraucht."

Wie ein gewaltiger Donnerschlag jagen die Geschosse aus den Rohren und schlagen drüben am Berg in die polnischen Schützenstellungen. Fontänen von Holz und Erde wirbeln krachend durch die Luft. Volltreffer! Der

Jubel der Sturmtruppen begleitet jeden Schuß.

Langsam beginnt die polnische Front zu wanken. Wie die Wölfe stürzen sich die kleinen Trupps der Freikorpskämpfer immer wieder den polnischen Linien entgegen, die Schritt für Schritt zurückweichen müssen.

Die Polen fliehen! Ihre zurückflutenden Reste laufen mitten in die Maschinengewehre der nachrückenden Reserve.

Da braust oben vom Berg unglaublicher Jubel: Vom Turm der Michaeliskirche flattert die schwarz-weiß-rote Fahne des Freikorps Oberland!

Die Schlacht ist entschieden. Der Annaberg ist fest in deutscher Hand. Ein teuer bezahlter Sieg: An den Hängen und Wegen liegen die toten Freikorpskameraden. Gefallen für die Freiheit ihres Volkes und die Einheit ihres Landes sind sie für immer unvergeßlicher Beweis für den selbstlosen Einsatz der deutschen Freikorps.

* * *

Der Verlust des Annaberges schmerzte den Polen politisch und militärisch. Mit ihm verlor er nicht nur eine strategisch wichtige Schlüsselstellung, sondern zugleich ein weithin sichtbares Zeichen seiner Stärke.

Korfanty tobte und befahl seinen Truppen die unverzügliche Wiedereroberung, doch der polnische Gegenangriff am 23. Mai schlug fehl. Im Gegenteil: Im Nachsetzen zerschlagen die deutschen Freikorps im Vorstoß auf Slawentzitz, Ujest und Kandrzin die neuangelegten Ausgangsstellungen der Aufständischen, befreien weite Teile Oberschlesiens von der polnischen Besatzung und spalten die gegnerischen Verbände.

Die Siegeszuversicht der Polen ist endgültig gebrochen. In aller Stille oder offen meuternd verlassen viele von ihnen die Korfantyarmee.

Jetzt sehen die Freikorps ihre Chance, ganz Oberschlesien zu befreien und in das oberschlesische Industriegebiet vorzustoßen. Ebenso wie nach den Kämpfen im Baltikum und der Niederschlagung des Spartakistenaufstandes melden sich nun wieder die Politiker zu Wort. Diesmal ist es der Völkerbund. Allen Verbrechen und Morden der Polen an den Deutschen hat er schweigend zugesehen; jetzt sind es die Polen, die unterliegen, und prompt schlägt sein Gewissen.

Unter dem Druck der Engländer und Franzosen erläßt der deutsche Reichspräsident eine Verordnung, wonach die Rekrutierung von Freiwilligen verboten ist. Jeder, der eine solche Organisation gründet oder ihr angehört, wird mit einer Gefängnisstrafe oder einer Geldstrafe bis zu 100.000 DM bestraft. Damit sind die Freikorps isoliert und vom Nachschub abgeschnitten. Le Rond stellt sich jetzt offen auf die Seite Korfantys und fordert die Deutschen zur Räumung des Annaberges auf. Die Freikorps lehnen ab. Ende Mai treffen wieder sechs britische Bataillone in Oberschlesien ein.

Berlin ist unfähig und anscheinend nicht willens, gegenüber den alliierten Siegern eine klare Linie durchzustehen. Trotz der eindeutigen Abstimmung, trotz der Siege der Freikorps treffen schließlich die Kabinette und ihre Marionetten die Entscheidung: Oberschlesien wird zwischen Deutschland und Polen aufgeteilt. Der östliche Teil mit all seinen Zink- und Bleigruben, mit 85 % der Steinkohlevorräte, mit 67 % der Roheisengewinnung und mit 50 % der Bevölkerung wird Polen zugeschlagen. Gerechtigkeit der Sieger! Ein offener Schlag in das Gesicht jedes Deutschen! Das Reich ist nurmehr Spielball in den Händen der Alliierten.

Die Freikorps werden gezwungen, sich aus Oberschlesien zurückzuziehen und ins Reich zurückzukehren. Gegen den Druck der Regierung und der Interalliierten Kommission sind sie machtlos. Unter Überwachung der Engländer verlassen die letzten Freikorpssoldaten im August 1921 Oberschlesien und kehren ins Reich zurück. Wie schon zuvor versuchen einige Freikorpsführer, zumindest einen Stamm ihrer Truppen zusammenzuhalten. Die meisten Freikorps jedoch lösen sich endgültig auf. Schlageter selbst geht, zusammen mit einigen Freunden, zunächst nach Danzig, das durch das Versailler Diktat vom Reich abgetrennt und zur 'freien Stadt' erklärt worden war. Seitdem versucht der Pole mit allen Mitteln, Danzig in seine Macht zu bekommen. Zusammen mit Heinz gelingt es Schlageter, sich in den engsten Kreis des polnischen Geheimdienstes einzuschleusen und die Pläne der Polen zu durchkreuzen.

Januar 1923. Einmarsch der französischen Besatzungstruppen in Essen

Der 'passive' Widerstand. Sperrung des Rhein-Herne-Kanals durch einen selbstversenkten Kohlefrachter.

Wenig später veröffentlicht die 'Gazeta Danska', die polnische Zeitung in Danzig, Schlageters Steckbrief. Sein kaltblütiges Auftreten gefährdete die polnischen Pläne allzu stark. Der drohenden Verhaftung entzieht er sich durch sofortige Flucht nach Berlin, wo er zusammen mit Kameraden in der Linkstraße eine Export- und Importfirma eröffnet.

* * *

Doch die Zeiten erlauben keine langen Atempausen. Während Deutschland unter den ungeheuren Reparationen leidet, die seine Wirtschaft mehr und mehr niederdrücken, während Tag für Tag endlose Kohlenzüge in Erfüllung der Siegerforderungen nach Frankreich rollen, suchen die französischen Imperialisten eine neue Gelegenheit, ihre Macht auszuweiten. Die ungeheuren Landgewinne des Versailler Diktatfriedens haben ihre imperialistischen Gelüste noch immer nicht gestillt. Der französische Staatspräsident Raimond Poincare, seit jeher erbitterter Gegner Deutschlands, wartet schon lange auf eine günstige Gelegenheit, um seine Truppen über den Rhein in das Herz der deutschen Industrie, das Ruhrgebiet, einmarschieren zu lassen, dessen reiche Bodenschätze und Industrieanlagen ihn reizen. Als die deutsche Regierung den astronomischen Forderungen an Kohlelieferungen für Frankreich nicht in voller Höhe nachkommen kann, sieht er seine Stunde gekommen. Am 3. Januar 1923 kündigte die französische Regierung in einer Note an den deutschen Botschafter in Paris an, daß sie eine Gruppe von Ingenieuren und Verwaltungsbeamten in das Ruhrgebiet entsenden würde, die die vertraglichen Lieferungen — so nannten die Franzosen die aufgezwungenen Reparationslieferungen — deutscher Ruhrkohle an Frankreich überwachen sollten.

Zum 'Schutz dieser Ingenieure' — so die infame offizielle Begründung der französischen Regierung — marschierten am Morgen des 11. Januar 1923 fünf französische Divisionen, schwere Artillerie, Panzer, Minenwerfer und Flugzeuge — unterstützt von einem kleinen Kontingent belgischer Truppen — in das waffenlose Deutschland ein. Nur ein Jahr nach dem Verlust der oberschlesischen

Industriegebiete sollte Deutschland nun in einem zweiten Schritt um sein wichtigstes Wirtschaftszentrum beraubt werden.

Mit diesem militärischen Einfall schrieb der französische Imperialismus ein neues Kapitel der deutschen Nachkriegsgeschichte. Der Anlaß zu diesem Schritt war ebenso nichtig, wie die tiefere Wurzel von Poincares Befehl klar war: Er wollte die französische Vorherrschaft in Europa durch die gewaltsame Angliederung des Ruhrgebietes an Frankreich ausbauen und sichern.

Diese Gründe legte bereits am 6. März 1923 der amtierende deutsche Reichskanzler, Wilhelm Cuno, in einer Rede vor dem Reichstag schonungslos offen:

"Recht und Vertrag sind mit dem Einmarsch der Truppen ins Ruhrgebiet gebrochen worden ... Es handelt sich um jenes alte Ziel, das seit mehr als 400 Jahren der französischen Politik eigen ist ... Es ist die Politik, die am erfolgreichsten Ludwig der Vierzehnte und Napoleon der Erste, die nicht minder deutlich aber auch andere Gewalthaber Frankreichs betrieben haben, bis auf den heutigen Tag."

Die Ungeheuerlichkeit der französischen Aktion wurde im weiteren Verlauf seiner Rede immer deutlicher, in der er die wahren Größen der bisher geleisteten Opfer Deutschlands schonungslos offenlegte:

"Jede deutsche Regierung hat das ihre getan, ihre Leistungsaufgaben im Rahmen des Möglichen zu erfüllen. Seelisch erschöpft und zerrissen, wirtschaftlich geschwächt, hat Deutschland vom Waffenstillstand an ungeheure Werte aus seiner Wirtschaft an die Gläubiger des Vertrages gegeben. Vom 11. November 1918 bis 30. September 1922 hat es Reichs- und Staatseigentum in den abgetretenen Gebieten im Wert von 5,6 Goldmilliarden, die Saargruben im Werte von einer Goldmilliarde übereignet, militärische Rücklaßgüter von 4,2 Milliarden übergeben, See- und Binnenschiffe im Wert von 6 Milliarden, Kohle und Koks im Werte von 2,3 Milliarden, hat deutsches Eigentum im Auslande blutenden Herzens aufgegeben im Werte von 11,7 Milliarden, Forderungen an seine ehemaligen Kriegsverbündeten abgetreten und so eine Gesamtleistung von 45,6 Goldmilliarden erreicht. Gleichzeitig wurde die Abrüstung durchgeführt, die

Kriegsindustrie ihrer Ausrüstung entblößt. Die deutschen Leistungen und die staatlichen Verluste machen so bis zum 30. September 1922 den Betrag von 56,5 Goldmilliarden aus, eine Summe, die beim heutigen Dollarstand dem unausdenkbaren Betrag von 285 Billionen Papiermark entspricht. Wer in der Welt kennt diese Ziffern? Die Staatsmänner der Alliierten kennen sie wohl, die Völker aber kennen sie noch immer nicht."

Während die deutsche Regierung zu verhandeln versuchte und Poincare alle deutschen Angebote kompromißlos zurückwies, besetzten die französischen Truppen das Ruhrgebiet.

Der Oberbefehlshaber der französischen Invasionstruppen, General Degoutte, erstellte jeden Tag einen 'Heeresbefehl', in dem er der französischen Regierung meldete, welche 'Linie' er genommen habe. Die Besetzung des Ruhrgebietes war angesichts der Wehrlosigkeit Deutschlands und der militärischen Stärke der Besatzungstruppen in wenigen Tagen abgeschlossen.

Jede Verordnung der Franzosen war ein offener und bewußter Schlag ins Gesicht der hungernden und wehrlosen deutschen Bevölkerung. Während deutsche Kinder starben, weil selbst die lebensnotwendigsten Nahrungsmittel fehlten, mußten ab sofort für jeden französischen Besatzungsoffizier drei, für jeden französischen Besatzungssoldaten ein und für jeden mitgebrachten französischen Hund ebenfalls ein Liter Vollmilch abgeliefert werden.

Die Erbitterung der deutschen Bevölkerung wuchs von Tag zu Tag. Als Willkür und Gewaltakte der Franzosen immer weiter zunahmen, handelte die deutsche Regierung. Sie rief ihre Botschafter aus Paris und Brüssel ab und erließ am 19. Januar an die Beamten in den besetzten Gebieten die Anweisung "Anordnungen der besetzenden Mächte keinerlei Folge zu geben".

Die Begründung nennt die Dinge beim Namen: "Die Aktion der französischen und belgischen Regierung im Ruhrgebiet stellt eine schwere Verletzung des Völkerrechts und des Vertrages von Versailles dar; infolgedessen sind Befehle und Anordungen, die in Verfolg dieser Aktion an deutsche Beamte ergehen, rechtsunwirksam."

Die Ruhrbevölkerung stand geschlossen gegen den

Feind. Die Ausrufung des 'passiven Widerstandes' durch die deutsche Reichsregierung vereinigte alle Schichten in ihrer Solidarität gegen die französischen Besatzungstruppen. Bergleute weigerten sich, in die Zechen einzufahren, Eisenbahner verließen ihre Züge und die Schiffer setzten ihre Schiffe unter Wasser: Der 'passive Widerstand' lähmte das ganze Revier, der Abtransport deutscher Güter nach Frankreich kam zum völligen Stillstand.

Auf diesen gewaltfreien, 'passiven Widerstand' reagierten die französischen Besatzer mit brutaler Härte. Ausweisungen und Verhaftungen häuften sich; Einlieferungen in Gefängnisse und Zuchthäuser, rücksichtsloser Gebrauch von Waffen bestimmten den Alltag.

Gewalt und Mord prägten das Bild der französischen Besatzung an Rhein und Ruhr. Täglich fielen deutsche Zivilisten den Kugeln der Franzosen zum Opfer.

Allein in Essen verloren am Ostersamstag des Jahres 1923 dreizehn Krupp-Arbeiter das Leben, als sie sich gewaltfrei weigerten, werkseigene Lastkraftwagen an die Franzosen auszuliefern. Rücksichtslos und ohne Warnung feuerten die Besatzungssoldaten auf Befehl des Leutnants Durieux in die Menge und richteten ein Blutbad unter den Arbeitern an. Und immer noch hatte der französische Besatzungsterror seinen Höhepunkt nicht erreicht.

Nach einer genauen Zusammenstellung aller aktenkundigen Vorfälle im Reichsministerium für die besetzten Gebiete wurden innerhalb der ersten 19 Monate der französischen Besetzung 137 Deutsche ermordet und 603 — teilweise lebensgefährlich — verletzt.

Doch der Terror der französischen Imperialisten konnte den Freiheitswillen des deutschen Volkes nicht brechen; auch dann nicht, als ihre Verbrechen jedes denkbare Maß überschritten.

Als sich die Gewalttaten der Franzosen häuften und selbst vor Frauen und Kindern nicht haltmachten, als sich erste Separatistengruppen unter dem Schutz der Franzosen daranmachten, die Rheinlande vom Reich abzutrennen, und die deutsche Reichsregierung keine Möglichkeit hatte, diesen Verbrechen zu begegnen, bildeten sich überall im besetzten Land kleine Gruppen von Freiheitskämpfern, die gegen die brutale Unterdrückungspolitik der Besatzungstruppen vorgingen.

In ihren Reihen kämpften Bergarbeiter und ehemalige Soldaten, Kommunisten, Gewerkschafter und die Reste der deutschen Freikorps. Heinz Hauenstein, der alte Freikorpskämpfer aus Oberschlesien, rief die zuverlässigsten seiner alten Kameraden zusammen. Unter ihnen war auch Albert Leo Schlageter, der aus Berlin herbeieilte, um erneut die Freiheit des Deutschen Reiches zu verteidigen. Als arbeitssuchende Bergleute getarnt, sickerten sie in das besetzte Ruhrgebiet und bauten mit dortigen Freiheitskämpfern ein Netz zur Gegenwehr auf.

Schlageter übernimmt die Führung des Stoßtrupps Essen, dessen Aufgabe es ist, die wichtigen Transportwege von Düsseldorf nach Essen zu unterbrechen, auf denen die Franzosen ihre Beute aus dem Ruhrgebiet wegschaffen.

Gewalt gegen Sachen also, nicht gegen Personen.

Diese kleinen Zellen deutscher Freiheitskämpfer gehen vom 'passiven' zum 'aktiven' Widerstand über, weil sie erkennen, daß passiver Widerstand gegen die konsequent angewandte Gewalt der Besatzer auf Dauer keinen Sieg davontragen kann.

Die Kameraden beugen sich über den wackeligen kleinen Tisch. Eine nackte Glühbirne wirft schwankend ihr Licht auf die ausgebreitete Landkarte: ein undurchdringlicher Haufen von Städten und Namen konzentriert auf kleinstem Raum — das Ruhrgebiet.

"Heute ist der 12. März. Unsere Aufgabe ist es, am 15., in drei Tagen also, die Eisenbahnbrücke bei Kalkum zu sprengen."

Schlageter sucht einen Augenblick auf der Karte. Sein Finger tippt auf eine bestimmte Stelle. "Hier, genau hier, ist sie. Die Eisenbahnbrücke über den Harbach. Wir unterbrechen damit die Bahnlinie von Duisburg nach Düsseldorf", sein rechter Zeigefinger zieht dabei eine unsichtbare Linie über die ausgebreitete Karte, "und bringen den Franzosen um seine wichtigste Möglichkeit zum Abtransport unserer Kohle."

"Donnerwetter! Das wird den Franzosen wurmen, ein toller Plan." Die Freunde sind begeistert. "Und nun zu den Einzelheiten: Feder und Zimmermann sichern.

König und Krause gehen mit mir bis zur Brücke. Ihr anderen verteilt Euch im weiteren Umkreis und haltet die Augen offen, der Franzose schläft nicht. Hauenstein läßt morgen durch Hayn den Sprengstoff von Wuppertal zu uns bringen. Wir treffen uns erst wieder am 15. Bis dahin keine Einzelaktionen, dafür steht einfach zuviel auf dem Spiel."

Alleine oder zu zweit verlassen sie nach und nach Krauses Wohnung und tauchen in das Dunkel der Nacht.

* * *

Lautlos huschen die Männer durch die Dunkelheit. Der Märzwind ist noch kalt. Der Atem bildet kleine weiße Wölkchen vor ihren Gesichtern. Noch ein paar Schritte und sie sehen den Bahndamm. Als ein langgezogener Wall zieht er sich durch die graue Landschaft. "Da ist es", flüstert Schlageter und zeigt auf eine Stelle, die etwas höher liegt als der eigentliche Schienenstrang. "Von jetzt an doppelte Vorsicht!" Fröstelnd kauern sich die Männer unter die kahlen Äste einiger Buchen, beobachten angestrengt das Gelände. Es ist nahezu lautlos. Kein französischer Wachtposten, der die Brücke sichert.

"Wir haben Glück." Sofort huschen Feder und Zimmermann in die Dunkelheit, um die Seiten zu sichern. Die Minuten vergehen, alles bleibt ruhig. "Also los!"

Langsam robben sich Schlageter, König und Krause näher an den Bahndamm. "Verdammt flaches Gelände", flucht König leise, "nicht mal ein Strauch. Wir liegen hier wie auf dem Präsentierteller."

"Nur ruhig bleiben, gleich haben wir es geschafft." Ringsum Stille, nur der Harbach plätschert leise. "Richtig idyllisch." Krauses Spott ist unübertroffen.

"Kopf runter!" Die Stille der Nacht wird jäh zerrissen. Donnernd nähert sich ein Kohlenzug. Rumpelnd überspringen die schweren Eisenräder der hochbeladenen, offenen Kohlenwaggons die Bahnschwellen. Französische Stahlhelme glänzen im Schein des aufgehenden Mondes.

"Verflucht, das hat uns gerade noch gefehlt: Franzosen!" Wie zwei feurige Augen huschen die Lichter der Lokomotive durch die Nacht, erfassen die leblosen Gestalten, entreißen sie für Sekunden der Dunkelheit und fliegen schon über sie hinweg.

"Gott sei Dank !" Dröhnend rauschen die schweren Wagen über die Brücke, wirbeln den Staub zwischen den Schienensträngen zu schmutzigen Wolken auf. Schotter rasselt den Damm hinunter. Rumpelnd verschwindet der Zug in der Dämmerung.

"Das war verdammt knapp, jetzt los !" Die Drei springen auf und drücken sich in den Schatten der Brücke. "Rauf ! Schnell !" Schlageter springt auf und gibt die Anweisungen. Ächzend schieben sie eine der schweren Bohlen um Zentimeter zur Seite.

"Die Sprengladung ... Bohle zurück ... Feuer !" Weißglühend frißt sich die helle Flamme an der Zündschnur hoch.

"Nichts wie weg !" Die Drei rutschen den steilen Bahndamm herunter, schon sind sie zurück bei den wartenden Kameraden. Dann ohrenbetäubender Lärm ! Feuerrot flammt es drüben am Bahndamm auf. Krachend fliegen die Eisenbahnschienen auseinander, wirbeln schwere Bohlen durch die Luft.

Freiheitskampf im Ruhrgebiet.

* * *

"Hast Du schon gelesen ?" Aufgeregt breitet Becker die zerknitterte Zeitung vor dem verdutzten Schlageter aus, blättert wild einige Seiten um und pocht hektisch auf einen schwarz umrandeten Text: "Dein Steckbrief ! Sie suchen Dich und Krause !" Tatsächlich, da steht sein Name. Schlageter nimmt die Zeitung und liest:

"Kaiserswert, 5. April 1923. Eisenbahnsprengung in Kalkum. Am 15. März 1923, abends gegen 8 Uhr, wurden die Eisenbahngeleise über den Harbach, Gemeinde Kalkum, gesprengt. Als Täter kommen wahrscheinlich zwei junge Leute in Frage, die wie folgt beschrieben werden. Familienname mutmaßlich Fr. v. Krampe oder von Krause und Albert Leo Schlagstein oder Schlageter, der eine 20-25 Jahre alt, 1,60 groß, schlank, dunkelblond, ohne Bart, volles Gesicht, Gang und Haltung aufrecht. Spricht ausländische Mundart (kein Rheinländer),

gekleidet mit schwarzen Schnürschuhen, braunen Sprot-
strümpfen, grauem Fischhautmantel mit Gürtel und heller Sportmütze. Der andere 20-25 Jahre alt. 1,80 groß,
schwächlich, blond ohne Bart, längliches Gesicht, Gang
und Haltung aufrecht, Rheinländer, trug Kneifer. Kleidung: schwarze Schnürschuhe, grauer Regenmantel und
heller Schnitthut. Infolge des Attentats sind angesehene
Bürger als Geiseln durch die Besatzungsbehörden ins Gefängnis gebracht worden und sollen erst bei Ermittlung
der Täter in Freiheit gesetzt werden. Es wird daher um
Zustellung geeigneter Ermittlungen nach den Tätern und
um evtl. schleunige Mitteilung an die unterzeichnete Po-
lizeibehörde ersucht. Die Polizeiverwaltung von Kaiserswert." Nachdenklich läßt er die Zeitung sinken.

"Na!" platzt Becker los, "was sagst Du nun? Die
Angaben sind einfach zu genau, da muß einer gequatscht
haben. Verdammter Mist aber auch." Becker ist aufge-
bracht und flucht wild vor sich hin.

"Langsam Becker, beruhige Dich erstmal. Wir müssen nachdenken." "Nachdenken! Nachdenken!" kon-
tert Becker, "dafür bleibt keine Zeit mehr. Du mußt auf
alle Fälle sofort verschwinden. Jetzt sind nicht nur die
Franzosen hinter Dir her, jetzt hast Du auch noch die
preußische Polizei am Hals!"

Schlageter überlegt fieberhaft. Was Becker sagt, ist
nicht wegzuwischen. Irgendeiner muß den Franzosen Informationen zugespielt haben. Die Sache ist gefährlich.
Auf der anderen Seite die Kameraden, die täglichen
Schikanen der Franzosen, der Ruhrkampf. "Erst müssen
wir noch den Prinzen Friedrich Wilhelm von der Lippe
aus dem Gefängnis holen, dann können wir weiter sehen."

"Das ist Wahnsinn", starrt Becker ihn an, "die
Franzosen haben Einblick in unsere Organisation bekommen. Sie wissen, wie Du aussiehst, wer Du bist. Du
kannst jeden Tag verhaftet werden."

"Das ist nichts Neues, wir wußten immer, was wir
riskieren. Wenn wir jetzt gehen, ist der Prinz verloren.
Und denk an unser Volk, die wehrlosen Frauen und Kinder. Wir können nicht einfach alle weggehen, wenn
Gefahr droht."

* * *

Zur Ausführung seiner Pläne sollte es nicht mehr kommen. Am 7. April, zwei Tage nach der Veröffentlichung des Steckbriefes wird Albert Leo Schlageter im Hotel Union in Essen verhaftet. Unter strengen Sicherheitsvorkehrungen verschleppen ihn die Franzosen am nächsten Tag in das Gefängnis von Essen-Werden.

Trotz der starken Bewachung gelingt es ihm am 14. April aus dem Gefängnis heraus einen Kassiber an Heinz zu schmuggeln, in dem er seine Lage schildert und die Kameraden vor Verrätern in den eigenen Reihen warnt. Jedoch zu spät. Die französischen Besatzer sind gut unterrichtet. Innerhalb weniger Tage verhaften sie mit Ausnahme von Heinz und Feder die ganze Gruppe.

Über die Frage, wie es zu Schlageters Verhaftung kommen konnte, ist seit seinem Tod kontrovers diskutiert worden. Zahlreiche Hinweise und nicht zuletzt die Aussage des Spezialkommissars der französischen Kriminalpolizei, Barthelet, vor dem französischen Kriegsgericht bestätigen aber nachhaltig, was Schlageter selbst zunächst nur vermutete.

Wilhelm Schneider, ein Mann, über den man bis heute nichts Genaues weiß, soll den Franzosen als Spitzel gedient und ihnen den Aufenthaltsort Schlageters und seiner Kameraden gegen Bezahlung verraten haben.

Der Haß der Franzosen war ungeheuer. Der 'aktive Widerstand' hatte die gesamte Ruhrbevölkerung mobilisiert und den Abtransport deutscher Güter auf ein absolutes Minimum geschraubt. Kanäle und Eisenbahnlinien waren gesprengt, und die Erbitterung der Bevölkerung gegen die Besatzung stieg von Tag zu Tag.

Während der Verhöre entlastete Schlageter seine Kameraden und nahm die Verantwortung für alle Aktionen auf sich. Die Mitbeteiligung schob er auf Kameraden, die außer Reichweite der französischen Besatzungspolizei waren.

Die Franzosen hatten ihr Opfer und der Prozeß gegen Schlageter und seine Kameraden ließ nicht lange auf sich warten. In der Anklageschrift vom 6. Mai warf ihnen das französische Militärgericht vor, "vom März bis April 1923 im Ruhrgebiet Nachrichten gesammelt und subversive Schriftstücke verteilt zu haben; dies zum Zwecke von Attentaten gegen Personen der Besatzungstruppen,

Beamte der Alliierten oder von ihnen abhängige Personen."

Desweiteren lastet man ihnen die Sprengstoffattentate am Bahnhof in Essen-Hügel am 12. März, in Kalkum am 15. März und in Werden-Kettwig Anfang April an.

Ihre Verteidiger, Dr. Sengstock, Dr. Marx und Dr. Müller erhalten ihre Ladung zum Prozeß, der auf Dienstag, den 8. Mai, morgens um 8 Uhr angesetzt war, erst im Laufe des Sonntagvormittag in einem gewöhnlichem Brief in ihre Kanzleien zugestellt. Sie lesen ihn also erst am Montag, den 7. Mai, einen Tag vor dem ersten Prozeßtermin.

Ein ungewöhnliches Zustellungsverfahren durch die Franzosen, das allein dazu dient, die Vorbereitungszeit der Verteidiger auf ein Minimum zu reduzieren. Es ist für sie unmöglich, sich innerhalb eines Tages in die umfangreichen, in französischer Sprache gehaltenen Akten einzulesen. Ungewöhnlich auch deshalb, weil in allen ähnlichen vorausliegenden oder nachfolgenden Fällen den Verteidigern die Ladung zu einem Gerichtstermin stets durch Ordonnanzen der französischen Gerichte persönlich überbracht und von ihnen quittiert werden mußte.

Die Verhandlung gegen Schlageter und die Mitangeklagten fand vor dem Düsseldorfer Landgericht in der Mühlenstraße statt. Das französische Kriegsgericht bestand aus dem Vorsitzenden, dem französischen Oberst Blondel, und vier weiteren französischen Offizieren. Angebliche Geständnisse wiesen alle Angeklagten während der Verhandlung zurück. Übereinstimmend erklärten alle, von den französischen Beamten schwer mißhandelt und zu Aussagen erpreßt worden zu sein, die mit der Wahrheit nicht übereinstimmten.

Schlageter nahm als einziger zu den Vorwürfen Stellung: "Ich achte Menschenleben und habe dies stets getan. Die Stelle der Sprengung bei Kalkum war so ausgesucht, daß Menschenleben im Personen- und Güterverkehr nicht gefährdet werden konnten. Mir kam es darauf an, die Eisenbahnverbindung als solche zu unterbinden, aber nicht, Menschen zu töten. Für das, was ich getan habe, stehe ich ein, ich bin bereit, die Folgen meiner Handlung zu tragen."

Nach diesen Worten Schlageters zog sich das Gericht für etwa zwanzig Minuten zur Beratung zurück. Unmittelbar danach verlas es ein etwa 30 Seiten starkes, maschinengeschriebenes Urteil. Die Tatsache, daß kein wirklich objektiv prüfendes Gericht in einer solch kurzen Zeit ein Urteil fällen und es auf dreißig Schreibmaschinenseiten festhalten kann, beweist nachdrücklich, daß das Urteil schon vor dem Prozeß feststand und ein reiner Racheakt der französischen Besatzungsmacht gegen die deutschen Freiheitskämpfer war. Alle Mitangeklagten erhielten hohe Gefängnisstrafen oder langjährige Zwangsarbeitsstrafen. Albert Leo Schlageter selbst wurde wegen Spionage und Sabotage zum Tode verurteilt. Die französische Besatzungsmacht wollte ihr Opfer!

Nach Bekanntwerden des Urteils erfaßt ein Sturm der Entrüstung das ganze Land. Der päpstliche Delegierte in Essen, Vertreter des Deutschen Roten Kreuzes, der Erzbischof von Köln, die Königin von Schweden und viele andere appellieren an die französische Regierung und bitten um eine Milderung des Urteils. Die Deutsche Reichsregierung klagt Frankreich der willkürlichen Gewaltanwendung an und schickt folgende Protestnote an den französischen Präsidenten: "Französische Kriegsgerichte haben kein Recht, auf deutschem Boden, den sie widerrechtlich besetzt haben, über die Freiheit oder gar über Leben und Tod von Deutschen zu befinden ... Die Deutsche Reichsregierung protestiert feierlich gegen diesen Mißbrauch der Gewalt, für den die französische Regierung die Verantwortung trägt."

Währenddessen treiben Heinz Hauenstein und die noch nicht verhafteten Ruhrkämpfer Pläne zur Befreiung Schlageters aus dem Gefängnis voran. Schon sind alle Schritte bis aufs kleinste vorbereitet, als Polizeiinspektor Roemer auf Befehl des amtierenden sozialdemokratischen preußischen Innenministers, Carl Severing, Heinz Hauenstein und zwei weitere Ruhrkämpfer in Barmen verhaftet.

Lähmendes Entsetzen breitet sich unter den Freunden aus: Damit sind alle Pläne gescheitert. Schlageters Schicksal nimmt seinen Lauf.

Die Verteidiger arbeiten fieberhaft. Als am 18. Mai ihre Revision durch das französische Kriegsgericht abgelehnt wird, unternehmen sie einen letzten Versuch zur Rettung Schlageters: Sie legen dem amtierenden Oberbefehlshaber des französischen Brückenkopfes Düsseldorf, General Simon, zwei Augenzeugenberichte vor, aus denen hervorgeht, daß Schlageter im Juni 1921 in Ratibor unter Einsatz des eigenen Lebens einen französischen Leutnant aus den Händen einer aufgebrachten Volksmenge befreit hat und nur einige Wochen später zwölf französische Soldaten in Groß-Udjest unter persönlichem Einsatz davor bewahrte, erschossen zu werden. General Simon ist von diesen Unterlagen zutiefst beeindruckt und schickt sie sofort durch Kurier an den französischen Präsidenten Poincare.

Zur gleichen Zeit tagt in Paris die französische Deputiertenkammer zur Frage der Ruhrpolitik. Andre Tardieu, langjähriger Propagandachef des schwerindustriellen 'Comite des Forges' und heftiger Gegner Poincares, wirft dem französischen Präsidenten in der Frage der Ruhrpolitik eine allzu nachgiebige und weiche Haltung vor und fordert härteste Maßnahmen gegen die widerspenstigen Deutschen.

Die Abgeordneten sind von dem Schreckensbild, das Tardieu von den Ruhrkämpfern entwirft, beeindruckt und wenden sich gegen Poincares Politik.

Um seine politische Macht nicht zu verlieren, entschließt sich Poincare zu einer Lüge, die den Deputierten zeigen soll, wie hart er in der Ruhrfrage durchzugreifen bereit ist. Er bittet um das Wort und weist die Angriffe gegen ihn mit folgender Lüge zurück: "Sie werfen mir Feigheit vor? Und das wagen gerade Sie mir zu sagen in dieser Stunde, da ich soeben nach Düsseldorf den Befehl zur Erschießung Schlageters gab?"

Es war eine Lüge, weil Poincare zu dieser Stunde den Befehl zur Erschießung Schlageters noch gar nicht gegeben hatte. Seine Behauptung war nichts anderes, als ein ebenso schäbiger, wie skrupelloser innenpolitischer Schachzug, um die Abgeordneten von seiner Härte zu überzeugen und auf seine Seite zu ziehen.

Als ihn am Abend der Brief von General Simon mit dem Entlastungsmaterial für Schlageter erreicht, war es ihm gar nicht mehr möglich, Gerechtigkeit walten zu lassen und das Urteil gegen Schlageter aufzuheben.

Unter dem Druck seiner eigenen Worte im Parlament und mit eiskalter Berechnung unterzeichnete Poincare am Abend nach der Debatte und nicht, wie er den Deputierten vorgelogen hatte, am Tage den Vollstreckungsbefehl zur Erschießung Schlageters.

Schlageters Schicksal war besiegelt: Eine Rettung war jetzt ausgeschlossen.

* * *

In der Nacht vom 25. auf den 26. Mai wird der Düsseldorfer Gefängnispfarrer Faßbender, der Schlageter betreute, durch den Leiter der französischen Gefängnisabteilung, Caron, aus dem Schlaf gerissen. Von ihm erfährt er, daß Schlageter um 4 Uhr in der Frühe erschossen werden soll. Zusammen mit dem zweiten Gefängnisgeistlichen, Roggendorff, und Rechtsanwalt Sengstock betritt er um halb drei das Gefängnis.

Trotz ihrer Bitten werden sie nicht zu Schlageter vorgelassen. Erst als um 3 Uhr 10 der französische Staatsanwalt, Oberleutnant Dumoulin, im Gefängnis erscheint, wird Schlageter geweckt. Schlageter nimmt die Eröffnung des Vollstreckungsbefehls vollkommen ruhig auf und schreibt einen Abschiedsbrief an seine Eltern.

Wenig später sein letzter Gang.

Gesichert von Kavallerie bringt ihn ein Lastkraftwagen zur nahegelegenen Golzheimer Heide. Kühl schlägt ihm die Nachtluft entgegen. Die französischen Schergen treiben Schlageter in die nahe gelegene Sandgrube und binden ihn an einen Holzpfahl.

Der neue Tag bricht eben an, als das Exekutionskommando vor dem aufrecht stehenden Schlageter antritt.

Französische Kommandos erschallen ! Klirren der Bajonette, das harte Schnappen der Gewehrschlösser.

"Allons !"

Scharf peitschen die Schüsse durch die Stille. Albert Leo Schlageter ist tot.

Seine letzten Worte sind uns erhalten: "Leben sie wohl ! Grüßen sie mir Eltern, Geschwister und Verwandte, meine Freunde und mein Deutschland !"

Der 'Schlageter-Kurs' der KPD
von Uwe Sauermann

Die Scheinwerfer eines Lastautos beleuchten grell den Todgeweihten. Ein französisches Peloton steht zur Exekution bereit. Schlageter ruft Deutschland an und fordert es auf, zu erwachen, zu entbrennen. Es sind seine letzten Worte. Der französische Kommandant ruft: "A mon commandement — feu!" — Die Feuergarbe der Salve zerfetzt Schlageters Herz. Er fällt und mit ihm der Vorhang. Das Publikum erhebt sich wie ein Mann von den Plätzen, singt das Deutschland- und das Horst-Wessel-Lied und bricht sodann in einen orkanartigen Beifall aus. Premierenbesucher Joseph Goebbels ist zufrieden: Ein besseres Geburtstagsgeschenk konnte er seinem Führer nicht bieten, als diese glanzvolle Aufführung des Schlageter-Schauspiels von Hanns Johst. Dieser Abend des 20. April 1933, dessen war er sich sicher, würde in die Theatergeschichte eingehen.

Hanns Johst, der dieses Stück 'Adolf Hitler in liebender Verehrung und unwandelbarer Treue' widmete, hat in seinem Übereifer vielleicht nicht einmal geahnt, daß er mit diesem eher flachen und kitschigen, als erhebenden Schauspiel ganzen Generationen das Andenken an seinen Helden verdunkelte. Der aufdringliche Schlageter-Kult der nationalsozialistischen Propagandaexperten hat geschafft, was den französischen Militärs 1923 nicht gelang: Schlageters Tat und Tod mit dem Makel der Peinlichkeit zu behaften.

Albert Leo Schlageter — das war nach 1945 ein durch den Ersten Weltkrieg aus der rechten Bahn geworfener Bürgersohn, ein Landsknecht reaktionärer Mächte und hirnloser Schlagetot. Hatte nicht sogar Johst einem Kameraden Schlageters die gar nicht witzig gemeinte Bemerkung in den Mund gelegt: "Wenn ich Kultur höre — entsichere ich meinen Browning"?

Albert Leo Schlageter wurde im Dritten Reich als eines der ersten 'Blutopfer' der Bewegung gefeiert. Nach dem zweiten Weltkrieg betrieb man diesen Mißbrauch des Namens Schlageter weiter. Er blieb der 'Erste Soldat des Dritten Reiches' und ein Vorläufer Horst Wessels. Selbst dort, wo er zum Schluß wirkte und den Tod fand, sah man in ihm alles andere als einen Kämpfer gegen die Fremdherrschaft. Auf der Golzheimer Heide bei Düsseldorf sind nicht nur alle Spuren des NS-'Denkmals' verwischt worden, sondern auch jede Erinnerung an Schlageter selbst. Wer heute auf die Idee käme, über den Toten ein gutes Wort zu verlieren, der müßte mit lautem Protest rechnen. Der schrillste Widerspruch käme sicher von seiten der Kommunisten. Dabei hätte gerade die Kommunistische Partei allen Grund, in Schlageter mehr zu sehen, als einen verunglückten SA-Rabauken. Sein Name könnte sie an eine Zeit erinnern, als ihre proletarischen Kämpfer gemeinsam mit nationalen Idealisten gegen Fremdherrschaft und Separatismus fochten. Vor allem aber würden die Kommunisten, wenn sie ihre eigene Parteigeschichte studieren würden, auf ein merkwürdiges Kapitel stoßen: auf den 'Schlageter-Kurs der KPD'.

* * *

Albert Leo Schlageter war tot. Die rechte Presse feierte ihn als Märtyrer, und die Linken verbreiteten sich über die Sinnlosigkeit seiner Tat. Die Erregung war noch nicht gänzlich abgeflaut, als drei Wochen nach dem Begräbnis der Tote erneut in die Schlagzeilen geriet. Es war etwas Unfaßbares geschehen. In der Sitzung der Erweiterten Exekutive der Kommunistischen Internationale hatte Karl Radek, Mitglied des Zentralkomitees der Kommunistischen Partei Sowjetrußlands und Mitglied des Präsidiums der Komintern, nach einer Rede Klara Zetkins das Wort ergriffen und Schlageter als 'Märtyrer des deutschen Nationalismus' geehrt, den 'Schergen des französischen Imperialismus' erschossen hätten. Es war der gleiche Radek, der vorher seine deutschen Genossen eindringlich vor jeder Art von 'Nationalbolschewismus' gewarnt hatte.

Die Zeitungen schäumten. Vor allem die sozialdemokratische Presse glaubte, nun endlich einem gefährlichen Komplott auf die Spur gekommen zu sein. Radek habe ausgerechnet diesen Schlageter zum 'Nationalhelden' gemacht, wütete der 'Vorwärts'. Die 'Leipziger Volkszeitung' warf Radek gar vor, er verharmlose die 'faschistischen Wölfe'. Zwar bot die Rede, las man sie gründlich, keinen Anlaß für solche Kritik, aber allein schon die Tatsache, daß sie Schlageter und seine nationalistischen Freunde als (fehlgeleitete) *Idealisten* ansprach und nicht als 'Kreaturen des Großkapitals' in den Abgrund trat, wie das sonst vielfach üblich war, sicherte dieser Rede eine Wirkungsgeschichte, die über die Aufregung des 'Vorwärts' weit hinausreichte. Selbst heute noch wird sie gern und häufig zitiert, wenn es gilt, den Kommunisten einen 'nationalistischen Sündenfall' vorzuhalten. Aber es verweisen auch immer wieder Leute auf Radeks Rede, die darin auch jetzt noch eine Verheißung erblikken. Allerdings ist mittlerweile kaum jemand in der Lage, daraus mehr als die Schlagwörter vom 'Wanderer ins Nichts' und vom 'mutigen Soldaten der Konterrevolution' zu zitieren.

* * *

An wen richtete sich die Rede Radeks? Sie ist zwar vor Genossen gehalten worden, aber sie war ganz offensichtlich eine 'Schaufensterrede', nicht dazu bestimmt, das eigene Lager für den Nationalismus zu erwärmen, sondern die deutsche bürgerliche Rechte zu beeinflussen. Das geht schon aus den schmeichelhaften Attributen hervor, mit denen er — für einen Kommunisten ganz stilwidrig — die deutschen Nationalisten versah. So hielt er es immerhin für möglich, daß 'die Kreise der deutschen Faschisten' dem deutschen Volke, also auch der Arbeiterklasse, 'ehrlich' dienen wollten. Den Beweis dafür, daß sie es aufrichtig meinten, habe zumindest Schlageter selbst durch den 'Weg der Todesgefahr, den er wählte', geliefert. Aber wer weiterliest, merkt sogleich, daß die eigentlichen Adressaten nicht die nationalistischen Intellektuellen und Einzelkämpfer waren, sondern die 'nationalistischen kleinbürgerlichen Massen'. Die 'faschistischen' Führer wurden zwar als Gesprächspartner und vielleicht auch als zeitweilige Verbündete akzeptiert, aber sie waren eben doch 'Klassengegner'.

In einem Aufsatz (1) hat Karl Radek verdeutlicht,

was er mit seinem Appell an die kleinbürgerlichen Massen bezweckt hat. Der 'Faschismus', also der antikommunistische Nationalismus, sei durch das bedrückende Versailler Diktat und die Wirtschaftskrise zu einer politischen Bewegung 'breiter Massen des proletarisierten Kleinbürgertums' geworden. Mit anderen Worten: die Erwartung der bolschewistischen Führer, Deutschland werde nach dem verlorenen Krieg den gleichen Weg einschlagen, den Rußland in einer ähnlichen Situation 1917 gegangen war, hatte sich nicht erfüllt. In diesem Fall hätte sich Deutschland, so rechnete jedenfalls Lenin, dem weltrevolutionären Lager angeschlossen und damit auch die damals noch von allen Seiten bedrohte russische Sowjetregierung abgesichert. Stattdessen hatte der deutsche Umsturz von 1918 eine Republik hervorgebracht, die trotz ihrer Knebelung durch die Versailler Mächte mehr dem Westen als dem Osten zuneigte. Die Kommunistische Partei, die vorgab, für die gesamte Arbeiterklasse zu sprechen, war weit davon entfernt, auf diese für Sowjetrußland beängstigende Entwicklung einwirken zu können. Es galt deshalb, der kommunistischen Politik jenseits der Arbeiterschaft, die zum großen Teil im Einflußbereich der westorientierten Sozialdemokratie lag, eine breitere Basis zu schaffen. Die 'kleinbürgerlichen Massen', jene Schichten des Volkes, die durch das wirtschaftliche Chaos buchstäblich 'enterbt' worden waren, mußten gewonnen werden. Gerade sie waren aber auch der Boden für den Nationalismus, der sich beharrlich weigerte, aus der Proletarisierung der Mehrheit der Bevölkerung Konsequenzen zu ziehen, die im Sinne der Kommunistischen Internationale gewesen wären.

Wie wollte Radek diese Massen gewinnen? "Die Kommunistische Partei muß imstande sein, in den kleinbürgerlichen Massen den großen heiligen Glauben an die Möglichkeit der Überwindung der Not zu erwecken, in ihnen die Überzeugung zu erwecken, daß sie zusammen mit der Arbeiterklasse imstande sind, die Not zu überwinden und die Grundlagen für ein neues Leben in Deutschland zu schaffen. Wird die deutsche Arbeiterklasse nicht imstande sein, den großen kleinbürgerlichen Massen diesen Glauben beizubringen, so wird sie geschla-

Werbeplakate deutscher Freikorps, wie sie nach dem 1. Weltkrieg überall in Deutschland zu sehen waren.

gen werden oder wenigstens für lange Zeit ihren Sieg hinausschieben müssen." Oder anders herum, mit dem Blick auf die 'kleinbürgerlichen Volksmassen': sei es der KPD nicht möglich, diese von der Fähigkeit der Arbeiterklasse zu überzeugen, das 'nationale Joch', den Versailler Vertrag, abzuschütteln, dann würden die 'berechtigten nationalen Gefühle' dieser Schichten von der Reaktion mißbraucht und gegen die Arbeiterklasse eingesetzt werden. Sie mit dem Gedanken zu befreunden, daß 'der Kommunismus nicht ihr Feind, sondern der Stern ist, der ihnen den Weg des Sieges' zeige, war für Radek das Gebot der Stunde.

* * *

Leo Schlageter, der Wanderer ins Nichts

(Karl Radek, auf der Sitzung der Erweiterten Exekutive der Kommunistischen Internationale am 20.6. 1923)

Wir haben das weitausgreifende und tiefeindringende Referat der Genossin Zetkin angehört über den internationalen Faschismus, diesen Hammer, der — bestimmt auf das Haupt des Proletariats zerschmetternd niederzufallen — in erster Linie die kleinbürgerlichen Schichten treffen wird, die ihn im Interesse des Großkapitals schwingen. Ich kann diese Rede unserer greisen Führerin weder erweitern noch ergänzen. Ich konnte sie nicht einmal gut verfolgen, weil mir immerfort vor den Augen der Leichnam des deutschen Faschisten stand, unseres Klassengegners, der zum Tode verurteilt und erschossen wurde von den Schergen des französischen Imperialismus, dieser starken Organisation eines anderen Teiles unserer Klassenfeinde. Während der ganzen Rede der Genossin Zetkin über die Widersprüche des Faschismus schwirrte mir im Kopf der Name Schlageter herum und sein tragisches Geschick. Wir sollen seiner gedenken hier, wo wir politisch zum Faschismus Stellung nehmen. Die Geschicke dieses Märtyrers des deutschen Nationalismus sollen nicht verschwiegen, nicht mit einer abwerfenden Phrase erledigt werden. Sie haben uns, sie haben dem deutschen Volke vieles zu sagen.

Wir sind keine sentimentalen Romantiker, die an der Leiche die Feindschaft vergessen und wir sind keine Diplomaten die sagen: am Grabe Gutes reden oder schweigen. Schlageter, der mutige Soldat der Konterrevolution, verdient es von uns, Soldaten der Revolution, männlich-ehrlich gewürdigt zu werden. Sein Gesinnungsgenosse Freksa hat im Jahre 1920 einen Roman veröffentlicht, in dem er das Leben eines im Kampfe gegen Spartakus gefallenen Offiziers schildert. Freksa nannte den Roman: Der Wanderer ins Nichts.

Wenn die Kreise der deutschen Faschisten, die ehrlich dem deutschen Volke dienen wollen, den Sinn der Geschicke Schlageters nicht verstehen werden, so ist Schlageter umsonst gefallen und dann sollten sie auf ein Denkmal schreiben: Der Wanderer ins Nichts.

Deutschland lag auf dem Boden, geschlagen, nur Narren glaubten, daß die siegreiche kapitalistische Entente das deutsche Volk anders behandeln wird, als das siegreiche deutsche Kapital das russische, das rumänische Volk behandelt hat. Nur Narren oder Feiglinge, die die Wahrheit fürchteten, konnten an die Verheißungen Wilsons, an die Erklärungen glauben, daß nur der Kaiser, nicht das deutsche Volk für die Niederlage zu zahlen haben wird. Im Osten stand ein Volk im Kampfe. Hungernd, frierend rang es gegen die Entente an vierzehn Fronten: Sowjetrußland. Eine dieser Fronten war gebildet von deutschen Offizieren und deutschen Soldaten. Im Freikorps Medem, das Riga stürmte, kämpfte Schlageter. Wir wissen nicht, ob der junge Offizier den Sinn seiner Tat verstanden hat. Der damalige deutsche Regierungskommissar, der Sozialdemokrat Winnig, und der General von der Goltz wußten, was sie taten. Sie wollten durch Schergendienste gegen das russische Volk der Entente Wohlwollen erobern. Damit die besiegte deutsche Bourgeoisie keine Kriegstribute den Siegern zahle, vermieteten sie junges deutsches Blut, das von der Kugel des Weltkriegs verschont worden ist, als ententistische Söldlinge gegen das russische Volk. Wir wissen nicht, was Schlageter über diese Zeit dachte. Sein Führer Medem hat später eingesehen, daß er durchs Baltikum ins Nichts wanderte. Haben das alle deutschen Nationalisten verstanden? Bei der Totenfeier Schlageters in München sprach General Ludendorff, derselbe Ludendorff, der sich bis auf heute England wie Frankreich als Obrist im Kreuzzug gegen Rußland anbietet. Schlageter wird beweint von der Stinnes-Presse. Herr Stinnes wurde eben in der Alpina Montana der Kompagnon von Schneider-Creusot, des Waffenschmiedes der Mörder Schlageters. Gegen wen wollen die Deutschvölkischen kämpfen: gegen das Entente-Kapital oder das russische Volk? Mit wem wollen sie sich verbinden? Mit den russischen Arbeitern und Bauern zur gemeinsamen Abschüttlung des Joches des Ententekapitals oder mit dem Ententenkapital zur Versklavung des deutschen und russischen Volkes?

Schlageter ist tot. Er kann die Frage nicht beantworten. An seinem Grabe haben seine Kampfgenossen die Fortführung seines Kampfes geschworen. Sie müssen antworten: gegen wen, an wessen Seite?

Schlageter ging vom Baltikum nach dem Ruhrgebiet. Nicht erst im Jahre 1923, schon im Jahre 1920. Wißt ihr, was das bedeutet? Er nahm teil an dem Überfall auf die Ruhrarbeiter durch das deutsche Kapital, er kämpfte in den Reihen der Truppen, die die Ruhrbergleute den Eisen- und Kohlenkönigen zu unterwerfen hatten. Watters Truppen, in deren Reihen er kämpfte, schossen mit denselben Bleikugeln, mit denen General Degoutte die Ruhrarbeiter beruhigte. Wir haben keine Ursache anzunehmen, daß Schlageter aus egoistischen Gründen die hungernden Bergarbeiter niederwerfen half.

Der Weg der Todesgefahr, den er wählte, spricht und zeugt für ihn, sagt, daß er überzeugt war, dem deutschen Volke zu dienen. Aber Schlageter glaubte, daß er am besten dem Volke dient, wenn er hilft die Herrschaft der Klassen aufzurichten, die bisher das deutsche Volk geführt und in dieses namenlose Unglück gebracht haben. Schlageter sah in der Arbeiterklasse den Pöbel, der regiert werden muß. Und er war ganz gewiß einer Meinung mit dem Grafen Reventlow, der da gelassen sagt, jeder Kampf gegen die Entente sei unmöglich, solange der innere Feind nicht niedergeschlagen ist. Der innere Feind aber war für Schlageter die revolutionäre Arbeiterklasse. Schlageter konnte mit eigenen Augen die Folgen dieser Politik sehen, als er ins Ruhrgebiet im Jahre 1923 während der Ruhrbesetzung kam. Er konnte sehen, daß, wenn auch die Arbeiter gegen den französischen Imperialismus einig dastehen, kein einiges Volk an der Ruhr kämpft und kämpfen kann. Er konnte sehen das tiefe Mißtrauen, das die Arbeiter zu der deutschen Regierung, zu der deutschen Bourgeoisie haben. Er konnte sehen, wie der tiefe Zwiespalt der Nation ihre Verteidigungskraft lähmt. Er konnte mehr sehen. Seine Gesinnungsgenossen klagen über die Passivität des deutschen Volkes. Wie kann eine niedergeschlagene Arbeiterklasse aktiv sein? Wie kann eine Arbeiterklasse aktiv sein, die man entwaffnet hat, von der man fordert, daß sie sich von Schiebern und Spekulanten ausbeuten läßt? Oder sollte die Aktivität der deutschen Arbeitermasse vielleicht durch die Aktivität der deutschen Bourgeoisie ersetzt werden? Schlageter las in den Zeitungen, wie dieselben Leute, die als Gönner der völkischen Bewegung auftreten, Devisen ins Ausland schieben, um das Reich arm, sich aber reich zu machen. Schlageter hatte ganz gewiß keine Hoffnung auf diese Parasiten und es war ihm erspart, in den Zeitungen zu lesen, wie sich die Vertreter der deutschen Bourgeoisie, wie sich Dr. Lutterbeck an seine Henker mit der Bitte wandte, sie sollen doch den Königen von Stahl und Eisen erlauben, die hungernden Söhne des deutschen Volkes, die Männer, die den Widerstand an der Ruhr durchführen, mit Maschinengewehren zu Paaren zu treiben.

Jetzt, wo der deutsche Widerstand durch den Schurkenstreich Dr. Lutterbecks und noch mehr durch die Wirtschaftspolitik der besitzenden Klasse zu einem Spott geworden ist, fragen wir die ehrlichen patriotischen Massen, die gegen die französische imperialistische Invasion kämpfen wollen: Wie wollt ihr kämpfen, auf wen wollt ihr euch stützen? Der Kampf gegen den ententistischen Imperialismus ist ein Krieg, selbst wenn in ihm die Kanonen schweigen. Man kann keinen Krieg an der Front führen, wenn man das Hinterland im Aufruhr hat. Man kann im Hinterland eine Minderheit niederhalten. Die Mehrheit des deutschen Volkes besteht aus arbeitenden Menschen, die kämpfen müssen gegen Not und das Elend, das die deutsche Bourgeoisie über sie bringt. Wenn sich die patriotischen Kreise Deutschlands nicht entscheiden, die Sache dieser Mehrheit der Nation zu der ihrigen zu machen und so eine Front herzustellen gegen das ententistische und das deutsche Kapital, dann war der Weg Schlageters ein Weg ins Nichts, dann würde Deutschland angesichts der ausländischen Invasion, der dauernden Gefahr seitens der Sieger zum Felde blutiger innerer Kämpfe, und es würde dem Feinde ein leichtes sein, es zu zerschlagen und zu zerstükkeln.

Als nach Jena Gneisenau und Scharnhorst sich fragten, wie man das deutsche Volk aus seiner Erniedrigung herausbringen kann, da beantworteten sie die Frage: Nur, indem man den Bauern freimacht aus der Hörigkeit und Sklaverei der Junker. Nur der freie Rücken des deutschen Bauern kann die Grundlage bilden für die Befreiung Deutschlands. Was die deutsche Bauernschaft am Anfang des 19. Jahrhunderts war, das ist für die Geschicke der deutschen Nation am Anfang des 20. Jahrhunderts die deutsche Arbeiterklasse. Nur mit ihr zusammen kann man Deutschland von den Fesseln der Sklaverei befreien, nicht gegen sie.

Vom Kampf sprechen die Genossen Schlageters an seinem Grabe. Den Kampf weiterzuführen, schwören sie. Der Kampf richtet sich gegen einen Feind, der bis an die Zähne bewaffnet ist, während Deutschland entwaffnet, während Deutschland zermürbt ist. Soll das Wort vom Kampfe keine Phrase sein, soll er nicht nur aus Sprengkolonnen bestehen, die Brücken zerstören, aber nicht den Feind in die Luft sprengen können, die Züge zum Entgleisen bringen, aber nicht den Siegeszug des Ententekapitals aufhalten können, so erfordert dieser Kampf die Erfüllung einer Reihe von Vorbedingungen. Er fordert von dem deutschen Volke, daß es bricht mit denen, die es nicht nur in die Niederlage hineingeführt haben, sondern die diese Niederlage, die Wehrlosigkeit des deutschen Volkes verewigen, indem sie die Mehrheit des deutschen Volkes als den Feind behandeln. Er erfordert den Bruch mit den Leuten und den Parteien, deren Gesicht wie ein Medusengesicht auf die anderen Völker wirkt und sie gegen das deutsche Volk mobilisiert. Nur, wenn die deutsche Sache die des deutschen

Volkes ist, nur wenn die deutsche Sache im Kampf um die Rechte des deutschen Volkes besteht, wird sie dem deutschen Volke tätige Freunde werben. Das stärkste Volk kann nicht ohne Freunde bestehen, um so weniger ein geschlagenes, von Feinden umgebenes Volk. Will Deutschland imstande sein, zu kämpfen, so muß es eine Einheitsfront der Arbeitenden darstellen, so müssen die Kopfarbeiter sich mit den Handarbeitern vereinigen zu einer eisernen Phalanx. Die Lage der Kopfarbeiter erfordert diese Einigung. Nur alte Vorurteile stehen ihr im Wege. Vereinigt zu einem siegreichen, arbeitenden Volk, wird Deutschland imstande sein, große Quellen der Energie und des Widerstandes zu entdecken, die jedes Hindernis überwinden werden. Die Sache des Volkes zur Sache der Nation gemacht, macht die Sache der Nation zur Sache des Volkes. Geeinigt zu einem Volk der kämpfenden Arbeit, wird es Hilfe anderer Völker finden, die um ihre Existenz kämpfen. Wer in diesem Sinne den Kampf nicht vorbereitet, der ist fähig zu Verzweiflungstaten, nicht fähig aber zum wirklichen Kampfe.

Dies hat die Kommunistische Partei Deutschlands, dies hat die Kommunistische Internationale an dem Grabe Schlageters zu sagen. Sie hat nichts zu verhüllen, denn nur die volle Wahrheit ist imstande, sich den Weg zu den tief leidenden, innerlich zerrissenen, suchenden nationalen Massen Deutschlands zu bahnen. Die Kommunistische Partei Deutschlands muß offen den nationalistischen kleinbürgerlichen Massen sagen: Wer im Dienste der Schieber, der Spekulanten, der Herren von Eisen und Kohle versuchen will, das deutsche Volk zu versklaven, es in Abenteuer zu stürzen, der wird auf den Widerstand der deutschen kommunistischen Arbeiter stoßen. Sie werden auf Gewalt mit Gewalt antworten. Wer aus Unverständnis sich mit den Söldlingen des Kapitals verbinden wird, den werden wir mit allen Mitteln bekämpfen. Aber wir glauben, daß die große Mehrheit der national empfindenden Massen nicht in das Lager des Kapitals, sondern in das Lager der Arbeit gehört. Wir wollen und wir werden zu diesen Massen den Weg suchen und den Weg finden. Wir werden alles tun, daß Männer wie Schlageter, die bereit waren, für eine allgemeine Sache in den Tod zu gehen, nicht Wanderer

ins Nichts, sondern Wanderer in eine bessere Zukunft
der gesamten Menschheit werden, daß sie ihr heißes
uneigennütziges Blut nicht verspritzen, um die Profite
der Kohlen- und Eisenbarone, sondern um die Sache des
großen arbeitenden deutschen Volkes, das ein Glied in
der Familie der um ihre Befreiung kämpfenden Völker
ist. Die Kommunistische Partei wird diese Wahrheit den
breitesten Massen des deutschen Volkes sagen, denn sie
ist die Partei der kämpfenden Proletarier, die um ihre
Befreiung kämpfen, um die Befreiung, die identisch ist
mit der Freiheit ihres gesamten Volkes, mit der Freiheit
all dessen, was arbeitet und leidet in Deutschland. Schla-
geter kann nicht mehr diese Wahrheit vernehmen. Wir
sind sicher, daß Hunderte Schlageters sie vernehmen und
sie verstehen werden. (Internationaler Arbeiterverlag,
Berlin, 1923)

* * *

Die Rede Karl Radeks zielte auf das nationale, verarmte Kleinbürgertum. In der Kommunistischen Partei
Deutschlands fand dieser nationalistische Zungenschlag
zwar nicht ungeteilten Beifall, aber ihre Agitatoren und
die Parteipresse bemühten sich dennoch mit großem
Aufwand, den von Radek gewiesenen neuen Kurs plausibel zu machen. Dabei konnten sie sogar darauf hinweisen, daß sich der nationalistische Wille bereits bewährt
habe. Schließlich hatte es sich schon herumgesprochen,
daß im besetzten Ruhrgebiet Kommunisten Schulter an
Schulter mit Nationalisten gegen die Franzosen kämpften. Einen Erfolg konnte der kommunistische Vorstoß
zu den Herzen der 'kleinbürgerlichen Massen' aber nur
haben, wenn auch ein Teil ihrer anerkannten Führer auf
Radeks Angebot einging und es in den eigenen Publikationen diskutierte. Das geschah auch tatsächlich. Zwar
nahm die vergangenheitsorientierte deutschnationale
Presse kaum Notiz von der kommunistischen Propagandaoffensive, aber in einigen konservativ-revolutionären
Zeitschriften fanden Radeks Worte einen lauten Widerhall.

Schon zehn Tage nach der Schlageter-Rede veröffentlichte der damalige völkische Reichstagsabgeordnete

Ernst Graf zu Reventlow (1869 -1943) in seiner Wochenschrift 'Der Reichswart' einen langen Kommentar: 'Mit Radek?'. Drei Tage später folgte unter der Überschrift 'Der Wanderer ins Nichts' ein Aufsatz Arthur Moeller van den Brucks (1876 - 1925) in der Wochenzeitung 'Gewissen'.

Daß sich gerade diese Autoren zur Stellungnahme gedrängt fühlten, ist nicht verwunderlich. Graf Reventlow, ein phantasievoller, etwas sprunghafter und stets gegen den Strom schwimmender politischer Publizist (auch im Dritten Reich war er, obwohl prominentes Parteimitglied, ein oft verdächtiger Außenseiter), hatte schon anläßlich des russisch-polnischen Krieges 1920 ein Bündnis mit Sowjetrußland zu Lasten Polens gefordert. Die Ostorientierung Moeller van den Brucks war eine Konsequenz seiner Weltanschauung, welche dem verrotteten Westen die 'jungen Völker' entgegensetzte und die Zukunft im erwachenden Osten sah. Daß man sich aber ernsthaft mit Äußerungen eines kommunistischen Parteivertreters auseinandersetzte, obwohl man innenpolitisch nur wenige Berührungspunkte mit den 'Roten' aufwies, hatte einen besonderen Grund.

Karl Radek hatte in dem erläuternden Aufsatz zu seiner Schlageter-Rede geschrieben: "Ich habe immer menschliche Achtung für jeden, der für seine Idee sein Leben einsetzt, mag es auch mein Klassengegner sein, den ich bis aufs äußerste bekämpfen werde." Keine Achtung habe er dagegen vor den Sozialdemokraten, die für nichts 'ihre Persönlichkeit einzusetzen wagen und die nur wie alte Weiber zu heulen verstehen'. Genau dieses Gefühl teilte Radek mit Nationalisten wie Moeller van den Bruck. Schon vor Schlageters Tod und dem neuen Kurs der KPD konnte man im 'Gewissen' lesen, daß die Nationalisten etwas Gemeinsames mit dem Radikalismus der deutschen Kommunisten verbinde. (2) Die Haltung der proletarischen Kämpfer und ihr 'gesundes Empfinden', das jeden sozialdemokratischen und pazifistischen 'Schwindel' instinktiv ablehne, habe zu einer 'weltanschaulichen Gemeinsamkeit' geführt, die schwerer wiege, als es politische Gemeinsamkeiten könnten — "wenn diese auch unter Umständen daraus folgen". Den deutschen Kommunisten wurde auch bereitwillig zugestanden, sie hätten vom russischen Beispiel gelernt, "daß es auch für Revolutionäre so etwas wie Außenpolitik" gibt. Das unterscheide sie in den Augen der in erster Linie außenpolitisch orientierten Nationalisten vorteilhaft von der Anhängerschaft der SPD. Als Radek am 20. Juni 1923 den Dialog mit den 'Faschisten' eröffnete, war der Boden also schon bereitet.

* * *

In einer ersten Stellungnahme bekräftigte Graf Reventlow am 30. Juni in seinem 'Reichswart' (3) die nationalistische Hochachtung für Kommunisten. Sie seien ehrlich und voller Idealismus; man könne mit ihnen aufrichtig reden, "was mit Sozialdemokraten und Demokraten nicht möglich" sei. Aber die Führer der KPD versuchten immer wieder, die Arbeiterschaft gegen die angeblich reaktionären Völkischen (4) aufzuhetzen. Solange dies so sei, schrieb Reventlow, müsse man vor den Sirenenklängen der Komintern auf der Hut sein. Meine es Radek ernst, dann solle er erst einmal für eine Entspannung der Beziehungen zwischen der KPD und den Völkischen sorgen. Stelle die Kommunistische Partei ihre Beschimpfungen ein, dann sei eine Zusammenarbeit möglich. Allerdings werde sich die völkische Bewegung nicht unter die Führung Moskaus begeben. "Wir Völkischen sind ohne Vorurteile, annehmen Beistand, von wo er sich bietet, denken aber nicht daran, dafür unsere völkische 'Substanz' aufzugeben ..."

Dieser Kommentar des Grafen ließ deutlich erkennen, daß Radeks Gedenkrede auf Schlageter ihn nicht nur mit Freude erfüllte. Ihm war klar, daß Radek sich in erster Linie an die 'Kleinbürger' wenden wollte, die auch seine Abonnenten und Anhänger waren. Auf diese Bedenken ging der kommunistische Funktionär Paul Frölich aus naheliegenden Gründen nicht ein, als er seine 'Antwort auf den Grafen E. Reventlow' (5) verfaßte.

Frölich kam es zunächst darauf an, die Ernsthaftigkeit des von Reventlow in Anspruch genommenen Antikapitalismus in Frage zu stellen. Konnte jemand Sozialist sein, der vom Klassenkampf nichts wissen wollte?

Und was den Internationalismus angehe, den Reventlow als den inneren Feind bezeichnet hatte, der niedergerungen werden müsse, bevor die Aufgabe der nationalen Befreiung in Angriff genommen werden könne: die Kommunisten seien nun einmal internationalistisch gesinnt. Wolle Reventlow auch sie zu Todfeinden erklären? So könne man dessen Antwort an Radek offenbar nicht interpretieren. Dem Grafen, der ja selbst von seiner Vorurteilslosigkeit im Umgang mit der KPD geschrieben hatte, komme es doch wohl darauf an, zu erfahren, ob der Kommunismus mit den nationalen Interessen Deutschlands in Einklang zu bringen sei oder nicht. Frölich antwortete mit einer bemerkenswerten Feststellung. Der Kommunismus werde den Nationalismus stets bekämpfen, "wo er als Maske für reaktionäre Bestrebungen auftritt". Der nicht solchermaßen verfälschte Nationalismus, das wird man daraus folgern können, war dagegen nicht zu verachten. Es verdient festgehalten zu werden, daß Frölich damit die Möglichkeit einer nationalistischen Gesinnung, die nicht kapitalistischen Interessen verhaftet war, freimütig einräumte. Er ließ sich aber, wie übrigens auch Radek, nicht auf eine Diskussion über die weltanschaulichen Grundlagen von Marxismus und Nationalismus ein. Im Moment ging es ja auch nur um Aktionen gegen den gemeinsamen Feind. Deshalb durfte Frölich sich damit begnügen, pragmatisch zu argumentieren. Er wisse, schrieb er, daß die nationale Unterdrückung Deutschlands vor allem die Arbeiter treffe. Aus diesem Grunde sei die KPD für das nationale Aufbegehren gegen den Versailler Vertrag. Deshalb habe sie sich auch aktiv am Ruhrkampf beteiligt, während die Unternehmer ständig Verrat übten. Wenn die Völkischen den Nationalismus nicht als 'Maske' benutzen und stattdessen gegen den 'wirklichen inneren Feind des deutschen Volkes', nämlich die Kapitalisten und die Reaktionäre, aufmarschieren wollten, dann könne man zusammenarbeiten. "Wer ohne Ranküne ein Stück Weg mit uns marschieren kann, der wird uns bereit finden."

* * *

Am 2. August 1923 erschien in der 'Roten Fahne', dem Parteiorgan der KPD, ein Aufsatz (6), der Aufsehen erregte. Es war nicht so sehr der Inhalt des Artikels, sondern der Name der Verfassers, der alle politischen Lager in Deutschland in nicht geringe Unruhe versetzte. So weit war die Zusammenarbeit der Radikalen also schon gediehen: die 'Rote Fahne' veröffentlichte an prominenter Stelle einen Beitrag des rechtsradikalen Reichstagsabgeordneten Graf Reventlow!

Es handelte sich um eine umfangreiche Erwiderung des Grafen auf die 'Antwort' Paul Frölichs. Mit diesem Abdruck hatte die KPD-Führung Schluß gemacht mit der bisherigen Form des Dialogs, der recht einseitig im Hinblick auf die zu gewinnenden 'kleinbürgerlichen Massen' der Nationalisten geführt worden war. Die proletarische Anhängerschaft der KPD war bis zu diesem Zeitpunkt von kritischen Entgegnungen der Gegenseite verschont worden. Nun sprach alles dafür, daß es der Kommunistischen Partei ernst war mit ihrem Vorstoß, daß sie ein aufrichtiges Gespräch suchte. Schließlich war es sehr riskant, den ungeschulten Lesern der Parteizeitung Gedanken von Leuten vorzusetzen, die von sich behaupteten, ebenfalls Sozialisten und Antikapitalisten zu sein, die sogar die KPD zu übertrumpfen suchten, indem sie ihr Inkonsequenz und außenpolitische Abhängigkeit vorwarfen.

Reventlow ließ sich von dem Entgegenkommen der 'Roten Fahne' nicht milde stimmen. Ob der Kommunismus die nationalen Interessen Deutschlands gefährde? Natürlich — bis jetzt! Vor Radeks Schlageter-Rede sei die KPD 'vehement antideutsch, antinational' gewesen. Deshalb brauche sie sich nicht darüber zu wundern, wenn ihre neue Haltung 'zunächst starker Skepsis begegnet'. Tatsächlich habe die kommunistische Presse auch nach dem 20. Juni nicht aufgehört, die Völkischen mit offensichtlichen Reaktionären, die es natürlich auch gebe, in einen Topf zu werfen. Dies könne er, schrieb Reventlow, 'nicht loyal finden'. Wenn die Rede Radeks eine neue Strategie und nicht nur eine Taktik verkündet habe, dann solle man nicht versuchen, 'die Völkischen von ihren Führern zu trennen'. Zur Sache selbst habe er zu sagen, daß die nationale Befreiungspolitik gegenüber

Frankreich 'wesentlich auch davon abhängen (wird), ob es möglich wird, mit dem Kommunismus zu einer Kooperation zu gelangen'. Es gehe um eine 'innerliche Verbindung der großen Masse mit dem Geschick des Reichs'. Darin stimme er mit Frölich überein. Aber 1813 (Radek hatte diesen Vergleich gezogen) sei Preußen eben nicht unter die Diktatur der Bauern gestellt worden; die Bauern seien befreit worden, und damit sei der Freiheitskrieg möglich geworden. Im Falle der Arbeiter müsse jetzt ebenso verfahren werden. Werfe in dieser Situation der Kommunismus mit seiner Forderung nach der Diktatur des Proletariats die 'Machtfrage' auf, so sei eine weitere Diskussion 'unnötig und der Fall klar'. Auch zur möglichen Ostorientierung der deutschen Politik nahm Reventlow Stellung. In seiner Erwiderung auf Radeks Schlageter-Rede hatte er auf die verpaßte Gelegenheit einer deutsch-russischen Zusammenarbeit anläßlich des Polen-Krieges hingewiesen. Frölich hatte ihm geantwortet: "Glauben Sie, daß diese Gelegenheit für immer vorbei ist?" Nein, räumte Reventlow nun ein, "das glaube ich nicht unbedingt". Im Augenblick sehe er aber nicht, in welcher Weise Sowjetrußland "für die Befreiung Deutschlands aus französischer Gewalt in absehbarer Zeit wirksame Hilfe leisten könnte, auch wenn es wollte".

Graf Reventlow hat auch in der Folgezeit, selbst im Dritten Reich, für eine nüchterne deutsche Ostpolitik geworben, die nicht von antibolschewistischen Kreuzzugsideen geprägt sein sollte. Aber er war nie der Meinung, daß man die Schicksale Rußlands und Deutschlands zusammenketten könnte. Das unterschied ihn von den Nationalbolschewisten der ersten Nachkriegszeit und der frühen dreißiger Jahre, die von einer antiversailler Weltrevolution träumten, die den Feind im Westen hinwegfegen sollte. Reventlow war auch zu sehr Tagespolitiker, um die Ostideologie und prinzipielle Rußlandfreundlichkeit Moeller van den Brucks verstehen und teilen zu können. Dieser konservativ-revolutionäre Denker sollte aber den kommunistisch-nationalistischen Dialog auf ein Niveau heben, das es heute überhaupt rechtfertigt, sich ausführlich mit den Auseinandersetzungen um den 'Schlageter-Kurs' der KPD zu beschäftigen.

Radek hatte Schlageter als einen 'Wanderer ins Nichts' bezeichnet. Auch Moeller van den Bruck wählte diese Überschrift, als er am 2. Juli in dem 'einzigen denkenden Organ der deutschen nationalistischen Kreise' (Radek), dem 'Gewissen', auf die Schlageter-Rede antwortete (7). Er begann mit dem Versuch einer Erklärung des Kurswechsels der Komintern und versetzte sich dabei in die Lage Sowjetrußlands. Die Möglichkeit einer Weltrevolution sei in weite Ferne gerückt. Innenpolitisch sei Sowjetrußland gefestigt, außenpolitisch aber ohnmächtig. Keine Rede könne davon sein, daß die Epoche des Kapitalismus vor ihrem Abschluß stehe. Im Gegenteil; der Weltkrieg habe eine neue Art von Kapitalismus hervorgebracht, da die Unterscheidung von Kapital und Arbeit nicht mehr wesentlich sei. In dem nun entstehenden 'gemeinschaftlich gebundenen Unternehmerkapitalismus' sei das 'Kapital', das mit der 'Arbeit' zusammenfalle, nicht mehr 'Geld'; es bedeute vielmehr 'Macht, Verfügungskraft, Bewegungsfreiheit'. Dieser neue Kapitalismus setze an die Stelle der 'Ausbeutung Vieler die Arbeit Aller '. Der Kommunismus könne ihm deshalb nicht mehr beikommen. 'Eine Ausbeutung der ganzen Erde bereitet sich vor, an der alle souveränen Völker in dem Grade einen Anteil nehmen werden, in dem ihre geistige und auf Arbeit gerichtete Entwicklung sie dazu befähigt. Sowjetrußland wird sich in dieses System einfügen müssen, muß sich ihm schon heute einfügen. Wenn Sowjetrußland aber die Mitarbeit verweigert, dann steigt die Möglichkeit auf . . ., daß der Weltkapitalismus den einzigen sozialistischen Staat außenpolitisch einkreist und schließlich erdrückt.' Um das zu verhindern, suche Radek nach einem letzten Ausweg. Er wolle das kapitalistische Lager spalten, indem er die Gegensätze zwischen dem als Volk ausgebeuteten Deutschland und dem ausbeutenden Frankreich nutze. Deshalb habe Radek in seiner Schlageter-Rede die deutschen Nationalisten auffällig oft gefragt, mit welcher Seite sie sich in ihrem Freiheitskampf verbinden wollten.

Die Antwort fiel Moeller leicht: "Selbstverständlich ist es schon aus raumpolitischen Gründen das Gegebene, daß das deutsche Volk sich in einem Weltkampfe, den Deutschland gegen den Westen, den Ententekapitalismus, den Weltkapitalismus führt, auf den Osten 'stützt' — nicht auf irgendeine Regierung, sondern auf den Osten als solchen, und damit auf Rußland." Schon 1918 habe man in Deutschland gefühlt, daß beide Völker in ihrem Kampf gegen die sich abzeichnende Versailler Ordnung zusammengehörten. Bisher habe Rußland aber die "Unterwerfung der deutschen Wirtschaft unter den Bolschewismus zur Voraussetzung des Zusammengehens gemacht. In diesem Fall wäre Deutschland aber völlig zusammengebrochen und auch für russische Zwekke unbrauchbar geworden.

Hat sich die kommunistische Einstellung nun geändert? Das müsse bezweifelt werden, meinte Moeller. "Der Kommunismus ist auf eine marxistische und materialistische Geschichtsphilosophie festgelegt, die ihn für alle möglichen Möglichkeiten geistig ausrüstete, aber am wenigsten für nationale Möglichkeiten." Die nationalistische Geschichtsphilosophie habe der marxistischen viel voraus. Sie wisse "um bestimmte psychologische und politische Gesetze, denen die Völker unterworfen sind" und nach denen sich jeder Freiheitskampf vollziehe, nämlich in jeder Situation und Zeit anders. Das Reden von der proletarischen Weltrevolution verbreite dagegen Illusionismus. Es werde der besonderen Lage Deutschlands nicht gerecht. Natürlich könne der Freiheitskampf nur mit dem Proletariat geführt werden. Aber die Arbeiter seien nicht dazu geeignet, sich an die Spitze des Kampfes zu stellen. Sie bildeten zwar die zahlenmäßige Mehrheit des Volkes, aber "eine Mehrheit kann sich nicht führen. Nur das Bewußtsein kann führen, ein Bewußtsein, wie es Schlageter besaß". Radek könne im übrigen davon ausgehen, daß die 'hunderte Schlageters', die er am Schluß seiner Rede erwähnt hatte, nichts anderes wollten als Schlageter selbst: die "Freiheit all dessen, was arbeitet und leidet in Deutschland".

Das Proletariat sei nicht identisch mit der Nation. Mache der Kommunismus so weiter wie bisher, dann könne es "eher so kommen, daß das deutsche Proletariat vor lauter Klassenkampf seinen Freiheitskampf verliert". Die von Radek angesprochenen 'Kopfarbeiter' und nicht die marxistischen 'Handarbeiter' müßten "die Sache des Volkes als ihre eigene führen".

Moellers Aufsatz war eine im Ton recht freundschaftliche, aber dennoch eine unmißverständliche Absage an Radek. Moeller van den Bruck räumte lediglich ein, daß der antiversailler Kampf nicht gegen das Proletariat geführt werden könne, sondern sich auf alle vorhandenen Kräfte stützen müsse. Anders als Reventlow nahm er das kommunistische Bündnisangebot nicht ausdrücklich an. Wohl hielt auch er Rußland für den natürlichsten Bundesgenossen Deutschlands, er war aber nicht bereit, diese Verbindung anders als unter außenpolitischen Gesichtspunkten zu betrachten.

* * *

Eigentlich hätten die Kommunisten das Gespräch mit den Nationalisten um die Zeitschrift 'Gewissen' jetzt abbrechen können. Die Fronten waren geklärt und Radeks Vorstoß war, soweit er den 'faschistischen' Intellektuellen gegolten hatte, gescheitert. Schon eine Woche später konnten Moeller van den Bruck und die erstaunten Nationalisten jedoch in der 'Roten Fahne' einen ausführlichen Artikel (8) lesen. "Dem 'Gewissen' zur Antwort" war er überschrieben, und verfaßt hatte ihn nicht Paul Frölich oder ein anderer KPD-Funktionär, sondern Karl Radek persönlich.

Radek sah durchaus, daß der Dialog nach dem so wenig entgegenkommenden Aufsatz Moellers schwierig, vielleicht für die Kommunisten auch peinlich geworden war: "Mögen die sozialdemokratische und die bürgerliche Presse, diese Organe des deutschen Zerfalls, über einen faschistisch-kommunistischen Block faseln, das wird mich nicht davon abhalten, zu versuchen, eine Klärung darüber herbeizuführen, wo die Elemente des deutschen Faschismus stehen, von denen ich annehme, daß sie nicht gewillt sind, *bewußt* den Interessen der deutschen Reaktion und des deutschen Kapitals zu dienen, sondern von denen ich annehme, daß sie bemüht sind, den Weg zu suchen, zu dem Neuen, ohne das der deutsche Zerfall, die Zermürbung des deutschen Volkes nicht aufzuhalten ist." Aber vielleicht glaubte Radek, seinen

Abtransport deutscher Kohlen nach Frankreich. Der Zug wird von einem französischen Posten bewacht.

eigenen Genossen noch mehr Erläuterungen schuldig zu sein. Schließlich war nicht nur der sozialdemokratische 'Vorwärts' verwirrt. Auch innerhalb der KPD waren die Stimmen nicht leiser geworden, die fragten, welchen Zweck die Anbiederung an die Nationalisten haben sollte. Hatte man nicht den 'Faschismus' bisher bekämpft, ohne Unterschiede zu machen, die nur die klaren Fronten des Klassenkampfes verwischen konnten? Mußte die eigene Anhängerschaft nicht irre werden an den ungewohnten Differenzierungen? Radek entschloß sich also, seiner Antwort an das 'Gewissen' einige klärende Sätze über den Zweck dieser Diskussion vorauszuschicken.

Man könne nicht, wie die Hamburger 'Nationalbolschewisten' des Jahres 1919 um Heinrich Laufenberg und Fritz Wolffheim es versucht hätten, "mit Ideen listen" und 'Mixturen' aus ihnen machen. Die KPD bleibe eine international ausgerichtete revolutionäre Arbeiterbewegung. Aber man müsse auf der anderen Seite sehen, daß der 'Faschismus' eine Massenbewegung geworden sei. Man habe ihn zu bekämpfen, wenn er den Kommunismus angreife, solle sich aber gleichzeitig fragen, "ob es nicht Dinge gibt, die uns einigen mit den nichtkommunistischen, aber . . . sozialleidenden Massen der nationalen deutschen Bewegung". Vielleicht könne es dann zu einer Zusammenarbeit kommen, die sich aus der Gemeinsamkeit der Interessen ergebe. Der Zweck seiner Schlageter-Rede sei es gewesen, "die deutschen kommunistischen Arbeiter zu warnen vor dem stupiden Standpunkt der Sozialdemokratie dem Faschismus gegenüber, der eine Mischung tödlicher Angst und blödsinniger Brutalität ist, sie anzuleiten, zu der kleinbürgerlichen nationalistischen Masse den Weg zu suchen". Außerdem, schrieb Radek, habe er von den aufrichtigen und volksverbundenen nationalistischen Intellektuellen wissen wollen, was sie konkret wollten und auf welchen Wegen sie es zu erreichen glaubten. An Weltanschauungsfragen, erklärte er Moeller van den Bruck, sei er in diesem Zusammenhang weniger interessiert. Moeller möge ihm aber folgende Fragen beantworten:

1. Welche Außenpolitik schlägt der deutsche Nationalismus vor? Ist er mit Radek der Meinung, daß ein deutscher Verteidigungskrieg gegen Frankreich zur Zeit

aussichtslos wäre? Was will er stattdessen unternehmen? Wie stellt er sich insbesondere zur Zahlung der Tribute, die aus dem Versailler Vertrag resultieren?

2. Wie soll die Innenpolitik des Kreises um das 'Gewissen' aussehen? Werden die Kosten, die zur Erfüllung des Versailler Vertrages und zum Ruhrkampf nötig sind, den Arbeitern aufgebürdet werden oder will man die Industrie dazu heranziehen, indem man die Erfassung wirklich aller Sachwerte betreibt? Sind die Nationalisten bereit, die Regierung denen zu überlassen, die Deutschland nicht länger als 'Objekt der Ausbeutung privatkapitalistischer Cliquen' behandelt sehen möchten, nämlich den (industriellen und geistigen) Arbeitern und den Bauern?

Moeller van den Bruck beantwortete am 30. Juli 1923 im 'Gewissen' nicht alle Fragen Radeks. Aber er bemühte sich doch, seinem Gesprächspartner mehr entgegenzukommen, als er es in seinem ersten Kommentar getan hatte.

* * *

Wirklichkeit

"Sowjetrußland hat in dieser verlogenen Zeit immer mit großer Deutlichkeit gesprochen. Es war nicht die großartige Offenheit, mit der Bismarck der 'vermeintlichen Schlauheit' eine 'frappierende Wahrheit' entgegensetzte. Es war vielmehr eine besondere bolschewistische, machiavellistische, nihilistische Deutlichkeit, war ein aktiviertes Nitschewo, war der Mut, Staatsmännern, namentlich des Westens, nicht nur in das Gesicht zu sagen, daß man ihre Handlungsweise bis in den letzten Hintergedanken durchschaute — sondern auch jetzt noch die Gelegenheit zu benutzen, um für die eigene Sache in der Welt zu werben.

Sowjetrußland hat damit einen neuen Ton der politischen Aussprache geschaffen, der seit dem ersten Aufrufe 'An Alle' allmählich unrevolutionärer, maßvoller, vorsichtiger geworden ist, der aber auch jetzt noch, wenn Radek sich an deutsche Kommunisten und deutsche Nationalisten wendet und konkrete Fragen stellt, um konkrete Antworten zu bekommen, mit dem Anspruche auf jene Offenheit hervortritt, die, wie Radek sagt, sich noch immer "als das beste Mittel jeder größeren Politik gezeigt hat". Offenheit will Wirklichkeit. Sie will nicht Wahrheit. Die Wirklichkeit ist unser einziger fester und unnehmbarer Besitz. Der 'Wahrheit' dagegen ist es ergangen, wie es der 'Freiheit' und wie es der 'Gerechtigkeit' erging. Sie wurde im Begriffe so abgebraucht, daß nur noch der Schwindler mit ihr falschmünzt und der Tor auf sie hereinfällt. Wahrheit, die ehemals eine christliche Gewißheit war, nach der ein Mensch handelte oder nicht handelte, wurde in der Folge eine moralische Forderung der Aufklärung, die das Göttliche vermenschlichte und dadurch vernichtete. Für den westlichen Menschen ist wahr, was ihm nutzt. Der deutsche Mensch hält sich noch immer mit einer gefährlichen Geneigtheit bei einer Wahrheit 'an sich' auf. Der neue Mensch wird wieder die Wahrheit 'in sich' verspüren — aber er wird sie in der Wirklichkeit suchen und finden.

Schon diese Zusammenhänge weisen auf die enge Verbundenheit aller konkret-politischen Fragen mit dem hin, was Radek die 'Weltanschauungsfragen' nennt. Radek will diese Weltanschauungsfragen auf die Gelegenheit einer besonderen Aussprache verschieben. Dies ist vom deutschen Standpunkte aus nicht möglich. Fragen lassen sich nicht in mittelbare und unmittelbare, geistige und praktische zerdenken. Die einen ragen in die anderen unmittelbar hinein. Praktische Fragestellung ohne geistige Fragestellung und umgekehrt, geistige ohne praktische, würde eine halbe Fragestellung sein. Ganze Fragen beziehen sich auf den Menschen, auf Völker und Völkergegensätze, auf das Lebendige der Dinge. Wir wollen ganze Antworten geben.

*

Radek fragt nach der Außenpolitik des deutschen Nationalismus.

Politik hängt von den Situationen ab. Man kann sich über die nicht hinwegsetzen, wenn sich die Völker nicht alsbald in der Wirklichkeit blutig oder dumm schlagen sollen. Wir pflegen als die Bekenner einer idealistischen Geschichtsanschauung alle Situationen auf den Willen des Menschen zurückzuführen, während die An-

hänger der materialistischen Geschichtsauffassung der Macht der Umstände vertrauen und auf die Zwangsläufigkeit der Entwicklung bauen. Aber sehr eigentlich ist, daß wir die größeren Realisten sind und vor allem eine Scheu vor Illusionen verspüren, die wir, nachdem die Menschen sich so manche gemacht haben, wenigstens uns nicht mehr machen wollen — während der Rationalist und materialistische Utopist sich den Ablauf der Dinge gemäß der Theorie, nach ihrer Doktrin und in vorgefaßten Propagandakonturen vorstellt. Wir fragen immer: wann kann der Wille des Menschen einsetzen? Wir erkennen in Wirklichkeit den Stoff dieses Willens, für den die Zeit erfüllt und die Voraussetzungen der Dinge bereit und reif sein müssen. Radek schrieb unlängst: mit Ideen kann man nicht listen. So schrieb der Idealist in Radek. Nun, die liberale Bourgeoisie hat sich mit ihren Maximen während dreier Jahrhunderte ein schnödestes Nutznießertum und zuletzt noch den Frieden von Versailles zusammengelistet. Aber nie und nimmer und nirgendwo kann man mit dem Wirklichen listen. Die Wirklichkeit ist ohne Spiegelfechterei. So antwortet der Realist in uns.

Auch Radek fragt nach der Situation. Er fragt, ob nach unserer Meinung für Deutschland die Möglichkeit besteht, 'in nächster Zeit einen Verteidigungskrieg wagen zu können'. Wir antworten: Nein! Und wir setzen hinzu, daß wir diese Möglichkeit nicht nur nicht für die 'nächste Zeit' sehen, sondern für eine ganz unabsehbare Zeit nicht — aus Gründen der militärpolitischen, wirtschaftlichen und seelischen Situation in Deutschland, über die wir mit Radek einig sind. Aber inzwischen beobachten wir die Situation. Wir beobachten die Wandlungen der außenpolitischen Konstellation, über die wir in diesem Zusammenhange nicht zu sprechen brauchen, und diejenigen der innenpolitischen Konstellation, die wir in den Vordergrund stellen wollen. Wir beobachten die Wandlungen im eigenen nationalistischen Umkreise und erkennen hier, daß fast früher, als nach der Revolution erwartet werden konnte, ein zunächst sehr erkärliches Reaktionärstum zu einer bloßen Velleität hinabsinkt und an der Stelle in den Deutschen, auf die es ankommt, ein neues Bewußtsein sich bildet, das es in

Deutschland vordem nicht gab. Und wir beobachten nicht zuletzt die Wandlungen in einem Proletariat, die sich in einfachen, denkungewohnten oder durch Demagogie verdorbenen Köpfen sehr viel langsamer vollziehen, die aber voraussehen lassen, daß auch die deutschen Arbeiter die politische Welt nicht immer so ansehen werden, wie man sie ihnen am 9. November vorstellte — sondern so, wie sie sich seit dem 11. Januar darstellt. Im Parteibereiche herrschen noch immer die unterschiedlichen Parteigesichtspunkte. Aber an der Ruhr nahm der Abwehrkampf eine Wendung, die ganz gewiß nicht 'Verteidigungskrieg' bedeutet, die jedoch dem Klassenkampfgedanken eine sehr bemerkenswerte außenpolitische Anwendung mit ebenso bemerkenswerter innenpolitischer Rückwirkung dadurch gibt, daß die Arbeiter in den einzelnen Betrieben die einzelnen Werke als 'ihre' Sache zu verteidigen beginnen. Wie, wenn Arbeiter und Unternehmer erkennen, daß sie eine gemeinsame Sache verteidigen?

Der Weltkapitalismus mag noch so verfilzt sein, daß sich überall dort, wo er nicht arbeitet, sondern ausbeutet, das bekannte Ungeziefer bildet. Aber dort, wo Wirtschaft wider Wirtschaft steht und die eine Nation die andere wirtschaftlich auszubeuten sucht, indem sie dieselbe militärpolitisch unterdrückt, richten sich nationale Gegensätze auf, über die hinweg es keine Verständigung gibt. Wenn man an einer freien Ruhr wieder zur freien Arbeit zurückkehren könnte, dann würde sich im Ergebnisse des gemeinsamen Erlebnisses jenes Verbundenheitsgefühl in eine neue Wirtschaftsgesinnung umsetzen lassen, die wenigstens an dieser Stelle der Erde den Klassenkampfgedanken endet. Nur: die Ruhr wird nicht frei werden. Der Kampf wird weitergehen: in Formen, die immer heftiger und, worauf wir gefaßt sein müssen, die schließlich so national wie bolschewistisch sein werden. Freilich, und sehr merkwürdigerweise: hier berühren wir einen Punkt, über den wir einer ganz anderen Meinung sind, als sie gerade der Bolschewist Radek zu haben scheint.

*

Wir sagen mit Ausdrücklichkeit: 'scheint'. Denn zunächst bestehen Widersprüche, die Radek erst klären müßte und auf die wir von unserer Seite nur hinweisen können.

Diese Widersprüche ergeben sich nicht aus den Fragen, die Radek an das 'Gewissen' gerichtet hat. Diese Fragen sind durchaus unmißverständlich, eindeutig, einfach. Aber die Widersprüche ergeben sich, wenn wir die Stellung vergleichen, die Radek bisdahin zum Reparationsproblem einnahm. In seinem 'Dem Gewissen zur Antwort' fragt Radek: "Was ist Frankreich gegenüber zu tun in der nächsten Zeit, in den nächsten Monaten, in den nächsten Jahren?" Und er antwortet für seinen Teil, indem er von den 'Tributen' spricht, die Deutschland werde zahlen müssen, und davon, daß "man die Franzosen aus dem Ruhrgebiet nur hinauskriegen könne, indem man große materielle Opfer bringe". Aber noch in der Sitzung der Moskauer Exekutive, in einer der Reden, von denen die Aussprache mit dem 'Gewissen' ausging, sprach Radek davon, "daß der Sieg Frankreich nichts bringen werde, denn Deutschland hat in den nächsten Jahren, selbst wenn es wollte, nichts, um seine Schulden zu bezahlen." Im Gegensatze dazu steht also Radek in seinen Fragen an das 'Gewissen' auf dem Standpunkte der Erfüllungspolitik—auf demselben Standpunkte, auf dem sonst nur Pazifisten, frankophile Allerweltsdemokraten und zweieinhalbprozentige Sozialisten stehen. Wir gaben Radek sehr recht, wenn er sagt, daß "der große Schrei gegen die Erfüllungspolitik noch keine politische Antwort ist". Aber auch der Ruf nach der Erfüllungspolitik scheint uns keine politische Antwort zu sein und als Fragestellung überhaupt nicht in Betracht zu kommen, wenn die Dinge so liegen, daß die Gegenseite überhaupt keine Erfüllung will und Frankreich an der Ruhr, am Rhein und an der Saar gar keine wirtschaftlichen Ziele hat, über die sich reden ließe, sondern politische Ziele, von denen es nicht ablassen wird. Und allerdings ist unsere Meinung, daß die französischen Absichten in dieser Richtung liegen, und daß wir zumal in Deutschland sehr viel weiter sein würden, wenn es nicht eine Richtung gäbe, die sich noch immer Selbsttäuschungen hingibt, vielmehr auch hier von der Wirklichkeit ausginge. Die englische Politik mag versuchen, Frankreich vor der Welt in ein moralisches Unrecht zu stellen. Die *deutsche Politik kann nur von dem Willen zum Unrecht als einer französischen Tatsache ausgehen.*

Auch Poincare hat unlängst eine Frage vorgelegt — eine Frage, die er in der etwas durchsichtigen Absicht stellte, auf sie eine vorgefaßte Antwort geben zu können. Er fragte patzig, indem er sich gegen den Vorwurf des Annektionismus wandte, was Frankreich denn im Frieden von Versailles erreicht habe. Und er antwortete mit der Stirn, die diesen Großbürger ziert: nichts! Frankreich, behauptet er, habe doch nur zurückgenommen, was es im Frieden von Frankfurt verlor, aber darüber hinaus habe es sich "auch nicht einen Zoll Landes" angeeignet. Das ist so buchstabenrichtig, wie es wirklichkeitsfern war. Sind den Franzosen nicht alle Wünsche einer vierundvierzigjährigen Revanchepolitik erfüllt worden? Besaß Frankreich je diesen Spielraum an der Saar, mit einer Abstimmung erst in fünfzehn Jahren? Besaß es je diese Stellung am Rhein? Selbstverständlich will Frankreich auch Geld, weil die Franzosen dieses Geld brauchen. Aber vor allem will Frankreich Land, Machtaufrichtung, Sicherung in alle Zukunft, einen rheinisch-westfälischen Vasallenstaat und die Zertrümmerung des deutschen Reiches. Vermöchte Deutschland überhaupt durch Zahlung oder Leistung das Land zu retten? Oder würde die französische Politik, nachdem sie von Deutschland nahm, was Deutschland ihr gab, nicht am Ende die Einlösung der Pfänder unter irgend einem neuen Vorwande verweigern, wenn eine deutsche Regierung mit ihr Ernst machte, ganz gleich, ob die Abzahlerin eine kapitalistische oder eine proletarische Regierung ist? Es gibt da keine Garantie!

So ist die Situation. Sie kann sich ändern, gewiß, und dann eine andere Politik verlangen. Sieht sich die deutsche Lage zwischen Frankreich und Rußland mit einem Male anders vom Westen aus und anders vom Osten aus an? Deutschland muß immer darauf gefaßt sein, daß sich zwischen Frankreich und Rußland bestimmte politische Beziehungen wieder herstellen, die von der Stellung zu England nahegelegt werden. Schon spüren wir, wie Frankreichs Interesse an Polen nachläßt und Frankreichs Interesse an Rußland sich verstärkt. Die französische Republik wird vor einer Verbindung mit dem Sowjetstaate so wenig zurückschrecken, wie sie vor der Berührung mit dem Zarismus zurückschreckte. Und nur der Sowjetstaat, meinen wir, dürfte die Rückwirkung auf die sechzig Parteien seiner kommunistischen Internationale scheuen, zu denen immerhin auch die deutsche kommunistische Partei gehört. Die deutschen Arbeiter, die im Westen betrogen werden, wollen nicht auch noch durch den Osten enttäuscht sein. Oder gehört auch diese Prüfung zu ihrer Nationalisierung?

Radek sprach in Moskau von Deutschland als einer 'Ausbeutungskolonie Frankreichs'. Und er sprach davon, daß man "ein Gebiet, in dem die Revolution herrscht, nicht ausbeuten kann". Deshalb, so meinte er, wird das deutsche Proletariat nicht nur gegen den deutschen Nationalismus, sondern auch gegen den französischen Imperialismus kämpfen müssen.

Diese doppelparolige Perspektive, in der die ganze furchtbare, aber auch vorläufig hilflose Zwischenstellung des deutschen Proletariats zusammengedrängt erscheint, soll uns nicht der Antwort auf die Frage nach den 'großen Opfern' entheben, die gebracht werden müssen, um, wie Radek sagt, "die Franzosen aus dem Ruhrgebiet hinauszubringen". Sie würde dies tun, wenn Radek seine Frage nur innenpolitisch und für den Fall einer Erfüllungspolitik gestellt hätte, die sich nach unserer Meinung als unwirksam, völlig vergeblich, ganz sinn- und zwecklos herausstellen müßte. Aber Radek stellt seine Frage in deren zweiter Hälfte auch außenpolitisch und für den Fall eines 'Volkskampfes', den man allerdings nur dann 'gegen die Franzosen schüren' kann, wenn man, wie er wiederholt, 'große materielle Opfer bringt".

Wir antworten ihm, daß es kein Opfer gibt, das nicht von der Unternehmerschaft, von der Bourgeoisie, von den vermögenden Klassen, und wer nur immer als Besitzer von irgend welchen 'Sachwerten' in wirtschaftlichen Betracht kommt, um der Nation willen gebracht werden muß, um das Land zu befreien. Es wird die Probe auf die Daseinsberechtigung dieser Schichten im Körper der Nation sein. Vor hundert Jahren brachten Adel und Bürgertum Leben und Gold dar. Sie bestanden die Probe und verschafften sich eben dadurch noch einmal eine Daseinsberechtigung, auf der sich die bevorzug-

te Stellung gründete, die sie in der Folge einnahmen. Dies alles ist heute nicht anders, und die Darbringung der Sachwerte ist nur eine neue Formel für die gleiche Sache. Das Opfer der Sachwerte setzt eine bestimmte Gesinnung bei denen voraus, die das Opfer bringen. Der Materialist wird vielleicht einwenden, daß man mit Gesinnung noch keinen 'Volkskampf' schüren und führen kann. Wir sind der Überzeugung, daß nichts in der Welt ohne Gesinnung irgend einen Wert hat und daß, wenn sie dem Kapitalismus fehlen sollte, sie ihm zunächst beigebracht werden müßte.

Doch bleibt die Frage nach den Sachwerten die Frage nach ihrer Erfassung als 'praktischem Kampfprogramm', wie Radek sagt. Radek selbst spricht aus, was er unter 'Erfassung der Sachwerte' im deutschen Falle versteht, er spricht es klug aus, und vorsichtig, und unter schonender Berücksichtigung der deutschen Wirtschaftsverhältnisse. Er nennt: "Syndizierung der Industrie in den Händen des Staates, die zwar keine Verwaltung jedes industriellen Gebietes durch den Staat bedeutet, aber einen Wirtschaftsplan erfordert; die Ausschaltung jeder parasitären Produktion; die Ausnutzung der Gewinnung zur Tragung der Kosten des Kampfes". Zu den Parasiten können wir nur sagen, daß wir uns so bald wie möglich einen deutschen Staat wünschen, der ihnen dasjenige Ende macht, das sie seit 1914 als Kriegsgewinnler, Friedensgewinnler und jetzt als Widerstandsgewinnler verdienen. Aber Parasiten einer Wirtschaft sind nicht der Körper der Wirtschaft.

Radek fordert für diese Wirtschaft einen Wirtschaftsplan. Er wird damit keine 'Planwirtschaft' fordern, gegen die wir einigermaßen mißtrauisch sind, weil sie sich, wenigstens als Formel, als eine nur literarische und reformistische Forderung herausgestellt hat. Aber darüber sind wir mit Radek einig, daß die Situation eine große wirtschaftliche Strategie verlangt, die allein die Wirtschaft als eine Kampfkraft einzusetzen vermag, und unter deren Diktatur allein die 'Gewinne' zur 'Tragung der Kosten des Kampfes' ausgenutzt werden können. Es fragt sich nur, in wessen Hände die große wirtschaftliche Strategie gelegt werden soll?

Radek antwortet: in die Hände der Arbeiterregie-

rung. Und hier sind wir allerdings nach unserer Erfah-rung mit Menschen, nach unserer Bewertung der persön-lichen wie klassenmäßigen Kampfkräfte, die in Deutsch-land zur Verfügung stehen, und übrigens auch nach der Erfahrung und Bewertung, die sich aus den Lehren der russischen Revolution ergeben, einer sehr anderen Mei-nung. Radek sagt freilich, daß er mit dem Begriffe der Arbeiter "auch die geistigen Arbeiter erfasse". Aber wir hängen diese geistigen Arbeiter nicht hintenan, sondern setzen sie voran. Wir wissen, warum wir dies tun. Zu den geistigen Arbeitern gehört für uns der deutsche Unter-nehmer. Er gehört für uns in wirtschaftlichen Dingen in die vorderste Reihe. Er ist der Deutsche, der als Erster den Blick für die Erfindung der Maschinen, die Einrich-tung der Fabriken, die Entstehung einer Übervölkerung und der Verwendung in der Industrie aufbrachte und der noch heute den Blick für die wirtschaftlichen Zu-sammenhänge mitbringt, die dem Arbeiter notwendig fehlen. Dieser deutsche Wirtschaftsführer ist nicht von der Wurzel her Kapitalist, wie der westliche Ausbeuter. Er ist vielmehr Schaffer von Werten, über die wir verfü-gen und die wir einsetzen können. Wir werden auf ihn nicht verzichten, solange er ein Mann bleibt, der 'die Probe besteht'. Ein Mensch ist wichtiger als eine Dok-trin.

Auch Revolutionen sollen von einander lernen. Wir haben, wofern dies noch nötig war, von der russischen Revolution gelernt. Und diese russische Revolution hat von sich selbst gelernt. Lenin hat bekannt: "Ich bin zu der Überzeugung gekommen, daß alle Leistung auf Ein-zelpersönlichkeiten beruht, die der Masse die Methoden diktieren, die Notwendigkeit und Augenblicksverhält-nisse erfordern." Es war die Erkenntnis der Situation, die immer mächtiger ist als die Doktrin, und aus deren politischem oder wirtschaftlichem Dilemma nur die gei-stige Überlegenheit des undilettantischen Menschen, der die Situation überblickt und beherrscht, einen Ausweg zu weisen vermag. Alle Umstürzler leben zunächst von dem Kapital, das sie vorfinden, ohne die geringste Vor-aussicht. Es ist unter Umständen sehr leicht für eine Klas-se, die Sachwerte zu erfassen, aber sehr schwer, sie zu verwerten oder gar, für ihre Neuschöpfung zu sorgen.

Wir müssen noch einmal Lenin anführen: "Die Aktionen der Klassen entbehren ständig des gesunden Verstandes, weil sie keine Rücksichten auf spätere Ziele und Erfordernisse nehmen." Man soll Sachwerte nicht nehmen, sondern schaffen, und die geschaffenen Sachwerte, die man in einer Situation vorfindet, soll man für die Zwekke dieser Situationen verwenden: in unserem Falle, für die Zwecke des 'Volkskampfes', von dem Radek spricht. In diesem Volkskampfe ist die Erfassung der Sachwerte keine Frage der Klasse, sondern der Nation — ihr gehören die Sachwerte. Und wer in diesem Volkskampfe die Nation in den Klassenkampf treibt, der gibt eine Doppelparole aus, mit der am Ende nur erreicht wird, daß die Kampfmittel zerschlagen, unverwendungsfähig, unbrauchbar gemacht werden. Wir müssen Lenin zum dritten Male anführen: "Nur der stärkste Wille des einzelnen Individuums und die schöpferische Kraft des freien Intellektes können die noch fernliegenden Phasen des Kampfes bei Zeiten erkennen und alles Für und Wider mit Sorgfalt kalkulieren. Diese Tatsache, der wichtigste Faktor des sozialen Lebens, ist uns entgangen, mir und meinen Freunden". Aber Rußland hat diese Erkenntnis nachgeholt und um seiner Rettung als Staat willen, seine Wirtschaft den Spezialisten überlassen. Radek rät an, die deutsche Wirtschaft den deutschen Kommunisten zu überlassen. Glaubt Radek im Ernste, daß Deutsche von Intelligenz sich bereitfinden werden, nur um einer Doktrin willen, die noch nicht einmal die ihre ist, Wege zu gehen, die sich in Rußland bereits als Umwege herausgestellt haben? Die deutsche Wirtschaft ist vielleicht das komplizierteste Instrument der Welt. Sie will, zumal in einem Volkskampfe mit besonderer Vertrautheit besorgt und bedient sein. Und man wird sich nicht gerade an Deutsche wenden, die als Arbeiter vielleicht die intelligentesten der Welt, aber als Politiker die primitivsten sind.

Wir haben im 'Gewissen' von Anfang an darauf hingewiesen, daß jedes Volk seine Revolution auf seine Weise macht. Die sozialistisch-pazifistische Revolution von 1918 war eine Revolution der Gutgläubigkeit und nur zu deutsch. Die nationale Revolution, die Radek jetzt anrät, wird, wir hoffen es, deutscher sein, und intelligen-

ter. Sonst kommt es auf diesem Umwege allerdings dahin, daß 'die Geschichte', wie Radek sagt, "mit einem vollkommenen Zusammenbruch endet", der noch sehr viel katastrophischer ausfallen dürfte, als der russische ausfiel. Auch diese nationale Revolution setzt einen dritten Standpunkt voraus, der, um in den Vorstellungen einer Dialektik zu bleiben, die dem materialistischen Theoretiker vertraut ist, die theoretisch-marxistische und die praktisch-bolschewistische Stufe auf einer neuen deutschen und überhöhenden Stufe aufnimmt und fortsetzt.

Der Marxismus ist eine Mathematik. Aber das Leben ist fließend, ist selbstherrlich aus eigener Kraft und immer von jener 'Tradition aller toten Geschlechter' abhängig, die Marx als einen 'Alp auf dem Gehirn der Lebenden' empfand — während der Mensch, der aus ihr in die Zukunft hinein handelt, durch sie eher frei und sicher und schöpferisch wird. Die Mathematik des Marxismus geht in der Wirklichkeit nicht auf. Und immer verlangt hier dieses Leben ein Recht, das es auch in Rußland verlangte und schließlich erhalten hat.

Wir Deutsche sind zu sehr Skeptiker, um der Mathematik zu vertrauen. Wir fragen uns immer nur, ob auch, und wie, und wann in Deutschland das Leben sein Recht wird erlangen können.

*

So bleibt die Frage nach unserer Stellung zu Frankreich, zu Rußland und zu der deutschen Arbeiterschaft.

Wir haben durchaus die Zuversicht, daß zu irgend einem Zeitpunkte, wofern wir nicht vorher als Volkstum durch irgend eine Dummheit, und wäre es eine mathematische Dummheit zu Grunde gehen, die größere Lebenskraft des deutschen Volkes sich gegenüber derjenigen des französischen geltend machen, sich die Kraft der 70 Millionen gegenüber den 40 Millionen durchsetzen wird. Und unser Ziel ist, diesen Augenblick herbeizuführen, die 70 Millionen in einer einheitlichen Richtung zusammenzubringen, unter überzeugender Zustimmung der Massen wie aller Einzelnen. Aber wir geben uns keiner Selbsttäuschung darüber hin, daß wir von diesem Ziele noch sehr weit entfernt sind. Wir wollen von den deutschen Parteien gar nicht erst reden, die

noch immer die Rettung von Ausflüchten erwarten, und
derweile im Parlament ihre Sonderstandpunkte bekosen.
Aber auch die deutsche Arbeiterschaft ist nicht reif und
bereit, sich als nationale Arbeiterschaft zu konstituie-
ren. Auch sie hofft vielmehr in ihrer politischen Kind-
lichkeit immer noch, daß irgend eine proletarische Internationale eingreifen werde, die für uns genau so zu
den Illusionen gehört, wie der bürgerliche Völkerbund.
Es gibt, meinen wir, keine konkretere Tatsache, als die
Geistesverfassung der Menschen, mit denen man politisch rechnen muß. Und doch sind wir überzeugt, und
dies ist die Tragik unserer Situation, daß die 70 Millionen nur einen einzigen Willen zu fassen brauchen, um
von der Stunde an wieder frei zu werden — vielleicht
sogar nur durch die Wucht der geistigen Tatsache, die
wir als Bewußtsein der Welt auferlegen.

Eine bestimmte Situation, die unmittelbar an das
Ziel der einzigen Willensrichtung hätte heranführen können, ist seit 1918 bereits verfehlt worden, und wird
auch heute verfehlt. Seit der Revolution versichert man
sich im deutschen Volke, und versichert man der deutschen Arbeiterschaft, daß nur Rußland und Deutschland
zusammenzugehen brauchen, um den Vertrag von Versailles zu zerbrechen. An der Logik dieser Rechnung ist
nicht zu zweifeln. Aber auch hier ist die Wirklichkeit
mächtiger als die Logik. Eine Schuld liegt sicherlich bei
der deutschen Politik: aber sie liegt auch bei der russischen Politik, sofern man in beiden Fällen überhaupt
von Schuld sprechen kann, und nicht von Zwangslage
sprechen muß. Sowjetrußland hat die deutschrussische
Verständigung nicht paritätisch, sondern bolschewistisch
und parteikommunistisch betrieben, hat sich die deutsche Revolution nicht deutsch, sondern russisch vorge-
stellt, und dadurch die deutsche antibolschewistische
Bewegung erst möglich und notwendig gemacht. Darüber verfehlte Sowjetrußland die europäische Situation,
brachte sich in die außenpolitische Notlage, sich ohne
Bundesgenossen der Angriffe der Entente erwehren zu
müssen, und verlor schließlich den polnischen Krieg,
den es mit deutscher Hilfe hätte gewinnen können. In
der Folge hat Rußland sich national zu sichern verstanden. Es behauptet heute, ein Machtstaat zu sein, aber

Mahnmal zur Erinnerung an die Ermordung Albert Leo Schlageters auf der Golzheimer Heide.

ALBERT LEO SCHLAGETER

noch immer ist es außenpolitisch ohnmächtig, und muß stets befürchten, daß es, wenn erst Deutschland völlig zusammengebrochen und ausgeschaltet sein sollte, von der triumphierenden Bestie des Weltkapitalismus erneut bedrängt und schließlich erdrückt werden wird.

In Deutschland glauben jetzt nur noch deutsche Kommunisten an das russische Heil. Sie sind gewohnt, den Russen alles nachzumachen. Sie haben ihren Pazifismus, mit dem sie noch in die Revolution zogen, fast freudig aufgegeben und möchten nun die rote Armee nachahmen. Wir sind gewiß, daß sie auch den Ruf aufnehmen werden, der jetzt von Moskau aus an sie erging und ihnen ihre proletarische Sache als eine nationale Sache darstellt. Aber dies alles hat keinen Wert, wenn es nicht aus einer eigensten Initiative hervorgeht. Wir haben bis jetzt nicht erlebt, daß der deutsche Kommunismus auch nur eine einzige und eigentümliche Idee zu der revolutionären Problematik beigetragen hat. Es ist ein Kommunismus von Geführten, die auch nur Parteipolitik treiben. So ergibt sich diese merkwürdige Situation, daß immer nur eine Verständigung von Mensch zu Mensch möglich ist, aber nicht von Bewegung zu Bewegung. Radek nennt eine Redensart, daß "die Arbeiter die Ziele der deutschen nationalen Kreise verstehen müssen." Wir meinen, es gibt keine bittere, härtere, drängendere Notwendigkeit, als wenn sich das Proletariat so mit den Motiven des Nationalismus beschäftigte, wie der Nationalismus sich mit den Problemen des Kommunismus beschäftigt. Wissen um Dinge ist Waffe im Kampf. Sieger wird, wer seinen Gegner kannte. Und auch Verbündete sind nur möglich, wenn sie sich mit ihren Beweggründen wechselseitig vertraut gemacht haben. Wenn der deutsche Proletarier nicht immer wieder gegen Kräfte in der Nation anrennen will, die aus einer von ihm noch unbegriffenen Welt kommen, dann wird er sich mit der für ihn zunächst befremdlichen und unheimlichen Tatsache auseinandersetzen müssen, daß die 'breiten sozial-leidenden Massen' des Nationalismus, an die Radek sich wendet, daß alle diese Menschen von Intelligenz, diese geistigen Arbeiter, die heute mit Proletarisierung bedroht sind, gleichwohl nicht von materialistischen Motiven bestimmt werden. Es gibt geistige

Sachwerte, die erfaßt sein wollen!

Das deutsche Proletariat müßte nicht so tief in das politische Schicksal des deutschen Volkes mitverflochten sein, wenn nicht auch von ihm gelten sollte, was von diesem gilt: daß seine Entschlüsse immer zu früh oder zu spät fallen:

Wann wird die politische Situation sich ergeben, in der es kein 'zu spät' mehr gibt, sondern nur noch Entscheidungen zur rechten Zeit?"

* * *

Nach diesen Ausführungen Moeller van den Brucks gab es keine Fortsetzung des Dialogs mit Radek mehr. Zwar faßte dieser in der 'Roten Fahne' noch einmal seine Vorstellungen zusammen (9), aber eine Annäherung in Sachfragen blieb aus. Das Ende des kommunistisch-nationalistischen Abtastens wurde allerdings erst von einem weiteren Aufsatz des Grafen Reventlow markiert. Wieder erschien er in der 'Roten Fahne'.

* * *

Trennendes

"Ich bin der Ansicht der 'Roten Fahne', wenn sie schreibt, in der Diskussion dürfe nicht nur das Gemeinsame, sondern müsse auch das Trennende scharf hervorgehoben werden. In meinen Aufsätzen über die Frage des Bündnisses zwischen Deutschland und Sowjetrußland habe ich das getan. Die 'Rote Fahne' hebt einige dieser Punkte wiederum hervor, anscheinend im Glauben, es handele sich bei mir oder auf der völkischen Seite überhaupt um Unklarheiten. Die 'Rote Fahne' sagt: nur wenn die Sache der deutschen Nation verbunden werde mit der Sache der internationalen Revolution, könne sie gegen den Imperialismus bestehen. Das ist eine Behauptung wie irgendeine andere. Ein Beweis für die Richtigkeit wird nicht erbracht und ist auch nicht zu erbringen. Ich bestreite auch, daß Rußland deshalb sich hätte siegreich behaupten können, weil es das 'Banner der Weltrevolution aufpflanzte'. Wollte man sich

vorstellen, Rußland hätte das Banner der nationalen und sozialen Revolution aufgepflanzt, so würde es die Sympathie der anderen Unterdrückten nicht minder gefunden haben als seinerzeit die große französische Revolution, die sich trotz internationaler Anreger und Antriebe immer mehr zu einer gewaltigen nationalen Bewegung auswuchs. Die 'Rote Fahne' bezeichnet es als Illusion oder als bewußte Dienstleistung für den Kapitalismus, wenn behauptet werde, das völkische Deutschland könne sich selbst befreien. Ich bin anderer Ansicht, nämlich der folgenden: würde in Deutschland auf Grund einer gleichzeitigen sozialen Umgestaltung die Bevölkerung nicht allein äußerlich, sondern auch innerlich einig, so würde keine Unterdrückung von außen dieser ungeheuren Kraft widerstehen können, und Deutschland würde dazu nicht allein die Sympathie aller Unterdrückten auf seiner Seite haben, sondern alle Völker, die nicht selbst Unterdrücker wären. Ich kann nicht verstehen, inwiefern dieser Standpunkt 'unhaltbar' sein sollte. Ich kann auch nicht verstehen, warum ein sozial umgestaltetes Deutschland für seinen Kampf gegen die Unterdrückung nicht ebenfalls die volle Sympathie Rußlands finden sollte, auch dann, wenn dieses Deutschland sich nicht als Sektion der kommunistischen Internationale bezeichnete, noch eine solche wäre. Welches Interesse könnte, rein sachlich betrachtet, Rußland bestimmen, einem solchen Deutschland nicht sympathisch und hilfreich zur Seite zu stehen ? Es würde damit für seine eigene Sache kämpfen, umgekehrt sich ins eigene Fleisch schneiden, wenn es dem deutschen Volke sagte: wir helfen Dir nur, wenn Du Dich auf den Boden der Internationale stellst ! — Beiläufig bemerkt, dürfte der 'Roten Fahne' wohl bekannt sein, daß gerade jetzt in Rußland eine nationale Bewegung im starken Wachsen ist, die sich auf Wiederherstellung der Grenzen von 1916 richtet. Diese Bewegung ist national, dabei nicht imperialistisch. Sie beeinträchtigt in keiner Weise die in Rußland geltenden sozialen Grundsätze noch auch Rätesystem. Warum also will man in Moskau nicht das als für Deutschland billig betrachten, was dem heutigen Rußland mit allem Grunde als Recht und als nationale Notwendigkeit erscheint ?

Die 'Rote Fahne' und früher Radek sagen, die Völkischen und Nationalen in Deutschland würden, falls sie sich nicht 'den Arbeitern anschließen', sie mögen wollen oder nicht, mit dem Kapitalismus zur Unterdrückung der Arbeiterschaft gemeinsame Sache machen. Wollte man sich vorstellen, daß es so käme, so würden Moskau und der deutsche Kommunismus, und zwar sie allein, die Schuld davon tragen; nämlich deshalb, weil sie von den völkischen und nationalen Massen Deutschlands verlangt hätten, daß diese sich auf den Boden der Internationale und als Teil der kommunistischen Internationale den, wie die 'Rote Fahne' sagt: "Arbeitern anschlössen". Völkische Dienstleistung an den Kapitalismus wird aber ausgeschlossen sein, sobald die deutsche Bewegung gegen.den Kapitalismus zur sozialen Umgestaltung Deutschlands auf deutscher Grundlage tritt, beide unterstützt durch die Haltung Moskaus. Dieser Zusammenhang ist so klar; man muß sich wundern, daß man auf kommunistischer Seite ihn nicht erörtert.

Der Artikel der 'Roten Fahne' wiederholt, das Bündnis mit Sowjetrußland bedeute, daß Deutschland sich mit der Sache der Weltrevolution verbünde. Das bedingt auch eine innere Umwälzung in Deutschland. Aber davon will Reventlow verständlich mit Sowjetrußland auswärtige Politik treiben, wie mit jeder anderen Macht 'Bedingung wäre, eben so verständlich, daß Deutschland keine innerpolitischen Preise dafür zahlte'. Es war und bleibt immer ein grundlegender Fehler für ein Volk, in der auswärtigen Politik innerpolitische Preise zu zahlen, ganz einerlei, um was für innere Verhältnisse es sich handelt; ein Volk muß vollkommen frei sein und frei handeln, um seine inneren Verhältnisse zu bestimmen. Diese Freiheit ist eines der höchsten Güter auch jedes einzelnen Volksgenossen, und es ist stets zu schwerstem Schaden für einen Staat und ein Volk gewesen, wenn es auf diese Weise verzichtete. Eine innere Umwälzung als Preis für ein Bündnis mit Sowjetrußland zu zahlen, wäre ein solcher verhängnisvoller Fehler. Die innere soziale Umwälzung aber an sich und auf deutscher Grundlage halte ich allerdings nach wie vor für eine Notwendigkeit und für die Vorbedingung einer wirklichen inneren Einigung des deutschen Volkes, die ihrerseits wiederum die Vor-

*bedingung zur Befreiung Deutschlands von fremder Un-
terdrückung bedeutet.*

*Wie wir uns die Lösung der sozialen Frage vorstellen,
haben Radek und die 'Rote Fahne' gefragt, und sie sagen, sie hätten darauf bisher nur Deklamation zu hören
bekommen. Ich stelle mir darunter die Befreiung vom
Kapitalismus vor, und unter dieser hauptsächlich: Ände-
rung des Eigentumsbegriffs und des Eigentumsrechtes,
Nationalisierung der Banken, Trusts, staatliche Verfügung über den Grund und Boden usw.*

*Die Behauptung Radeks ist ganz unrichtig, die Völ-
kischen seien an die von ihm aufgeworfenen Fragen vom
außenpolitischen Standpunkt herangetreten. Was man
heute völkisch nennt, das gab es schon lange vor dem
Kriege in Gestalt der damaligen Deutsch-Sozialen usw.
Zur Zeit des Kriegsausbruches war die völkische Bewegung, wenn schon zersplittert, doch überall in Deutschland zu finden und im wachsen. Da war nicht das Außenpolitische das Leitmotiv, sondern es war der soziale Ge-
danke. Die völkische Bewegung ist jetzt, wie die Kommunisten wissen, stark und wird immer stärker. Schon bevor Radek seine Schlageter-Rede gehalten hat, wurde
die Frage von der Möglichkeit eines Zusammengehens
zwischen Völkischen und deutschen Kommunisten in
beiden Lagern besprochen. In dem Punkte sind und waren sich die Völkischen einig, daß von einem 'Anschluß'
an die Kommunisten, wie ihn auch die 'Rote Fahne' verlangt, nicht die Rede sein kann. Wer das auf der kommunistischen Seite glaubt, unterschätzt einmal die
wachsende Stärke der völkischen Bewegung, ferner ihre
unbrechbare Verankerung in dem völkischen Gedanken.
Dieser schließt den Internationalismus als Basis aus.
Ebenso unabänderlich ist er in seiner Stellung dem Ju-
dentum gegenüber. Unser Kampf gegen den Kapitalismus und andere antisoziale Erscheinungen freilich richtet sich ohne Unterschied gegen Juden und gegen Deutsche, das sei ausdrücklich bemerkt. Die soziale Umwälzung, die wir für notwendig halten, muß deutlich sein
und bleiben. Was nicht deutsch ist, gehört nicht hinein.
Wohl aber können wir uns eben von diesem reinen deutschen Boden aus Beziehungen und Zusammenarbeiten
mit anderen Kräften und Mächten vorstellen, die in ih-*

rem Bereich Ähnliches tuen und wollen wie wir. Der augenblickliche Standpunkt des deutschen Kommunismus ist unlogisch und vom sozialen Standpunkt unverständlich, wenn er nämlich erklärt, eine soziale Umwälzung in Deutschland könne er nur mitmachen und unterstützen, wenn sie auf internationalistischer Basis sich vollzöge; und das gleiche gelte von einem deutschen Befreiungskampf nach außen. Was Moskau anlangt, so läge es, wie gesagt, im eminenten Interesse der Sowjetrepublik, für diesen Befreiungskampf Deutschlands mit allen Kräften einzutreten, einerlei, ob der deutsche Kampf gegen den Kapitalismus als ein rein nationaler oder internationalistischer aufgefaßt und durchgeführt würde.

Die 'Rote Fahne' sagt: der Soldat der roten Armee kämpfe für die Freiheit der Welt und sei deshalb besser als der andere. Ich meine, deutsche Arbeiter und andere deutsche Volksgenossen, die für die Befreiung Deutschlands kämpften, würden zum mindesten ebenso gut sein. Der soziale freiheitsliebende Mensch dient der Welt am besten, wenn er für die innere und äußere Freiheit seines eigenen Volks kämpft und dieses zunächst vor allem hochhält.

* * *

Der Artikel Reventlows betonte zwar das "Trennende" zwischen Kommunismus und Nationalismus bzw. völkischer Bewegung, aber er machte in dieser Diskussion, die seit der Schlageter-Rede Karl Radeks geführt worden war, die weitestgehenden innenpolitischen Zugeständnisse. Vielleicht wäre die Auseinandersetzung auf dieser Ebene noch eine Weile weitergegangen, wenn nicht der "Passive Widerstand" an der Ruhr am 26. September 1923 von der Reichsregierung abgebrochen worden wäre. Die Führer Sowjetrußlands sahen nun ein, daß der Kampf des gedemütigten Deutschland mit der westlichen Siegermacht nicht mehr den Punkt erreichen werde, von dem aus die Gegensätze im kapitalistischen Lager als unüberwindlich erscheinen mußten. Der Abbruch des Widerstandes gegen Frankreich ließ eine neue Politik der Weimarer Republik erahnen. Sie würde auch in Zukunft nicht aus der Versailler Ordnung auszubrechen versuchen, indem sie sich auf den Osten stützte. Vielmehr war damit zu rechnen, daß sie sich nach der nicht bestandenen Kraftprobe ihrem Schicksal fügen würde. Die KPD durfte ihr Spiel mit dem Feuer abbrechen.

Der Schlageter-Kurs der KPD scheint auf den ersten Blick kaum etwas mit den Taten des Nationalisten Albert Leo Schlageter zu tun zu haben. Weshalb wurde diese Strömung trotzdem in dieser Ausführlichkeit dargestellt?

Das kurze Leben Schlageters kann nicht als ein 'Heldenleben' bezeichnet werden. Dieser unruhige Geist ist nicht angetreten, um einer leuchtenden Idee zu folgen, die in jeder Situation der alles überstrahlende Leitstern gewesen wäre. Schlageter war eher ein Verzweifelter. In einer verworrenen Zeit wollte er, der Nationalist, seinem Volke dienen. Er wollte Deutschland von Feinden befreit sehen, aber er wußte es nicht zu verhindern, daß reaktionäre Kräfte, die alles andere als das Wohl der Nation im Sinn hatten, ihn und seine gläubigen Kameraden mißbrauchten. Ob er im Baltikum 'die Bolschewisten' bekämpfte oder sich im Ruhrgebiet mit 'den Roten' schlug, immer hatte sein Einsatz Schattenseiten. Einer seiner Biographen, Ernst von Salomon, hat später eingesehen, daß die Freikorps zwar das Gute wollten, infolge ihrer politischen Ahnungslosigkeit aber letztlich an den falschen Fronten kämpften. Als Schlageter 1920 gegen aufständische deutsche Arbeiter vorging, da ahnte er, daß dunkle Hintermänner seine Kameraden als Schutztruppe benutzten. Aber ihn trieb der Ordnungsinstinkt und das Gefühl, mit den kommunistischen Feinden der bürgerlichen Republik auch die Feinde der deutschen Unabhängigkeit treffen zu können. Insofern der Nationalist Schlageter sich ungewollt in den Dienst der Konterrevolution stellte, war er tatsächlich ein 'Wanderer ins Nichts'. Ob man diese Charakterisierung auch auf den Freiheitskämpfer des Jahres 1923 übertragen kann, ist jedoch sehr zweifelhaft.

Im besetzten Rheinland richtete sich der Kampf Schlageters gegen Unterdrücker. Darin war sich das ganze Volk einig; auch die kommunistischen Arbeiter, die nichts dabei fanden, sich den Franzosen Arm in Arm mit den Freikorpssoldaten entgegenzustellen. Ob Schlageter den Sinn dieser neuen Frontstellung klar erkannt hat, ob er bereit war, innenpolitische Konsequenzen daraus zu ziehen, wissen wir nicht.

Eine mögliche Konsequenz zogen die Führer der Kommunistischen Internationale. Sie erklärten, nun sei es an der Zeit, den Kampf gegen die äußeren *und* inneren Unterdrücker und Ausbeuter der Volksmassen, gegen die kapitalistischen Westmächte *und* die Reaktion zusammenzufassen. Daß die Kommunistische Internationale nur taktierte und eher sowjetrussische als deutsche Interessen im Auge hatte, steht auf einem anderen Blatt. Es interessiert in diesem Zusammenhang allein, daß sich deutsche Nationalisten fanden, die den Aufruf Karl Radeks beantworteten. Es ist wahr: Die Mehrheit der nationalen Bürgerlichen wies das Ansinnen der Kommunisten als plumpe Propaganda zurück. Für sie war Radek der Feind schlechthin. Graf Reventlow und Moeller van den Bruck unterschieden sich von ihnen dadurch, daß sie die Nation, das Wohl des deutschen Volkes in seiner Gesamtheit, über innenpolitische Ressentiments und Klasseninteressen stellten. Sie waren bereit, notfalls auch einen Pakt mit dem Teufel zu schließen. Ob sie sich dabei zu Recht auf Schlageter beriefen, sei dahingestellt. Anzunehmen ist aber, daß Albert Leo Schlageter diesen nationalrevolutionären Denkern näherstand als den liberalen Auch-Nationalen, die Reventlow und Moeller nie verzeihen konnten, daß sie sich einmal mit dem Kommunisten Radek eingelassen hatten.

Seit dem bemerkenswerten Disput sind sechzig Jahre vergangen. Die nationale Not, die damals Schlageter, Reventlow und Moeller van den Bruck zur Verzweiflung trieb, kommt uns angesichts der gegenwärtigen Lage fast erträglich vor. War damals Oberschlesien bedroht, so scheint heute ganz Ostdeutschland verloren. Die Rote Armee, die Schlageter im Baltikum bekämpfte, steht nun an der Elbe. Der französische Imperialismus hat zwar nicht nur am Rhein endgültig ausgespielt, aber dafür ist die Hälfte des deutschen Reichsgebiets und die Mehrheit des deutschen Volkes dem Gesetz der neuen Führungsmacht der westlichen Welt unterworfen. Ein Vergleich mit der Zeit Schlageters ist kaum möglich.

Auch deshalb nicht, weil die Sowjetunion — belehrt durch die Schrecken des Weltkrieges und festgelegt durch ihre Rolle als Bewahrerin des Systems von Jalta — heute kein Interesse mehr an einem weltrevolutionären Partner Deutschland zu haben scheint. Doch hatten bisher alle politischen 'Realitäten' eines gemeinsam: sie waren vergänglich. Wie die Zukunft Deutschlands aussieht, wird nicht zuletzt der entscheiden, der bereit ist, sich im Interesse der Nation über Bürgerkriegs- und Weltbürgerkriegsparteien zu erheben, Bündnispartner auch dort zu suchen, wo der bürgerliche 'Patriot' erschreckt zurückzuckt und nur einer Sache zu dienen: der Sache des Volkes.

(1) K. Radek: 'Der Faschismus, wir und die deutschen Sozialdemokraten'. In: Schlageter, eine Auseinandersetzung. Berlin, 1923
(2) Die diesbezüglichen Artikel wurden wiederabgedruckt in: Was sagt die 'Rote Fahne'? (Eine Broschüre der Reihe 'Ring-Flugschriften'), Bln., 1923
(3) Graf E. Reventlow: 'Mit Radek ?'. In: 'Reichswart' Nr. 26
(4) Reventlow war Reichstagsabgeordneter der Deutschvölkischen Freiheitspartei, als er diesen und seine folgenden Aufsätze schrieb. Deshalb sprach er von den 'Völkischen' und vermied, anders als Moeller, die übergreifende Bezeichnung 'Nationalisten'.
(5) P. Frölich: 'Eine Antwort auf den Grafen E. Reventlow'. In: Schlageter, eine Auseinandersetzung. Berlin, 1923
(6) Graf E. Reventlow: 'Ein Stück Wegs ?'. Wiederabgedruckt in: Ders.: Völkisch-kommunistische Einigung ? Leipzig, 1924
(7) A. Moeller van den Bruck: 'Der Wanderer ins Nichts'. In: 'Gewissen' Nr. 26 vom 2.7.1923
(8) K. Radek: 'Dem 'Gewissen' zur Antwort'. In: 'Rote Fahne' vom 10.7.1923
(9) K. Radek: 'Kommunismus und deutsche nationalistische Bewegung'. In: 'Rote Fahne' vom 16./18.8.1923